A Comprehensive Guide to Self-Defense

Gong Chen, EdD
San Jose State University

KENDALL/HUNT PUBLISHING COMPANY
4050 Westmark Drive P.O. Box 1840 Dubuque, Iowa 52004-1840

Cover image © 2004 PhotoDisc, Inc.

Copyright © 2004 by Gong Chen

ISBN 0-7575-1019-1

Printed in the United States of America
10 9 8 7 6 5 4 3 2 1

Dedication

To my father Ying Chen, mother Hui Ding, and aunt Zhi Chen;
wife Yuan Li, daughter Carol, and son Victor;
brothers and sisters Dong, Ming, and Fan;
other family members, for their everlasting love and support.

Contents

PART TWO. PREVENTION IN SELF-DEFENSE 61

PART FIVE. LIFETIME LEARNING AND APPLICATIONS IN SELF-DEFENSE 219

PART SIX. SKILL DEMONSTRATION IN VIDEO COMPACT DISC 237

Preface

As the world stepped into the twenty-first century, the threat of crime, leading with terrorism crimes, has spread throughout the world. Self-defense education has never been so essential to everyone in the United States and throughout the world. The reality of increasing violent crimes has created a huge market for self-defense education.

The first edition of this book, published in 1998, was designed to provide a comprehensive view and practical guidelines for university self-defense classes and university students. This second edition is still targeting university students, but the contents have expanded to k-12 grades, the community people, and the working populations. The purpose of the new book is to help students and community people become aware of the need for self-defense, to establish comprehensive knowledge of self-defense, to develop systematic self-defense mental strategies, to prepare overall self-defense physical skills, and to continue learning self-defense and apply what they learn from this book their entire lives.

This book is written based on theoretical analysis and practical applications of self-defense and relevant fields. It combines the fields of applied criminology, psychology, martial arts, crime prevention, and physical education to make self-defense a science. The contents of the curriculum are based on: 1) analysis of the nature of Self-defense; 2) analysis of processes of all crimes that self-defense concerns; 3) martial arts and applications; 4) analysis of crime data and thousand real life cases; 5) opinions from criminologists, police officers, martial art experts, and authors of crime prevention and self-defense; 6) a national study on nationwide university self-defense courses by the author; 7) a series of first-hand research on self-defense by the author; and 8) semester-based students' evaluations and modifications for twelve years, and classroom experiments on effectiveness of strategies and skills.

The major contents of this book have been applied in the instruction of self-defense in university classes since 1991. All physical skills have been tried for their effectiveness, useless skills have been eliminated from the classes, while new and approved effective skills have been added. Most of the mental strategies have been evaluated by students with regard to their effectiveness for their learning and applications in their lives.

This edition has five major parts and twenty chapters. Part one focuses on self-defense process, awareness for the rationales of self-defense, understanding the crime process and characteristics of each crime self-defense concern, and understanding the rights of self-defenders. The second part of the book discusses prevention procedures and strategies in self-defense. These procedures and strategies have been introduced from three perspectives: location-oriented prevention, crime-oriented prevention, and population-oriented prevention. The third part of the book introduces on-site response with non-fighting strategies. It includes specific back-away strategies, handling different crimes on-site, and handling everyday conflicts. The fourth part of the book introduces seven types of physical skills to prepare students to fight back in life-threatening situations. The fifth part of this book focuses on follow-up activities and lifetime learning and applications after students take a class.

The major changes in the second edition of the book include the following three aspects. **First,** much new content has been added to the new edition. New content includes: 1) the results and applications of new, first-hand research done by the author to support the theories, models, and practice of self-defense; 2) new self-defense theories and their applications created by the author and other experts; 3) updated statistics on crimes and prevention 4) prevention models and strategies on different types of crimes and for different populations of potential victims; 5) strategies of handling minor conflicts to avoid the upgrading of confrontations which often develop into severe crimes; and 6) applications of modern technology in crime prevention and self-defense. **Second,** an instructors' teaching manual provides information to prepare to be qualified instructors, where to find sources, how to design a specific curriculum, how to plan instruction schedules, how to teach effectively; it also contains detailed examples of curriculum and instruction that has been written separately for self-defense instructors. **Third,** a VCD tape with demonstration of all skills has been created to help students learn better from the actual motions.

All physical skills in photos and in motions are demonstrated by regular students in my self-defense classes. After 20-25 hours' training, most students can handle these skills very well and many of them can demonstrate standard skills. That means, the readers of this book can do the same after they learn and train properly. Besides all physical skills, major practice, combination drills, assignment, and skill tests are also demonstrated in the VCD. The VCD can be played on any DVD player, VCD player, PC computer, or Macintosh computer. When you use a PC, click on "My Computer" first, then click "NEW VCD", then click "MPEGAV", then click "AVSEQ01.DAT", and then select the "Windows Media Player" to play. When using a Macintosh, first click the "NEW VCD" on the screen, then click "MPEGAV", then click "AVSEQ01.DAT", and then select "QuickTime Player" to play.

I hope this book will help students learn self-defense more effectively, and I hope they are safe from crimes throughout their lives. Any feedback for the book is welcome. For more information about self-defense research, instruction, workshops, and instructor training programs, please contact the author through the following address.

Acknowledgments

I wish to express my great gratitude to:

Gloria Hsu for computerized editing for the book and the VCD, Curt Sennewald, Human Performance Staff, and the following students who demonstrated physical skills in the textbook and/or VCD

Alison Anderson	Audra Baker
David Boden	Leslie Calhoun
Tessie Carranza	Vincent Chan
Ming Chin	Matthew Cuecao
Stephanie Deleon	Lisa Doughty
Randy Fang	Jose Fernandez, Jr.
Long Hoang	Joanne Kabariti
Somchai Kalra	Sith Koopthavonrerk
Wen Chang Lee	Kathleen Lindsey
Steve J. Lived	Laurisa Killer
Cheong In Na	Beau Pierce
Tisha L. Ponder	Stacy Rappoport
Heather Rasmussen	Norman Rial
Julio Cesar Sanchez	Michelle Schukraft
Jenny M. Scott	Selena Hendrix-Smith
Jason Stipp	Carlos Torres
Merlin Valencia	Phillippe Zervogiannis

and students in my self-defense classes for helping with filming and providing feedback.

PART ONE

Introduction to Crimes and Self-Defense

- ➤ Introduction to Self-Defense and Crime Prevention

- ➤ The Rationales of Self-Defense

- ➤ Crime Process Analysis

- ➤ Different Crimes and Characteristics

- ➤ Legal Aspects and Services

Chapter 1
Introduction to Self-Defense and Crime Prevention

This chapter provides a basic introduction to self-defense. Included are discussions on the meaning and nature of self-defense and crime prevention, the major purposes and functions of self-defense education, a brief history and contemporary status of self-defense education, self-defense for university students, the process of crime prevention and self-defense, and major models of self-defense.

What Is Crime Prevention and Self-Defense?

People very often use the terms crime prevention and self-defense interchangeably. There are some differences between these two concepts, but there are also similarities. Their relationship is interrelated—there is self-defense in crime prevention and there is crime prevention in self-defense. Crime prevention has both broad and specific meanings. The broad implication of crime prevention means the effort of the whole society to reduce, control, and prevent violent crimes. For example, education has the function of preventing youth from joining gangs or choosing crime as a career, proper welfare will provide people necessary financial support so that they will not have to commit crimes for a living, police and other law enforcement systems limit criminals' freedom on the street, and neighborhood watch programs have the function of keeping the neighborhood safe from gangs and other crimes, etcetera. The basic function of broad crime prevention is to keep the society safe. The specific implication of crime prevention is to prevent crimes before they happen in personal self-defense process.

Self-defense is the personal effort to defend oneself with whatever force (skills or strategies) is reasonably necessary to prevent crimes before they happen or to deal with actual or threatened violent crime attacks. The function of self-defense is to keep oneself safe from crimes of violence. It can be classified as a section of the broad crime prevention process. For maximum protection of personal safety, it is essential that these two processes work together. Since this book focuses on the personal effort, the term "self-defense" will be used throughout the book.

Nature of Self-Defense

The nature of self-defense includes the following aspects: 1) It is always defensive and always a reaction to the criminal's actions. 2) It is very unpredictable when, where, and how the attacks will occur. 3) It is brutal, since attackers may use any violent methods. 4) It is complicated, and it involves many factors which determine the winning odd.

Self-defense is a battle between potential attackers (criminals) and defenders (victims). There are practically no limits to strategies, skills, and weapons employed by either party. To the criminals, it is a battle to get something for nothing or to cause damages to the victims. To defendants, it can be a battle concerning life and death, or guarding what they have earned through hard work.

Self-defense can be considered a sport game between attackers and defendants. This game requires not only physical skills and body conditioning, but also mental strategies and emotional effort. Defendants need to know how to prevent crimes beforehand, how to recognize potentially dangerous situations, how to make correct decisions when attacked, and how to use any physical skills and strategies necessary to win.

Self-defense is also like an investment in the stock market. It is very unpredictable, and it is not a fair competition. The criminals are not bound by laws or morals, and they have the freedom to do anything in any way at anytime and anywhere to anyone. On the other hand, however, defendants do not know exactly who the attacker will be, who the victims will be, where and when the attacks may happen, how the victims will be attacked, and what the attacker wants to do to the victims. Very often the defendants do not have enough time and information to make proper decisions when attacked; therefore the results of the self-defense is probably dependent up on chance. This is the biggest disadvantage for self-defense, and this unfair competition requires defendants to be on guard at all times and to prepare themselves overall to increase their chances of winning.

Purpose of Self-Defense Education

The major purposes of self-defense education are to develop awareness, knowledge, mental skills, strategies, physical skills and hands-on experience, and actual ability of students so that they can successfully avoid becoming victims of violent crimes and handle unarmed or armed attackers in life-threatening or other situations. Although self-defense education cannot guarantee that the students will be 100% safe after taking a self-defense course, systematic education and training in self-defense will dramatically reduce the chances of becoming a victim. That is the major function of self-defense education. The two major objectives of self-defense education are to make students mentally SMART and physically TOUGH in self-defense.

Development of Self-Defense Education

The phenomenon of self-defense actually started in the animal world, long before human beings existed. Due to the presence of both predators and prey, most animals developed self-defense mechanisms for their own survival. For example, octopi set up a screen to cover themselves before they escape, rabbits can run fast to get out of attacks, chameleons hide themselves in the environment, and beavers build their homes in safe places.

The behavior of self-defense in human beings started several thousand years ago. Records in the history of China indicate that several thousand years ago people already used skills and strategies to prevent burglaries and robberies. However, the concept of self-defense in the West started much later, somewhere around the 1600s, when people started to learn martial arts for self-protection purposes. The earliest documents which can be located in Western countries on self-defense also were in the 1600s. At that time, there were some discussions on the history of self-defense, and there were ideas on how to protect life and property. By the 1880s, there were many discussions on self-defense and the law. In 1905, the first book was published which tried to teach people how to fight back for self-protection, but the book basically focused only on the boxing aspects. In the 1940s, a few books were published to teach women how to protect themselves, and some martial arts types of self-defense occurred, such as jujitsu and judo self-defense. These books basically taught people how to use these martial arts for fighting back in self-defense. In the 1960s and 1970s, more self-defense books were published, yet most of them were still martial arts oriented. In the late 1970s and 1980s, self-defense books did not limit their concepts of self-defense to martial arts anymore; instead many books tried to teach people prevention and back-away strategies and skills, and more books focused on self-defense for women. Self-defense courses also started at many places. In China, Chinese Martial Arts (also called Wushu or Kungfu) has long been used as a way for fitness and self-defense and that was only the application aspect of Wushu, self-defense has not been taught as a course in schools, and books on self-defense were not published until later in the 1980s and 1990s. So far, most books published in China on self-defense covered only less organized skills. The only comprehensive self-defense book was published by Chen and Liu in 1999.

Contemporary Status of Self-Defense

The concept of self-defense became popular in the 1990s. More people have realized the importance of self-defense in their lives and have started attending self-defense training. This is due to several factors: the intensive reports on crimes in the media, the spread of crimes to almost every corner of this nation, the fear of becoming a victim of crime, and a lack of confidence in the law enforcement system that is meant to protect citizens. Since the 911 hijacking and bombing of the World Trade Center in New York in 2001, the need for self-defense has reached a historical high in the United States, and the self-defense literature has also expanded.

In the 1990s, several self-defense textbooks were published in an effort to teach people self-defense and crime prevention. Self-defense classes were offered at universities, community centers, and private martial arts studios. Some high schools and middle schools also started teaching students self-defense and crime prevention. Several types of self-defense equipment have become popular, such as personal alarms, mace, and pepper spray. It is impressive that people are gradually becoming aware of the need for self-defense as a part of their lives and more courses are being offered in schools.

Although self-defense is growing very rapidly across the nation, there are some problems which impair its further development. These problems include, but are not limited to the following.

1. Even though self-defense courses are offered in many places, there is a lack of a commonly recognized curriculum (Cummings 1992, Chen 1998). A study of nationwide university self-defense curriculum (Chen 1998) indicated significant differences in self-defense instruction. It seems that many classes were taught based on the personal perspective or background of the instructor, instead of being based on the analysis of the nature of self-defense and what should be taught in self-defense. Some classes focus on throwing skills, and some classes focus on kicks, punches, and blocks only. Some classes focus on skill development, and other classes focus on prevention. Some community self-defense classes taught oral self-defense only because these instructors believed that women are not strong enough to use physical skills. This may mislead the students to believe that they have learned everything about self-defense, when they have actually only learned a small part of it, and students are not well prepared for different life-threatening situations. Self-defense is very situational and students should be well prepared for all different kinds of situations with various types of strategies and skills.

A review of self-defense textbooks published in the 1980s and 1990s also indicated that self-defense textbook authors had different opinions on self-defense curriculum. It seems that unlike other sports, in which the curriculum has been established and class contents are commonly recognized, there is a lack of a common understanding in self-defense course structure or curriculum.

2. There are not many places people can go for systematic education in self-defense. Very often, self-defense is taught through short classes in community centers, workshops, presentations, speeches by police officers, or demonstrations.

3. Although there are many people teaching self-defense nationwide, there are no criteria for self-defense instructors, and there is no certification program for self-defense instructors. Therefore, it is not easy to evaluate the quality of instruction in self-defense.

4. There is a lack of systematic research in the field of self-defense. The theoretical aspects of self-defense develop very slowly. So far, many strategies and skills are being taught without research data to support their effectiveness. Furthermore, many skills taught in classes or demonstrated in some self-defense and martial arts books are not practical or useful for real fighting-back in self-defense. Book authors and instructors should try these skills first in close-to-real situations so that they can test their effectiveness before teaching or demonstrating them in the books.

5. There is a lack of connection between self-defense and the criminology profession. self-defense in nature basically is a combination of both criminal study and combative techniques. However, criminology professionals tend to concentrate on the crime research and neglect the applications of their knowledge in crime prevention and self-defense. On the other hand, self-defense instructors tend to teach physical movements without much knowledge of crimes and criminals.

6. The rate of regular people who have received formal self-defense education is very low. According to the author's studies, although 17.8 percent of university students indicated learned some self-defense, less than 1 percent of university students really took a formal self-defense class (Chen 2000). Although self-defense (together with martial arts) is a part of the curriculum in American high schools and middle schools, very few students had the chance to learn real self-defense due to the lack of classes (Chen, Fall 1999). Elementary school students basically have no chance to learn self-defense since it is not a part of the curriculum in America, and in reality, few students learned self-defense (Chen, Summer 1999).

Self-defense will continue to grow in the future and should become a life skill for everyone. The problems experienced by our society have led to greater development in the field of self-defense. We would like to see more people from various fields joining the effort to further develop self-defense education.

Self-Defense for College Students

University campuses, which used to be peaceful places for academic research and study, are not safe anymore (Whitaker et al 1993). Campus crimes are increasing at a very fast pace, and rape and prevention on campus have brought greater concerns. On the other hand, crimes at the workplace, where college graduates will spend most of their lifetime, is also increasing at a surprising speed and has become a top health/life threatening factor in the workplace.

Self-defense education plays an important role in ensuring the academic study, career success, and the entire life of university students. It is essential that students develop self-defense concepts and skills to prepare for the increasingly violent environment in schools and the workplace. Self-defense has become a very important part of student life, just like other skills such as language, computers, and mathematics. As a very important life skill, self-defense deserves a great deal of attention among college students, since self-defense is not systematically taught at the high school level, and there will not be place where they can receive systematic and comprehensive training in self-defense after they graduate from colleges and universities. So far, university self-defense remains the best self-defense education. The problem is that although college students rank self-defense as the most valuable course (Trimble and Hensley 1993, Wilkinson 1993 and 2000), only a small percentage of students have actually taken it (Chen 2000).

Major Solutions to Crimes—The Big Picture of Self-Defense

Crime prevention involves the effort of the whole society, and there are different models of crime prevention. Conklin (1999) introduced the ideological approaches to solving the crime problem from the criminological perspective. These approaches include: 1) the **conservative approach** which focus on better life, better discipline, more self-control, and more severe penalties; 2) the **liberal approach** which focuses on educational and vocational training, welfare assistance, job opportunities, non-discrimination, and community organizations; and 3) the **radical approach** which focuses on white-collar crimes and political correction, thus is less useful in solving the violent crimes. Conklin also presented a three-strategy model. The first strategy is the crime and criminal justice system, including the law, the police, the courts, and the prisons. The second strategy is situational crime prevention which includes three techniques. Technique one is to increase the offenders' effort by using target-hardening (locks), access-control (ID), deflection of offenders (close street), and control of facilitators (gun or alcohol). Technique two is to increase offenders' risks by using entry screening, formal surveillance (guards or alarm), surveillance of employees (doorman), and natural surveillance (neighborhood watch or environment design). Technique three is to reduce the rewards by using target removal (hide valuables), property identification, removal of inducement (no gender on phone list), and rules setting (zero-violence school). The third strategy is dealing with the causes of crime, including enhancing the social support available from families, schools, friends, employers, communities, and government.

There are other strategies people use to solve crime problems. Some of them are included in Conklin's model. One is the environmental design, which uses access control, entry screening, target hardening, locks, fences, signs, and natural surveillance such as improving lighting and trimming bushes, as well as surveillance. Another strategy is the facilitator control which includes limiting alcohol and guns, curfew, target removal, identifying property, and removing inducement. Another way is the technical development which includes closed circuit television system, alarm systems, metal detectors, stun guns, pepper spray, mace, bullet-proof jackets, wrist radio bands, technobras, and personal alarms.

Three Levels of Crime Prevention

Chen (February 1998) divided the crime prevention process into three levels from the self-defense perspective. These solutions involve the efforts of the whole society, including government, schools, law enforcement system, the community, and individuals. These three levels need to work together for the maximum effect in crime prevention.

Level One

The function of the first level is to reduce the number of would-be criminals. This involves the efforts of the government, schools, family, and other education sources. These solutions work from different perspectives.

Education

Formal education in schools educate students to become good citizens, develop better discipline and self-control, and prepare students for better careers, thus reducing the chance of the younger generation becoming would-be criminals. Other special education programs also help prevent youth from choosing crime as their careers. For example, the GEARUP program provides funds and support to low-income youth to help them prepare for college. The Drug Awareness Resistance Education (DARE) program in public schools will help reduce drug related crimes among youth. The Gang Resistance Education and Training (GREAT) Program supported by the Bureau of Alcohol, Tobacco, and Firearms along with the Federal Law Enforcement Training Center educate youth away from gangs and their activities. The National Youth Sport program provides low-income students opportunities and funding to engage in healthy activities and reduce their chances to be in unhealthy activities such as gangs and drugs. There are hundreds of programs like these in the country. Some programs deal with conflict resolution, some focus on anger control or stress management, and some stress laws and rule setting. On the other hand, corrective education will help to prevent former youth criminals from repeating their crime careers. All these education and programs help reduce would-be criminals.

Government

Providing decent jobs, job training, welfare, and favorable living conditions for regular people, especially people who are in poverty or unemployed will reduce their motives of committing robbery, burglary, or other crimes for a living, and it will also reduce anti-social behaviors. This certainly will reduce their opportunities of becoming potential would-be criminals.

Family

Family is the basic unit of the society, and there will be less criminals if all families can function well. The good role model of the parent as a good citizen, strong relationships among family members, love and respect in the family, responsibility for child education and guidance, and healthy family activities can dramatically reduce the chances of youth becoming criminals and developing violent behaviors.

Society

Equality and fairness in the society certainly can reduce the hate-related crimes as well as aggravated assaults. Everyone in this country needs to realize that some common social morals need to be followed by everybody in the society to make the world peaceful. Government officials, police officers, teachers, managers, and even regular people should understand the basic philosophy that treating others with respect and fairness will finally result in the return of a safe society and environment. They should not treat other people in ways that they do not want to be treated.

Level Two

The function of the second level is to threaten the criminals and limit their chances of committing crimes. Grossman (1998) suggested three major solutions at this level including strong police, death penalty, and three strikes. This level involves the following formal and informal law enforcement systems and communities:

The Police

Police along with FBI officers function in several ways in terms of crime prevention. One role of the police is as the safety guards for the society. Most criminals will not dare to attack people in public because of the existence of police officers, whether they are patrolling the streets or hiding in schools. Another role is to catch the criminals through investigation, secret witness, Internet chasing, and wanted lists in post offices and on television. The third role is their rescue function when people are attacked. Police are the biggest threat to criminals because criminals are afraid of being caught. Therefore, police are the biggest obstacle in the way of criminals. Private security guards in industries and business, and escort services at schools have a similar guarding function like the police. Last but not least, police officers also educate people about the crimes and criminals and how to deal with them. This makes crimes harder, since the victims are more aware of the potential risks.

Courts and Jails

The major function of courts and jails is to punish the criminals for their behaviors, and to deprive the freedoms of criminals so that they will not have opportunities to commit crimes again. They both work together to reduce the numbers of the criminals on the street. They both also have the psychological threatening power to deter the criminals from committing crimes due to the fear that they may be caught and sentenced to jails or death.

Community Organizations

Community organizations have different functions in preventing crimes. People who join Neighborhood Watch programs work together with police to keep the criminals away from their residential areas. Security companies work with residents to patrol and secure their residential areas. Gun control groups try to limit the facilitating factors of the crime. Gang prevention programs patrol the residential areas and keep in close touch with youth and would-be gang members to block the way of crimes.

The Criminology Studies and Self-Defense Experts

The experts of criminology studies investigate the patterns of crimes and criminals and make crime prevention more scientific and effective. On the other hand, self-defense experts and martial art experts prepare people mentally and physically for the potential attacks, which makes the crimes harder.

Level Three

The function of the third level is the individual effort to prevent crime and to protect oneself and one's family from violent crimes along with the help of some organizations. This process will make people aware of the dangers and provide training for people in order to reduce the chances of becoming victims and increase people's ability to handle the situations effectively. Self-defense training also makes it more difficult for criminals to commit crimes.

Self-Defense Classes

Self-defense classes are taught in schools, colleges, community centers, and industries. These classes provide basic training for people and prepare them for self-defense. Even though there are significant differences in the quality of the classes, some training is always better than nothing. Encouraging family members to join self-defense classes or teaching family members also can be a part of the self-defense training process.

Martial Arts

There are more than 15 popular martial arts taught and practiced in the United States. These martial arts teach people how to use physical skills for self-defense. Even though there are different styles of martial arts, they all teach some self-defense skills.

Special Training

There are some special training sessions for self-defense. They usually are short and focus on one special skill. For example, mace training usually takes several hours and people learn how to use mace for self-defense. Some classes offer training on using guns in self-defense and some train people on stun guns.

Supporting Organizations

In each state and even in some cities in the United States, there are organizations which provide support to regular people and crime victims. These groups include rape prevention and help, child abuse centers, domestic violence prevention and help centers, missing children help centers, and victims support centers and coalitions. These organizations are established to help people and victims in different ways, and people should take advantage of them.

The Learning Process of Self-Defense

The goals of learning self-defense basically include two aspects. The first is to become SMART in self-defense, and this is the mental aspect of self-defense. This goal is to develop students' mental and psychological ability to prevent the crime before it happens and to handle the situation with appropriate decisions. The second goal is to become TOUGH physically, and this is the physical aspect of self-defense. This goal is to develop students' body conditioning and physical combative ability so that they can deal with the actual attacks effectively and increase the odds of winning.

The learning of self-defense includes several steps which have proved very effective. The first step is to be aware of the importance of self-defense in everybody's life. The second step is to have a good understanding of the crimes, criminals, crime patterns, victims, and the process of self-defense. The third step is to develop and carry out prevention strategies and skills in everyday life. The fourth step is to understand your rights in self-defense and to develop abilities to handle different situations on site. The fifth step is to develop various combative skills which resemble the fighting-back situations in real self-defense and to develop appropriate body conditioning. The sixth step is to find ways to learn continuously after the class is over, and to carry out Self-defense concepts and actions throughout your lifetime.

Major Models of Self-Defense

Leung (1991) presented a self-defense model. This model includes the following five objectives in self-defense education: prevention, avoidance, deterrence, escape, and survival.

Cummings (1992) suggested the following "model objectives" for college self-defense courses. These objectives, in his opinion, should: 1) increase awareness of environment and self; 2) recognize potentially threatening situations and identify high-risk behaviors; 3) consider a variety of self-defense options for a given situation; 4) implement mental, vocal, and physical techniques; 5) identify resources; and 6) find ways to continue learning about self-defense after course completion.

Dr. Fein (1996) presented a three-level self-defense model. This model includes prevention, psychological defense, and physical defense.

Chen (1993) presented a model of physical skills of self-defense at the National Basic Instructional Program Convention at Raleigh, North Carolina. This new physical skill model summarized most self-defense fighting-back skills into seven different categories based on the analysis of the nature of self-defense and major martial art competitions, especially street fighting and ultimate fighting. The new model also stresses the combination and transition among theses seven types of skills to make the training close to the real-life self-defense situation. The seven types of skills include distance fighting, close fighting, throws, floor fighting, joint control, releasing, and special fighting which includes dealing with a gun, knife, and multiple attackers.

In 1996 at the Southwest AAHPERD Annual Convention, Chen (1996) presented a comprehensive curriculum for university self-defense courses based on his years of research and instruction of self-defense. This curriculum included awareness for the need of self-defense, understanding of the crime process, prevention principles and strategies at different locations, on-site mental responses, on-site physical skills, body conditioning and self-confidence development, understanding your rights and legal issues, lifetime learning and application strategies, and martial arts for self-defense. In 1998 Chen published his comprehensive textbook *A New Concept of Self-Defense* to carry out this new comprehensive curriculum. Carleton and Chen in 1999 published a series of self-defense articles for self-defense in public schools. These articles not only provided a comprehensive curriculum for public schools, but also provided advices for teacher preparation and teaching guidelines. Chen (June 2002) presented and published his newest comprehensive curriculum for university self-defense courses at the 44th International Council of Physical Education, Recreation, Sport and Dance World Congress in Taiwan.

REFERENCES

Carleton, N. and G. Chen. "Self-Defense through Physical Education I: How to Plan a Unit," *Strategies* 12(6): 31–37, May/June 1999.

Carleton, N. and G. Chen. "Self-Defense Through Physical Education II: Teacher Preparation and Equipment Needs" *Strategies* 12(6): 32–35, July 1999.

Carleton, N. and G. Chen. "Self-Defense Through Physical Education III: Implementation" *Strategies* 13(1): 33–36. September/October 1999.

Chen, G. *A Model of Physical Skills of Self-Defense.* A Paper Presented at National Basic Instructional Program Convention at Raleigh, North Carolina, September 1993.

Chen, G. A Complete University Self-Defense Curriculum. A Paper presented at The Southwest AAHPERD Annual Convention, Sacramento, CA. 1996.

Chen, G. *A New Concept of Self-Defense.* Dubuque: Kendall/Hunt Publishing Company, February 1998.

Chen, G. "A Study on Subjects Taught in American Nationwide University Self-Defense" Courses" Journal of ICHPERSD, XXXV (1), 28–33, 1998.

Chen, G. "How Much American Elementary School Students Know about Self-Defense" *Journal of International Council of Health, Physical Education, Recreation, Sport and Dance,* XXXV(4), 58–61, Summer 1999.

Chen, G. "A Study of Self-Defense Education of American High School Students" *Journal of International Council of Health, Physical Education, Recreation, Sport and Dance,* XXXVI(1), 36–41, Fall 1999.

Chen, G. "A Study of Self-Defense Education of American University Students. Journal of International Council of Health, Physical Education, Recreation, Sport and Dance XXXVI(1), 36-41, Fall 2000.

Chen, G., R. Zhang, and Y. Zhang. *A Comprehensive Curriculum for University Self-Defense Courses,* Taipei: The 44th ICHPERDSD World Conference Proceedings, 2002.

Conklin, J. E. *Criminology* (4th ed). New York: Macmillan Publishing Company, 1999.

Cummings, N. "Self-Defense Training for College Women." *Journal of American College Health* 40(4) 183–188, 1992.

Donziger S. R. *The Real War on Crime.* New York: Harper Collin Publishers, 1996

Fein, J. *How to Fight Back and Win.* Sebastotol: Torrance Publishing Company, 1996

Grossman, D. "Trained to Kill." *Christianity Today,* August 10, 1998.

Leung, D. *Self-defense: The Womanly Art of Self-Defense, Intuition, and Choice.* Tacoma: R & M Press, 1991.

Trimble, R. T., and L. D. Hensley. Survey of Basic Instruction Programs in Physical Education. Proceedings of The National Conference on Basic Instruction in Physical Education. Raleigh, NC, 1993.

Whitaker, L. C., and J. W. Pollard. *Campus Violence: Kinds, Causes, and Cures.* Binghamton: Haworth Press, Inc, 1993.

Wilkinson, S. Students needs in Activity Program at SJSU. A survey conducted by the Department of Human Performance, San Jose State University, San Jose, CA. 2000

Chapter 2
The Rationales of Self-Defense

This chapter explains the basic rationales of self-defense. The main purpose is to make people aware of the need for self-defense and self-defense education. Included are discussions on the theoretical and practical needs for self-defense, and analysis of existing solutions to crimes.

Position of Self-Defense in Human Life

The most important treasure for each human being is the physical life. The physical life is the carrier of the whole life process that includes health, wealth, self-actualization, self-esteem, career, education, family, enjoyment, and everything for a person. All of these are like many zeros which have no meaning at all with the number 1 in front of these zeros, and the number "1" is the physical life.

1,000,000

The life also looks like a balloon in which the rubber skin is the physical life which holds up the air that represents all other things in one's life. There is nothing left if the balloon is poped by a needle. As an old saying puts it, "if one is not breathing, nothing matters."

Human life is almost like a balloon and looks very strong and normally will live up to 70 or 80 years or older if nothing happens to it. However, some people live up to that old age while others die very early due to three life/health-threatening factors: accidents, diseases, and violent crimes. Our lives and health can be taken away easily by one of these three factors. The life seems hard to human beings.

Accidents

There are many kinds of accidents and these accidents can ruin people's life and health easily. Type one is **traffic accidents** and common car and motor bike accidents kill as many people as the gun (Cox 1997). Other traffic accidents include train crash and derailment, airplane crash, ship and boat turnovers, bike crash and fall, and snowmobile accidents. Type two is **exercise and sport accidents**. These accidents include death and injuries from boxing games and martial art competitions, regular sport injuries, rock climbing, car racing, shooting in hunting, falls, and skiing accidents. Type three is the **playground and recreation accidents**. These accidents can be falling, head being trapped, drowning, and attack by wild animals and insects. Type four is **military training accidents**. They include transportation accidents, firearm accidents, and ship turnovers, et cetera. Type five is **natural disasters**. Examples include tornadoes hurricanes, floods, snow fall, earthquake, forest and grass fires, landslides, volcanoes, and tsunami. Type six is firearm accidents due to the over-spread and abuse of firearms in the United States. Type seven is poisoning. Included are poison plants, food poisoning, over drinking, and use of drugs. Type eight is **medical accidents**. Included are use of wrong medicines, carelessness of doctors and nurses, and infected drugs. Type nine is **construction accidents**. Included are falling cranes and other objects, falling from a height, or being cut or hit by machines.

Victims of these accidents can be anyone, but most are males and youth. Accidents occur most often to residents in an urban center, most deaths occur in motor vehicle, more in injuries at home, and most accidents occur in a cyclical manner.

There are some classes which prepare people for some accidents, such as earthquake prevention and fire prevention. But no comprehensive class has been identified in the nation to prepare people for all different types of accidents, and prevention of accidents is less studied. To most people, the ways to prepare for include attending a special class, reading and trying the guidelines in brochures and books, and most importantly, taking precautions. (By the way, prevention of these accidents is not discussed in this book.)

Diseases

Disease is another life and health threatening factor people face today, and most people eventually die of one or more diseases. Among thousands of different types of diseases, cancer, AIDS, heart attack, strokes, and other inner organ and system diseases are the common killers. Establishment of a healthy and active life-style is the key to the prevention of health problems.

Crimes of Violence

The violent crime is the third factor that ruins people's life and health. These crimes include murder, aggressive assault, rape, robbery, burglary, terrorism attacks, wars, and riots. The consequences of violent crimes are similar to the accidents and diseases, but these crimes are committed intentionally. Prevention and preparing to deal with these violent crimes is the major focus of standard self-defense classes. Reducing the effect of this threat to human life and health is the only focus of this book. This is the big picture on the major function of self-defense—to protect one third of your life.

Theoretical Background of Self-Defense—Human Needs Theory

According to Abraham Maslow (1970), a psychologist nationally recognized for his theory of the human needs pyramid, human beings have different levels of needs. People must first meet basic physiological needs (such as food, drink, and sleep) before they can move to a higher level need such as self-esteem or self-actualization. The need for security represents the second basic level in Maslow's pyramid. This theory indicates that the need to protect oneself from the potential attacks from criminals plays a very important role in human lives.

Maslow's human need theory has established the theoretical basis for self-defense and its education—the security of life through crime prevention and self-defense is an important part of human existence. The reason is very simple: safety and security ensure life, and no achievement can be made without a physical life. People need other skills, such as computer or math, to achieve their life goals, but they also need self-defense skills to protect their life and what they have earned through their hard work. Unfortunately, this theory has been ignored by most people in terms of its implications in self-defense education.

The Reality Background—Crimes of Violence

Maslow's theory is supported by the real-life crime statistics. In 2001, based on the Uniform Crime Report, 15,980 people were murdered, 90,491 people were raped, 422,921 people were robbed, 907,219 people were assaulted, and 2,109,767 people were burglarized. A totally of 1.4 million Americans became victims of violent crimes (murder, assault, robbery, and forcible rape) and an additional 11.6 million Americans were victims of other dangerous crimes. In another word, currently one out of every 100 Americans will become the victim of a violent crime each year and one out of every ten Americans will become victims of some type of crimes. This number does not even include crimes that are unreported. About 25 percent households in the United States become the victims of crimes one or more times each year, and only about 50 percent of violent crimes are reported to the police (Meadows 1998). The experts indicate that unreported crimes account for as much as twice the reported cases and the actual number of victims should be much higher. On 911, several hundred passengers on four airplanes, several thousand people in the World Trade Center, and several hundred firefighters and police officers became victims in just one case of violent crime.

Based on the crime report, 83 percent of children under twelve years old will become victims of violent crimes during their lifetimes (Brewer 1994). It was predicted that at least 80 percent of American people would become a victim at least once during their lifetime and practically every individual in this country has a chance of becoming a victim of crime. According to a survey on rape which questioned 6,000 students from 32 colleges, representing various institutions of higher education, one-sixth of all college women will be raped before their graduation (Koss, et al. 1987). Crime also has become the first leading health threatening factor to the female working class, and the second leading factor to the male working class.

Based on the crime report and the cases in everyday life, anyone-rich or poor, business CEOs or elementary school students, men or women, old or young-will have the chance to become victims of violence. Crimes might happen to you anywhere including your home, workplace, recreational places or driving; and anytime day or night. You might be facing different types of criminals and attacks in different ways.

Crimes are spreading to every corner of society, and there is no place one can feel completely safe anymore. The fear of becoming victims of violent crimes has spread to every corner, every person, and every family in this country. The most prominent fears among woman (Brewer 1994) include being raped, their children being attacked, car breaking down during the night, an intruder in the house, being mugged at gunpoint, a bomb on their airplane, being poisoned by people, and attacked due to racial reason. Meadows (1998) indicated that 38 percent of the people in the United States worried about being assaulted, 35 percent were afraid of burglary; 23 percent had the fear of being beaten up, shot, or stabbed; and 19 percent were scared of being killed. Since the 911 event in 2001, people certainly have more fears than ever.

The Ever-Present Crimes and Criminals

Violent crime has become a part of society and the life of everybody. All violent crimes including murder, rape, assault, robbery and other crimes such as burglary, arson, and organized crime has existed in the history of China for several thousand years. These crimes never disappeared, no matter what the Chinese government has done to prevent and to punish. For the last two hundred years in the United States, violent crimes have prevailed, even though the patterns and dimensions of the crimes have changed over time. The crimes of violence have actually gotten worse in recent years and have much more destructive power than before.

The criminals of violent crimes also have been a part of the human being and they do not disappear either. Old criminals die but new criminals replace them like waves in the ocean. No matter how hard people and society try to eliminate them, they will not disappear. Just like cancers and other disease, crimes of violence threaten the life and health of human beings and the world will not be peaceful when criminals still exist. We have to accept the fact that violent crimes and criminals are a part of our lives, and we have to live with them in the same world, no matter whether we like it or not. Since we cannot eliminate them and we have to live with them, we have the chance to become their targets. We better be prepared to prevent them, otherwise we will suffer from the severe consequences of the violent crimes.

Consequences of Crimes to Victims

Crimes, especially violent crimes, have severe consequences to everyone in this country. Millions of people suffer from the loss of lives of family members and friends and the loss of property. The financial and emotional costs are too high for anyone to afford or ignore. The consequences of crimes include, but are not limited to, the following:

1. Physically: Crimes can cause death, physical injuries and pain, or permanent disability.
2. Psychologically and emotionally: Crimes spread the fear of becoming a victim and cause prolonged fear after someone become a victim. Crimes also cause stress and psychological pressure which have a negative influence on everyday life.
3. Financially: Crimes cause financial problems to the victims. These problems include loss of property, unpaid wages, hospitalization expenses, therapeutic services, loss of social security, loss of survivor's benefits, funeral costs, and replacement costs of stolen property, often well beyond the original prices (Conklin 1999). Studies indicate these costs to the victims and to society: $9,350 per aggravated assault, $2,940,000 per murder, $86,500 per rape, $19,000 per robbery, and $1,100 per burglary.
4. Socially: Crimes cause more social problems to victims. These problems include: the inability to trust others: fear of public places and streets; disruption of your home, school, or office atmosphere; a sense of less choice and freedom; the pressure to move to a safer place; and the need to quit a job or change schools (Conklin 1999).
5. Children: Crimes have very negative influences on children. Children usually show more mistrust of strangers, low self-esteem and confidence, hostility toward other children, more fights, a greater tendency to carry weapons, a distorted sense of time and thoughts or perception, nightmares, and prolonged lifetime effects (Conklin 1999).

The violent crimes also have severe consequences on society and the community. Crimes have been recognized as a major factor which impairs the development of this country. Crimes cost society billions of dollars every year in terms of treatment of crime-related injuries, costs of prevention, and expenses of strengthening law enforcement; reduction of the nation's economic output; decreased employment; increased consumer prices; and a reduction in per capita income (Conklin 1999). Crime has darkened the future of this country and affected the life of each individual within this country. The case of the 911 terrorism attack is a typical example.

How Close People Are to Becoming Victims of Violence

In university self-defense classes taught by the author in the United States, students were often asked the same question: "Did you ever think you may become victims of violence?" The answer from most people was "No". In everyday life, few people ever think about the possibility of themselves becoming victims of violence crimes until they actually become the victims, then it very often is too late to learn from the horrible experience. The cases on television and in newspapers often are treated by people as other people's bad luck, and the influence of the cases, no matter how terrifying they were, tend to be forgotten very soon. The result is that very few people actually prepare themselves for the prevention and handling of violent crimes. To regular people, the crime is far from them and it is for other people only, and it has nothing to do with them.

This feeling is not surprising since people tend to learn from their personal experience. These people never realize the fact that they may rub elbows with criminals very often in daily life, and very often they may just have missed becoming victims. Even I, myself, as an author of self-defense books and articles, dealing with statistics and cases everyday and being a self-defense instructor, never felt that crimes are close to me until a colleague was murdered in 1999 in San Jose,

California. This murder shocked me for almost a month, because I finally realized how close I have been to crime. In conversation with other friends, I was even more surprised to find out that many of them have had the experience of being victims.

The Department of Justice advised that "Every American now has a realistic chance of becoming a victim of violence" (Strong 1996). After eight years, the warning is still here but occurs much more frequently since the 911 terrorist high jacking and bombing of the World Trade Center in New York. The government warned that besides airlines and building, bridges, pipelines, and most recently, supermarkets and shopping centers are becoming the targets of terrorism attacks. What is coming next is unpredictable, since to terrorists and criminals, practically every part of the country is vulnerable to the attacks, including our schools. We better believe that crime is real, and it is close to everybody. And we better believe the warning. It is not a joke.

Pros and Cons of the Existing Solutions

Many people may still wonder why self-defense is needed while police officers, the FBI, courts, and jails are there to stop crimes and protect citizen lives. This attitude toward self-defense indicates that these people still live in a dream. An analysis of the current solutions to violent crimes may help them wake up, because the existing law enforcement systems do not always function effectively to protect each individual's safety (Merier 1989, Meddis and Davis 1993). Based on Snow (1995), only 21 percent of cases were solved, with murder (65 percent), robbery (24 percent), and burglary (14 percent). But if one considers that only a third of the crimes were reported to the police, the actual solution rate is much smaller. Based on the 2001 Uniform Crime Report, 62 percent of murders, 56 percent of aggravated assaults, 44 percent of rapes, 25 percent of robberies, and 46 percent of violent crime cases were solved.

Police Officers

Most people believed crime is a police problem, not theirs (Brewer 1994). Yes, the police officers (and FBI officers) are responsible for protecting civilians' lives, but they are generally not responsible for specific individuals' personal safety. In another words, they are not anyone's bodyguards. Police officers have been working very hard to reduce crimes and sometimes they have to sacrifice their lives and health in dealing with crimes; but very often the crimes are still out of their control due to various reasons. The major functions of the police in crime prevention are limited due to the following factors:

1. The ratio factor: The ratio of police officers to the general population usually is around 3:1000 (FBI Report 2000). That means that three police officer is in charge of one thousand people. It is impossible for that officer to watch and guard one thousand people at the same time.

2. The time and spatial factor: When the criminals attack people, they usually avoid the police, and they finish the attacks as fast as they can in case the police arrive at the scene. Therefore, it is very difficult for the police to get to the scene to stop crimes, even when some victims have a chance to call the police immediately before or after they have been attacked; it takes some time for the police to respond, while the attack may only last a few seconds. For example, a burglar usually takes less than five minutes to break in (Mantice 1992) while a street robbery usually only lasts for several seconds. In real life, few cases were reported where police officers made it at the scene before the attacks occurred or while the attacks were happening to save the victims. Furthermore, in many cases, the police are not given the opportunity to respond because the victims did not have sufficient time, or they cannot report at all.

3. The function factor: No criminals will inform the police that they plan to attack someone; therefore, the only way the police can help the victim on the spot is when they happen to be at the crime scene by chance or if they are really close to the location. Instead, the police can only protect potential victims in one of several ways. First, they have a threatening power which warns the criminals that the police will catch them if a crime is committed. This threatening power may scare some criminals, but not most of them. If these criminals still want to attack the victims, it is almost impossible for the police to stop them. It is rare for the police to know in advance what will happen to the victim and to arrive at the crime scene in time to protect the victim. Second, the police usually arrive only after a victim has been attacked. They take care of the victim, and then try to find the criminals. They might catch the criminals later on, but to the victim, it is just too late. Third, police officers some times educate people about crimes and prevention.

The Court

The function of the court in crime prevention is to punish the criminals for their crimes. These criminals usually are punished by fines, community service, or time in jail. The purposes of the punishment are either to scare the criminals so that they do not dare to commit crimes again or to lock them up so that they do not have the freedom to commit crimes again. However, the court has many problems in terms of protecting an individual's life.

1. The percentage of criminals caught: Only a small percentage of criminals end up in jail. Based on Russell (2000), only 9 percent of the rape offenders are arrested, more than 50 percent of rape prosecutions are dismissed before the trial, 25 percent of the convicted rapists never go to jail, 25 percent convicted rapists receive jail sentences, and 50 percent convicted rapists serve only an average of a year or less in jail. That means most criminals are still at large, and they are more likely to continue attacking people since they have not been punished. Only about 15 percent of burglars were arrested (Mantice 1992). Generally only 1-2 percent of all serious crimes were reported to police and lead to arrest, conviction, and imprisonment. Therefore, the formal sanctions of the criminal justice system are probably less important in controlling criminal behavior than informal sanctions (Conklin 1999)

2. Criminals out of jails: Most criminals arrested don't stay in jail forever. Some are released due to the lack of evidence (how many criminals leave evidence when committing crimes?) or a lawyer's defense, bail, or the limited space in jails. Once released, the cycle of crimes is more likely to continue.

3. Moderate punishment: The light punishment on crimes and criminals in this country often lets many criminals get free easily. The law usually limits what the victim can do in self-defense, but these limits have no effect on the criminals, therefore the criminals often have a great deal of freedom. The importance of the criminals' human rights, in many cases, outweighs that of victims. The moderate punishment to criminals only encourages the criminals to commit more crimes. It is estimated that about 80 percent of the criminals commit crimes again after they regain their freedom.

Neighborhood Watch

Neighborhood Watch is becoming popular and it is certainly effective in preventing crime through the efforts of the entire neighborhood. The problem is that your neighbor is not your personal watchdog. They may help when they see something is wrong, but more likely they may not see it at all because they have their own concerns, or sometimes they do not want to get involved if the risk to their own safety appears to be too great.

Education

Education is a long-term investment in crime prevention and self-defense. However, the function of education is very limited because: 1) some criminals are believed to be influenced by genetic factors and education can do little to change them, 2) the bad influences in the society where people grow up are irreversible, and these bad influences are much stronger than education. That is why the criminals never disappear.

Preparation

Since we have to live with criminals in the same world, we have to be prepared to prevent and deal with them so that we will have less chance of becoming victims. Just like any sport or war, a good preparation is the key to the winning. Without preparation, people put themselves at risk, and furthermore, they tend to feel hopeless and helpless when they are facing the attacks.

Based on the semester survey to university students in each self-defense class taught by the author during the last twelve years, all students indicated that they were more aware of the importance of self-defense, and the mental training changed their life styles to more being safety-oriented, and they indicated that they have reduced their chances of becoming victims. The physical skill training provided students more hands-on experience and self-confidence, and most students indicated that they are not afraid of using skills to defend themselves when attacked.

Brewer (1994) reported that victims indicated that self-defense helped them on all crimes of violence (59.6 percent), rape (63.3 percent), and assault (60.5 percent). However some victims indicated taking self-defense measures made the situation worse on all violent crimes (6.7 percent), rape (7.2 percent), and assault (6.4 percent). Ferguson (1994) indicated that 18 percent of woman said resistance worsened the situation, while 40 percent avoided injury or further injury, 38 percent managed to escape, and 22 percent scared off the attackers.

The Rationales of Self-Defense

Summarizing the above discussion from different perspectives, the following conclusions can be made. These conclusions indicate the rationales of self-defense and self-defense education. It explains why people need self-defense and its education.

1. Crimes of violence are a part of society, and criminals of violent crimes are a part of the human population, no matter whether we like it no not. We have to live with them, and the risk of becoming their victims is a part of our lives.
2. Violent crimes may happen to anyone, anywhere, at anytime, and in any form. Every individual has the risk of becoming a victim at some point during their lifetime. We have to prepare ourselves to prevent and to deal with it if we do not want to become victims.
3. The law enforcement systems cannot protect each individual's life or property effectively. It is the victim's responsibility to learn self-defense in order to protect his/her life, including family and property, against crimes. Thus self-defense is a part of our lives.
4. It is better to be well prepared before crime happens to you or your family. You can avoid being caught in life-threatening situations, feeling hopeless and helpless, or facing the consequence of serious crimes through crime prevention and self-defense. Self-defense education can reduce your chances of becoming a victim.
5. Self-defense is an important life skill. People need academic skills for a good career, well developed language skills for effective communication, and sufficient initiative in order to succeed in daily living. However, people also need to develop essential self-defense skills in order to protect the most important elements of our existence-life itself and property which has been obtained through hard work.
6. Self-defense education, a part of college education for the development of every student as a whole person, plays an important role in ensuring the academic study, career success, and the whole life of university students. Usually self-defense is not taught systematically before college, and it is an important life skill which students can use during their college years and more importantly, during many years after they graduate.

REFERENCES

Bayley, D.H. "Police Functions, Structure and Control in Western Europe and North America" In edited by N. Morris and M. Tony *Crime and Justice: An Annual Review of Research,* Vol. 1, Chicago: University of Chicago Press, 1979.

Brewer, J.D. *The dander from Strangers: Confronting the Threat of Assault.* New York: Insight Books, 1994.

Conklin, J. E. *Criminology,* 4th ed. New York: Macmillan Publishing Company, 1999.

Cox, V. *Guns, Violence, and Teens.* Springfield: Enslow Publishers, 1997.

Donziger S. R. *The Real War on Crime.* New York: Harper Collin Publishers, 1996.

Koss, M. P. et al. "The Scope of Rape: Incidence and Prevalence of Sexual Aggression and Victimization in a National Sample of Higher Education Students," *Journal of Consulting and Clinic Psychology* 55(2), 1987.

Mantice, J. *Bug Off!* Evanston: Walnut Grove Publishers, 1992.

Maslow, A. H. *Motivation and Personality,* 2nd ed. New York: Harper and Row, 1970.

Meadows, R.J. *Understanding Violence and Victimization.* Upper Saddle River: Simon & Schuster/A Viacom Company, 1998.

Meddis, S. V. and R. Davis. "Poll: Get Tougher on Crime." USA Today, October 28, pp1. 1993.

Merier, R. F. *Crime and Society.* Boston: MS: Allyn and Bacon, 1989.

Strong, S. Strong on Defense. New York: Pocket Books, 1996.

Russell, D.E.and R.M. Bolen. *The Epidemic of Rape and Child Sexual Abuse in the United States.* Thousand Oaks: Sage Publishing Inc, 2000.

Snow, R. L. *Protecting Your Life, Home, and Property: A Cop Shows You How.* New York. Plenum Press, 1995

Chapter 3
Crime Process Analysis

This chapter covers discussions on major crimes that self-defense concerns, the facilitating factors of crimes, and trends of crimes. It is essential that readers have a thorough knowledge of these topics so that they will know what they are dealing with in self-defense.

Types of Crimes

There are four major types of crimes based on the criminological analysis (Conklin 1999). The first type is **conventional crimes** which includes two major kinds: **crimes of violence** and **property crimes. Crimes of violence** are further classified as **murder, forcible rape, robbery**, and **assault** (simple assault and aggravated assault). These crimes cause to consequences to the victims physically and emotionally. **Property crimes** can be classified into **burglary, larceny, motor vehicle theft, arson, fraud,** and **vandalism**. These crimes cause consequences to the victims emotionally and financially.

The second type of crime is **white-collar crime.** This type of crime includes four kinds: 1) **Crimes by business** such as deceptive advertising, tax fraud, or bribery; 2) **Crimes by employees against business,** such as employee theft and expense account fraud; 3) **Crimes by government employees,** such as police brutality and bribe-taking by officials; 4) **Crimes by professionals,** such as medical quackery and healthcare fraud. These crimes cause consequences to the victims emotionally and financially.

The third type of crime is **organized crime**. It includes gang activities, terrorism, smuggling of immigrants or firearms, and drug trafficking. These crimes cause consequences to the victims physically, emotionally, and financially.

The fourth type of crime is **victimless crimes**. This type of crime includes drug use, gambling, prostitution, and pornography. These crimes cause consequences to the victims physically, emotionally, and financially. But in these crimes, the victims are the criminals themselves.

Crimes That Self-Defense Concerns

Although most of the crimes mentioned above may happen to potential victims and cause some consequences, the crime of violence resulting in physical injuries is more dangerous to people, and has more severe consequences. Therefore, crimes of violence become a greater concern of people. Some crimes such as burglary and organized crimes may cause physical and emotional damage to victims besides the financial loss.

The crimes self-defense concerns include murder, forcible rape, assault (especially aggravated assault), robbery, organized crimes, and burglary. Murder, forcible rape, and aggravated assault directly cause severe physical and emotional injuries, and therefore they become the major focus of self-defense and its education. Robbery, organized crimes, and burglary are very often associated with murder, aggravated assault, and forcible rape and usually have a severe psychological impact on the victim, although the basic purpose of robbery, organized crimes and burglary is to obtain valuables rather than to cause physical harm.

Very often several crimes are connected together, either because the criminals have multiple purposes when they attack the victim, or they see other opportunities then change their mind during the attack. For example, a victim of rape is often beaten or murdered, a victim of robbery may be murdered or raped during the course of the robbery, and a victim of burglary may be raped or murdered, etcetera.

Major Causes of Crimes

According to criminal statistics and real-life cases, the causes of crimes are significantly different depending on the types of crimes, and individual cases. A survey of 589 convicts indicated that belonging to a gang is the leading cause of crime, just behind drugs and alcohol combined, and unemployment (Snow 1995). Another survey indicated what people thought as the potential causes of crime (Maguire and Pastore 1994). These potential causes include influence of drugs, lack of moral training at home, availability of guns, influence of television violence, absence of father at home, poor quality of schools, lack of good jobs for young people, racism in the society, and decline of religion. Margolis (1997) believed that causes of teen crimes include gang activities, guns, drugs and alcohol, entertainment and media influence, lack of supervision, and minorities in disadvantage. Some believed the causes of crimes include violence on TV, poverty, and loose gun control (Grossman 1998). These results indicated the causes of crimes from a sociological perspective.

There are many reasons which drive the criminals to commit crimes from the individual perspective. Cases and statistics indicated that the individual reasons include the need for money and valuables for survival due to poverty, unemployment, or for support of drug use. Some crimes are triggered by the need to satisfy sexual desires and to control other people. Some people commit crimes due to the anger, hate, jealousy, revenge, retaliation, and discrimination. Some people commit crimes when they are frustrated, hopeless and helpless, and have a lack of self-control. The detailed reasons for committing crimes will be discussed in the next chapter.

Basic Process of Crimes

The crime process is more like a chain with several rings hooked each other. Basically, the criminals follow this basic process or pattern when committing crimes. A brief analysis of this process will help defendants understand the patterns of crimes and to prevent the process by taking away one or more rings from the chain. Any missing link will result in the failure of the crime against a certain victim.

Ring 1: The Criminal

The process starts with the criminals, who are the locomotives of each crime. The process will not exist without them.

Who are the criminals? Is there a profile for the criminals? Criminology experts and police experts have been trying to establish a profile or a model for criminals so that they can be recognized easily by regular people for prevention purposes and by police for solving the crime cases. But so far this effort is not successful, since criminals do not wear labels or identify themselves, and they do not look like the bad guys that audiences can recognize easily in movies. Actually, they often cover themselves very well and look just like common people. They look nice, well-mannered, and helpful in order to be trusted by their prey. They blend into the surroundings just like chameleons and they hide in the crowd without any clues and catch the victims off guard. It is very difficult to recognize potential attackers, and this is the greatest disadvantage for all self-defenders. Conversely, the attackers know where the victims are, as well as when and where and how they are going to engage in the attack.

The only exception is probably the pickpocket. In an interview by the author with police officers in China in 2000, police officers indicated that experienced police there usually have the ability to recognize the thieves conducting pickpocket in shopping malls, stores, and on the street. The basic clue is the thieves' eyes and their behaviors. Criminals' eyes move faster, very often, in different directions, and focus on people's purses and pockets. Their behaviors also have some patterns. In 2001, a magazine photographer in China, with the help of the police, caught many thieves in the camera and displayed in the public to warm people the tricks of thieves (Wang 2001).

The following discussion will analyze the criminal from several viewpoints to help students understand these potential crimes. Criminologists and police officers suggested several clues to help identify some potential criminals. These clues include people with criminal records, unemployed people, and people who tend to act impulsively.

Relationship with the victims

The relationship between the criminal and victim ranges from family members to total strangers, and different types of crimes have different patterns. Murder used to be common among family members, yet since the 1990s it is more likely that the victims will be killed by both people they know and strangers. Rape is committed about 50 percent of the time by strangers and about 50 percent of the time by acquaintances. Assault is committed by both, but less often by strangers and more commonly by acquaintances. Most robberies involve strangers since criminals feel that they have less chance of being recognized when robbing someone they do not know. About 40 percent burglaries were committed by people victims knew.

Gender of the criminals

Although criminals include both genders, males commit a greater percentage of the five major categories of crime. Based on recent statistics, males committed about 90.5 percent of the murders (based on the arrested rate), 98.8 percent of the forcible rapes, 90.7 percent of the robberies, 82.3 percent of the aggravated assaults, 88.9 percent of the burglaries, 66.7 percent of theft, 86.9 percent of motor theft, and 84.3 percent of arson (Conklin 1999).

Race of criminals

Criminals include all racial groups in this country, even though some groups show a relatively high rate of arrest. All groups of criminals have a tendency to commit crimes against victims of the same race. This is especially true in most murders and rapes.

Age of criminals

The existing cases indicate that ages of criminals range from as young as ten years old to eighty years of age. But most of the criminals are between the ages of sixteen and thirty four.

Social status of criminals

Criminals typically show various socioeconomic statuses, ranging from the poor to the very rich. However, there seems to be a slightly greater number of criminals from the poor segments of our society than those from the middle or upper classes.

Criminals can be classified into two categories from the self-defense perspective. The first type is the normal criminals. They either learned or were born to commit crimes. The second type is the regular people converted into criminals due to some circumstances. Most people have both the good and bad features in their mind. In normal circumstances, the good features take the control of the behaviors due to moral, educational, and the law enforcement considerations. But in some situations, the bad features take over the control, and then normal people can become criminals and commit crimes by surprise. For example, a good man may commit a rape when he sees an opportunity, and an argument can lead good people on both sides into a fight or murder.

Ring 2: The Crimes, Motives, and Triggering Factors

The second part of this chain is what the criminals want to do to the victims and their motives to commit such crimes. Crimes are their actions, motives are their main drives for the criminals to commit such crimes, and the triggering factors are the incidents which directly trigger the criminal's motives to commit crimes.

Actions

What the criminals want to do include murder, rape, robbery, assault, burglary, organized crimes, and combinations of any above crimes. These crimes can be divided into three types: hate oriented, money oriented, or sex oriented, and combinations of these three.

Triggering Factors

There are many reasons which stimulate the criminals to commit crimes. Current cases indicate a list of direct triggering factors for various crimes. These reasons include, but are not limited to, opportunity, loss of jobs, financial hardship, road rage, or arguments over small things.

These causes explain the various reasons criminals commit crimes from biological, psychological, socioeconomic, and spiritual perspectives. But the major motivations behind crime can be summarized into two types: the desire for valuables and hate.

Major Motives

Motive is a very important factor in crime prevention and self-defense. Generally speaking, every crime is committed because there is a motive behind it, and every criminal attacks the victim with one or more motives. Analysis of the major motives of criminals can help us have a better understanding of these criminals, and therefore learn how to prevent crime more effectively.

1. Strong desire for valuables. Valuables include money, materials, and the human body. This motive explains most robbery and burglary, as well as a certain percentage of rape cases (as well as larceny, white-collar crimes, most organized crimes, and victimless crime). This desire may arise for different reasons, such as greed for valuables, psychological satisfaction, survival, unemployment, or poverty. The triggering factors include seeing unguarded property, carelessness of the victims, or seeing other opportunities.

2. Hate oriented: This motive explains most of the murders and assaults, as well as a certain percentage of rape cases (also arson, vandalism, and some organized crimes). This motive may arise from different triggering factors: arguments, jealousy, mistreatment, psychological damage, suspicion, anger, humiliation, revenge, frustration, depression, competition, misunderstandings, sadness, discrimination, or the result of being bullied and rejected. Sometimes the criminal initiates the crime, and at other times it is the victim who starts the trouble. For example, tail-gating or treating other people badly may result in hate and a need for revenge.

Besides the above major motives, there are other minor motives which do not belong to the two major categories. Insecurity is a motive of crimes, and insecurity can be caused by being threatened by someone, being in another person's way (such as a drug smuggler), or when you are a witness to a crime. This motive explains some gang activities, organized crimes, and most murders committed by women. Inner satisfaction is another motive; seeking power or control is a good example of this motivation. This motive explains some cases of murder, assault, rape, and bullying.

Ring 3: Targets of Crimes—The Victims

The third section of the link is the target of the criminals. All criminal actions will fall onto some-one as the targeted victims. Although theoretically and practically everyone has the risk of becoming a victim of crimes, some individuals will have a greater chance, while others will have less chance. The chance of becoming a potential victim depends on many factors or combinations of these factors.

A. FACTORS OF VICTIMIZATION

Gender

There are some misunderstandings about self-defense. Very often people think that self-defense is just for women because women physically are weak in comparison to men. There are many self-defense courses entitled "self-defense for women" nationwide, but there is not a single course designed just for men. Actually males and females both have chances of becoming victims of violent crimes. Although women have a greater risk of becoming victims of rape, men more often than women become victims of murders. In 2001 for example, 10,503 men as apposed to only 3,214 women were murdered. Therefore, everyone needs self-defense, not only for themselves but possibly also for their children. For example, a father without self-defense training takes his eleven-year-old daughter on a hiking trip, and they are confronted by two criminals who want to rape the daughter. The father is in trouble because he can not flee and leave his daughter to these attackers, but he cannot win the battle and protect his daughter either, since he does not have necessary skills or strategies.

Age

Many people believe that older people have a greater chance of becoming victims of violent crime than young people. Actually, it is not true. For example, in the San Jose area in the 1990s, the youngest victim of rape was 3 months old and the oldest was 86 years old. The statistics indicated that people from 16 to 44 are at a higher risk than older individuals, but the range of victims was so broad that it covered almost any age.

Socioeconomic Status

People of different social status may have different chances of becoming a victim, and they may become victims of different types of crimes. Rich people may have a greater chance of robbery, while poor people may become victims of rape and assault. People working at retail stores at night may be at a greater risk of being robbed than people working during the daytime, and people whose work is related to encountering gang problems are at a greater risk than people working with computers.

Race

All different kinds of people became victims of crime, regardless of their ethnic background. The victims of crime include Whites, Blacks, Hispanics, Asians, or Native Americans. In other words, people of any race have a chance of becoming victims, although the crimes they face might be different. For example, Asians often become victims of burglary because criminals know they tend to hide their cash in the house; often the criminals have a clue that Asians tend to leave their shoes outside of the door when they are home, and it is easy for the criminals to identify if the house is empty or not. White women have the most chance of becoming rape victims.

Preparation

People who are prepared in crime prevention and self-defense have less chance of becoming victims than people who are not prepared. For example, a house equipped with an alarm and a big dog is less likely to be a target because it is sets up a strong deterrence to the criminals. People who have training on rape prevention will not put themselves in bad situations easily, and people with combative skill training will have more chance of getting away safely when attacked. Sometimes a person who has learned self-defense may also become a victim, but the chance is much less.

Physical Appearance

Physical appearance is a factor in victimization. Usually criminals tend to pick up vulnerable victims so that they will get what they want fast and safely without much resistance and risk. Therefore people who are not tall and strong tend to be chosen as the targets. The most obvious example will be bullied victims in schools. However, tall and strong people might have chances too, especially when they have the stuff the criminals want or the criminals really want to revenge. In these kinds of situations, strong appearance can only make the criminals use more violence and attack harder.

Life-style

Lifestyle plays a very importance role in victimization. People who are cautious about their safety and always do things in a safe way obviously have less chance than people who do not care much about self-defense. For example, people who have bad tempers and always create enemies will have more chance to become victims of murder and assault. Women who go to parties often and drink too much there become victims of rape easily. A manager who tends to treat his subordinates in a nasty way sure makes people hate him, and thus creates enemies easily.

B. How Vctims Are Selected

Most of the time, criminals pick their targets with specific purposes and criteria. Their criteria for choosing victims include one or more of the following elements.

1. Victims who possess two types of things the attacker desires. One type of thing is money, valuables, and other material things. People who have these things often become victims of robbery and burglary. The second type of thing is the physical body of the targets, especially women. These people often become the victims of rape. Men-especially white men-tend to become victims of rapes when they end up in jails for some reasons. As discussed before, this is one of the two major motives which trigger the criminals to commit crimes.

2. Victims whom the attackers hate and want to do something bad to. The hate can be triggered by criminals, such as discrimination against someone, or the victim might be in the way of doing things. The hate also can be triggered by the victim usually called precipitation, such as the husband threatens to kill the wife, and the wife has to kill the husband first as a self-defense. Sometime people bully the victims to a degree that the victims have to kill the bully for self-protection. About 25 percent of murders were victim-precipitated (Curtis 1974) and 38 percent in part by the victim (Voss and Hepburn 1968). Sometimes the victims are just scapegoats, for example, the victims belong to a certain race or an opposite gang. These victims tend to become victims of murder, assault, rape, family violence, and arson.

3. The vulnerability of victims. The vulnerable victim is more likely to become the target of crimes because it is much easier to attack a vulnerable person than someone who appears to be tough and assertive, and the criminals will face less risk of strong resistance. The vulnerability includes several aspects. Physical appearance is the first feature attackers will look for. Women and petite people often appear to be easy targets. The second feature the attackers look for is the preparedness of the victims. People who are unprepared can easily become victims. For example, a house with a security alarm and a dog has less chance of becoming a target of burglary than a house without them. The third feature is the location and timing where criminals have more advantage and less risk of being caught.

Each individual has different kinds of vulnerability, depending on gender, age, where he/she lives, and what he/she does. For example, high risk rape victims are university fresh-women, junior and senior high school girls, and young women alone. Lindquist (2000) listed factors that make a woman vulnerable to date rape. The list included a false sense of security, a false sense of intimacy, misleading appearance, drinking or taking drugs, allowing herself to become isolated, ignoring warning signals, and her inner guidance.

4. Random victims. Sometime the victims are not pre-selected. They are simply just randomly picked because the victim happens to be at the wrong place at the wrong time. One typical example is the passengers of the airplanes in the 911 hijacking and bombing in New York in 2001. Another example is victims of the school shooting in Columbine High School in 1999.

5. Victims may facilitate their own victimization through their behavior. Examples include visiting places where there are gangs and drug problems or taking risky activities such as hitchhiking, using or selling drugs, or prostituting (Meadows 1998).

Ring 4. Locations

The fourth section of the link is the locations of the crime—the spatial factor of the crime process. When criminals commit crimes, they tend to find appropriate places where they can approach victims easily and escape fast, where police are not present, help to the victims is less possible, the victims are more vulnerable.

Crimes may occur practically anywhere the victim is. Criminals can find the potential victims in their homes, schools, workplaces, parking lots, banks, shops, hospitals, recreational areas, restaurants, hotels, elevators, and on the transportation which connects these locations. But at some locations the chances are much less than at other locations. For example, houses in a good neighborhood usually have much less chance of burglary than houses in the downtown area of big cities. A woman is less likely to be robbed when working in daylight and at a crowed place than a woman who works alone during the night. On the other hand, however, larceny and purse/jewelry snatching tend to occur in crowded places where the criminals can hide in the crowd, approach targets easily and escape easily. Terrorist attacks also are more likely occur in crowded places.

Ring 5. The Timing of the Crime: The Temporal Factor

The fifth section of the process is the timing of the crimes, often referred to as the temporal factor. Crimes may occur at anytime of day and on any dates. The crime reports indicate that there is no significant difference in the crime rate on the dates of the year except burglary in the summer is little higher than winter time. However, in terms of the hours in a day, there is significant difference between daytime and evening time. There is relatively less chance of crime in broad daylight than the evening and night. Criminals like the darkness because it is easier to commit crimes, and there is less chance of being caught or identified. Parties and dates provide the opportunity for more rape crimes than other times. The times you are alone on the street represent a far greater chance of crime than when you stay with a group of people. At times when you are more prepared and aware there will be fewer opportunities for crimes to occur.

The temporal factor is often associated with the spatial factor and other factors. For example, a woman jogging in an isolated area in daylight may have a chance of being attacked. Some burglars like to visit houses at daylight when everyone is out for work or school and the house is empty. Terrorism attacks often take place in daytime and in crowed areas too.

Ring 6. Methods and Tricks of the Crimes

The sixth section of the process is the methods of the crimes. Criminals are very smart, and they know how to use tricks to make their acts effective and to have less chance of being identified and caught. The violence levels are different depending on the situations.

LEVELS OF ATTACKS

Crimes occur to victims at different levels. The intensity of crime may range from severe to moderate to mild: severe crimes include murder, rape, robbery, and aggravated assault; moderate crimes are such things as burglary, arson, and simple assault; and mild crimes include instances such as bullying or pick-pocketing. Brewer (1994), an experienced victimologist and self-defense consultant, brought up a four-level model of attack: the verbal insult, the threat, the physical beating, and the kill. The physical injuries caused by crimes can range from death, severe injury or disability, to minor injury. The psychological and emotional damage can range from short time to lifetime, and from mild and severe. The different types of crimes can involve the use of a gun, knife, and other weapons, or a barehanded attack.

THE METHODS OF ATTACKS IN CRIMES

Real life cases have shown that criminals used many different methods and tricks in committing crimes. Some methods and tricks are well known and some are new, and criminals will surely develop more and more new tricks as people become aware of their old methods and take precautions. These methods and tricks used by criminals in many cases can be classified into several types.

1. Sudden attacks: This kind of attack occurs suddenly, fast, and by surprise, and it gives victims no time to prepare and react. Examples include street robbery and parking lot robbery and rapes at isolated places and in victim houses during a burglary. One recent case indicated this type of trick. A woman was sitting in the car reading newspaper at Marina Food in Cupertino in California. A man suddenly opened her door and grabbed her purse then ran away before the lady realized what happened at a place which usually is safe (Channel 26 News, April 29, 2002). A woman at a clothing store got into the elevator with a lone man. He suddenly pushed the stop button and raped her, then threatened her with a gun not to tell (Snow 1995). A Chinese engineer was walking on the street at 11 pm in Detroit when an attacker walked by and suddenly stabbed the victim to death and ran away with his wallet in 1999. Another case is that a woman opened the door and stepped into her house. But the attacker who hid behind the bush suddenly jumped out and pushed her in. A couple years ago in San Jose, California, a girl walking to school in the morning was suddenly dragged into a van by two men and raped.

2. Out-power the victims: Another method used by criminals is to scare and out-power the victims so that the victims will cooperate instead of resist. It is very difficult to deal with armed attackers and multiple attackers, even for martial arts experts. A formal karate champion got into a fight with two armed men in a bar in California in the 1980s. The karate man gave the two guys a good lesson while his stomach was cut open; he was totally disabled. The major out-power methods include out-powering victims by using weapons, especially guns and knives, or outnumbering the victim with more attackers. The attackers obviously have more advantages when they have weapons and more people and preparation. The robbers in the United States tend to use weapons while robbers in China tend to outnumber the victim, even though they use non-firearms as well.

3. Use tricks: Another type of common method or strategy used by criminals is to use a variety of tricks to set up the scene then attack. One type of trick is abusing the sympathy of people. Examples include pretending to be sick or injured, such as using a cast or crutch to get help then attack the helper, carrying a baby and saying their car is broken and asking for a ride, pretending to have a flat tire and requesting to use your phone in your house, or faking to have heels caught an the elevator and snatching your wallet.

Another type of tricks is to dress up decent and trustworthy so that they can approach victims with ease. Examples include pretending to ask for directions when you are in the car or in the house and then robbing you, pretending that they are salesperson, repair person, or asking for fictitious people to get you open the door for them; dressing up like a police man to stop your car or get into your house; dressing up like pretty girls to attract victims; or calling you to a place while they burglarize your house. They may respond to your lost and found advertisement and trick you.

The third type of trick is to distract your attention while committing crimes. For example, one punk bumps into you purposely and drops his books and another snatches your purse or wallet while you are helping pick up the books. It is probable that one gigolo asks for directions and another snatches your purse from the passenger side of your car. One case indicated that the attacker was talking to the victim while the attacker's partner hit the victim with a baseball bat.

The fourth type of tricks is to create obstacles to force the victims to stop and step out to an open place where the attackers can approach the victims with ease. One trick is that the attacker drives in front of the victim and stops suddenly to cause accidents, most victims have to step out and deal with that. A similar trick is to bump the victim's back bumper in an isolated place to get the victim out to exchange the insurance information. Another way to stop the victim is to place a rock or a tree, or dig a hole in the road to force the victims out. This happened very often in China in recent years.

Another type of trick is to pretend to help people when they are in need, then attack them. When Terry Chateen's car broke down, a stranger named Steven Judy convinced her that there was no way he could fix the car and then gave her a ride to a creek bank, raped and murdered her, and then tossed her three children into the river and drowned them (Snow 1995).

Another trick criminals use is to fool the victims with promises. This way the victim falls into the trap step-by-step and victims usually lose their last chance to get out or fight out when they find out the criminals are cheating them. A perfect example is the 911 hijacking and bombing in New York. The hijackers fooled people to believe that there would not be any danger if they cooperated, just like the traditional hijacking, until the airplanes crashed in to the buildings.

One type of trick involves the use of substance to make victims lose their ability to control the situation. This is especially true in rape situations in the United States. The attackers like to trick women to over drink, use drugs, to put date rape drugs into their drinks. But in China now a days, drugs are often put into drinks on trains and criminals rob the victims easily this way. The police on duty have to warn passengers about the danger on all trains. In many murder situations, these types of drugs are used often too.

Using threat or harassment is one way to trick the victims. Extortion is a typical way to rip off small businesses. Threatening to give people a shot with the AIDS virus is now one way to get money from people on street in China. This type of tricks is common in school bullies.

Facilitating Factors of Crimes

Besides the basic process of the crimes, there are three facilitating factors which are often associated with these crimes. These factors have different functions of initiating or facilitating the crime process.

Alcohol

Alcohol presents in 1/3 to 2/3 of all murders and in 40 percent of sex offenses (Greenberg 1981). Another survey of homicides indicated 47 percent of victims and 64 percent of defendants used alcohol (Dawson and Langan 1994). Alcohol reduces inhibitions and triggers crime behaviors easily. Alcohol also reduces anxiety in criminals and builds up courage and a concept that how drank people can behave. Alcohol also throws victims off-guard psychologically and loses their consciousness and physical ability to resist the criminals (Conklin 1999).

Drugs

Drugs are associated with all crimes of violence. On the criminal's side, drugs make them lose consciousness and self-control ability and drug use also increases their need for more money since drugs are expensive. On the victim's side, using drugs throw them off-guard psychologically and lose their consciousness and physical ability to resist the criminals Research indicated that more than 75 percent of robbers are drug addicts who need money for their drug supplies (Snow 1995). But they only got an average $80 per robbery, therefore they need to commit more robberies, otherwise they could not behave the normal ways.

Firearms

Firearms are considered as the most important factor in facilitating crimes. Criminals with firearms are most dangerous and frightening to the victims, and thus make the crime process easier and lessen resistance. Firearms are legal and easy to obtain in the United States. Conklin (1999) indicated that there are 200 million firearms in the U.S. in private hands, 1/3 are handguns, and 40 percent of families have one or more guns. About 86 percent male in juvenile correction facilities and 30 percent high school students owned guns while gangs and drug dealers tend to carry guns. Compared to other countries where guns are illegal for the public, the United States has the highest percentage of gun murders in the world. According to Herbert (1994), the numbers of handgun murders in 1992 were 12 in Australia, 33 in Great Britain, 36 in Sweden, 60 in Japan, 91 in Switzerland, 128 in Canada, but 13,220 in the United States. The fatal injuries in assaults also indicated that the gun was leading with13 percent while knife assaults accounted for 3 percent and 1.7 percent with body parts. Firearms also lead to death 2-5 times more than knife in assaults.

Firearms were also used by defendants in self-defense. The victimization data indicated 55,000 cases each year, while a survey indicated 1.5-2.1 million each year with 3/4 occurring in/near victims' homes against burglary, robbery and assault, and in 1/4 of these cases, guns were actually fired. On the other hand, there are problems with using guns for self-defense. Most people cannot carry guns with them since it is illegal, and they do not want to violate the law while criminals can do anything they want. Furthermore, guns are often stolen by burglars, and having firearms at home causes more shooting or accidents at home. For example, a 14-year-old girl in Louisiana in 1994 was shot by her father when she jumped out from a closet to welcome her parent coming home at 1:00 pm.

Watching Crimes

Since the 1990s, crimes have shown several trends. Some trends lasted for a short time and some lasted long-term. The trends of crimes change over times. In the late 1990s, school shooting became a trend, and the beginning of the 2000s, it started with needle shots, which are becoming popular in China after one year, and followed with terrorism attacks. The trend now is terrorism across the world. It is important to watch these trends and to be aware of their significance and to be prepared.

The trends of crimes include, but are not limited to, the following aspects: 1) Crimes committed by youth. More and more crimes were committed by teenagers and some murders were even committed by children as young as ten years of age (Conklin 1999). 2) Carjacking. It is more dangerous than ever before when people are waiting for traffic signals, or waiting for help when their cars have broken down, or when getting in or out of their car at parking lots. 3) Crimes involving the use of firearms. It was estimated that there are 200 million guns in the United States, averaging one gun per person, and the use of guns is out of control. More and more crimes now involve weapons, either to make the crimes easier to commit or to eliminate witnesses. 4) Gang-related crimes. There are more gangs on the street, and they commit more crimes than ever before. These gangs are dangerous because they are often cold-blooded, use deadly weapons, and overwhelming group force is utilized to deal with the victim. These gangs can be drug related or race related, with race related gangs developing rapidly in this country during the last several decades. Gangs are operating in 94 percent of American cities and are spreading from large or medium cities to small towns. 5) Crimes at the workplace. There have been cases involving teachers and professors shot by students, managers killed by former employees, and people robbed at convenience stores. Workplace crimes have countered 1/6 of violent crimes in the United States and have become a top health-threatening factor in the workplace. 6) Hate crimes. Hate is a very important motivation in committing crime and it can get out of control easily. The number of hate related crimes is increasing due to many factors, such as increased population which results in limited job opportunities and resources, extreme stress created both at the workplace and in other life experiences, unfairness in society, and racial conflicts, etc.. 7) Terrorism. Since the 911 hijacking and bombing in New York in 2001, the threat of terrorism attacks has been increasing and has caused tremendous fear among people in the world. The danger and potential damages of terrorism attacks can be very severe due to the fact that the targets of terrorism attacks are all vulnerable and it is almost impossible to safely guard all of these places.

REFERENCES

Brantingham, P., and P. Brintingham. *Patterns in Crime.* New York: Macmillan Publishing Company, 1984.

Brewer, J.D. *The Dander from Strangers: Confronting the Threat of Assault.* New York: Insight Books, 1994.

Conklin, J. E. New Perspectives in Criminology. Boston: Allyn and Bacon, 1996.

Conklin, J. E. *Criminology* (6th ed.). MA: Needham Heights: Allyn and Bacon, 1999.

Curtis, L. A. *Criminal Violence: National Patterns and Behavior.* Lexington: D.C. Health, 1974.

Dawson, J. M., and P. A. Langan. *Murder in Families.* Washington D.C.: U.S. Department of Justice, July 1994.

Donziger S. R. *The Real War on Crime.* New York: Harper Collin Publishers, 1996.

Ellis, L. *Theories of Rape.* New York: Hemisphere Publishing Corporation, 1989.

Federal Bureau of Investigation Uniform Crime Report. Crime in the United States. U.S. Department of Justice, Washington, D.C., 1996.

Federal Bureau of Investigation Uniform Crime Report. Crime in the United States. U.S. Department of Justice, Washington, D.C., 1999.

Feldman, P. *The Psychology of Crime.* New York: Cambridge University Press, 1993.

Fike, R. A. *Staying Alive: Your Crime Prevention Guide.* Washington, DC: Acropolis Books. 1994.

Flowers, R. B. *Sex Crimes, Predators, Perpetrators, Prostitutes, and Victims.* Springfield: Charles Thomas Publisher, 2001.

Gelles, R. *Through a Sociological Lens: Social Structure and Family Violence.* Newbury Park: Sage, 1993.

Gong, A. X. *Underground Society in China.* China: Changchu, China: Shenhua Publisher, v302, pp6. 2001.

Greenberg, S.W. "Alcohol and Crime: A Methodological Critique of the Literature." In edited by James Collins, *Drinking and Crime.* New York: Guilford Press, 1981.

Grossman, D. "Trained to Kill." *Christianity Today.* August 10, 1998.

Herbert, B. "Guns In America: Deadly Data on Handguns." *New York Times*, March 2, 1994. p.A15.

Hickey, E. W. *Serial Murders and Their Victims.* CA: Wadsworth, 1997.

Jankowski, M. S. *Islands in the Street: Gangs and American Urban Society.* Berkeley: University of California Press, 1991.

Kenney, D.J., and J. O. Finckenauer. *Organized Crime in America.* Belmont: Wadsworth, 1995

Kushner, H. W. *Terrorism in America.* Springfield: Charles Thomas Publisher, 1998.

Lindquist, S. *The Date Rape Prevention Book.* Naperville: Sourcebook, 2000.

Levin, J., and J. McDevitt. *Hate Crimes.* New York: Plenum Press, 1993.

Maguire, K., and A.L. Pastore. *Sourcebook of Criminal Justice Statistics.* Washington D.C.: 1994.

Mann, C. R. *How Women Kill.* Albany: State University of New York Press, 1996.

Mantice, J. *Bug off!* Evanston: Walnut Grove Publishers, 1992.

Margolis, J. A. *Teen Crime Wave: A Growing Problem* Springfield. Enslow Publishers, 1997

Meadows, R. J. *Understanding Violence and Victimization.* Upper Saddle River: Simon & Schuster/A Viacom Company, 1998.

Merier, R. F. *Crime and Society.* Boston: Allyn and Bacon, 1989.

Miller, M. Copying with Weapons and Violence in School and on Your Street. New York: The Rosen Publishing Group, 1999.

Miller, M., and J. File. *Terrorism Factbook.* Peoria: Bollix Books, 2001.

Mount Auburn Hospital Prevention and Training center in Waltham and the Dating Violence Project. Cambridge, MA: Author, 1995.

"Report Cites Heavy Toll of Rapes on Young." New York Times. June 23, 1994.

Rand, M. *"Carjacking: A National Victimization Study."* Washington D.C.: Bureau of Justice Statistics, Department of Justice, 1994.

Rand, M. *Criminal Victimization in the United States.* Washington D.C.: Bureau of Justice Statistics, Department of Justice, 1997.

Reppetto, T.A. *Residential Crime.* Cambridge: Ballinger, pp16, 105, 1974.

Russell, D. E., and R. M. Bolen. *The Epidemic of Rape and Child Sexual Abuse in the United States.* Thousand Oaks: Sage Publishing Inc, 2000.

San Jose Police Record. San Jose, CA, 1994

Sanders, W. B. *Gangbangs and Drive-Bys: Grounded Culture and Juvenile Gang Violence.* New York: Adline de Gruyter, 1994

Skorneck, C. "683,000 Women Raped in 1990, New Government Study Finds." Boston Globe, April 24, 1992.

Snow, R. L. *Protecting Your Life, Home, and Property: A Cop Shows You How.* New York. Plenum Press, 1995.

Timrod, A.D., and M. R. Rand. *Violent Crimes by Strangers and Nonstrangers.* Washington D.C.: U.S. Department of Justice, 1987.

Voss, H.L. and Hepburn, J. R. "Patterns in Criminal Homicide in Chicago." *Journal of Criminal Law, Criminology, and Police Science, 59, 499–508, 1968.*

Wang, Y. D. "Photographer Caught Pocket-Lifters on Photos." *Youth Generation,* November, 2001.

Wolff, L. Gangs. San Diego: Lucent Book, 2000.

Chapter 4
Different Crimes and Characteristics

This chapter provides students with detailed discussion on characteristics of each major crime of violence self-defense targets. Like preparing for wars or sport games, a thorough understanding of the crime process gives defendants a greater advantage for winning. As a very famous Chinese military principle puts it: You have no chance of winning if you do not know either your opponent or yourself; you have only 50 percent chance of winning if you know one side (yourself or opponent); but you will have 100 percent chance of winning if you know both your opponent and yourself. The prevention strategies and principles are developed based on the detailed analysis of the process.

Crimes of Violence

Murder

Facts

Murder is the willful killing of a human being. There are three types of murder: single, serial, and mass murder. According to the newest report, 15,980 people were murdered in the United States in 2001, and the number of murder cases remains about the same every year. Murders account for 1.1 percent of all violent crimes. Even though there is always harsh penalties and less chance to get away (murder has the highest solution rate of all crimes), people still commit murders (Snow 1995). The consequences of a murder include the victim's life, the psychological influences (pain and emotional trauma) to the victim's family, and the financial cost to the victim's family and the government. The average cost per murder is $2,940,000 for medical expenses, funeral costs, lost productivity, and welfare or social security to the survivors (Conklin 1999)

Relationship of Offenders and Victims

Murders involve offenders and victims of any race, but typically victims tend to be murdered by offenders of the same race. According to the 2001 Uniform Crime Report, about 84 percent of the white victims were murdered by white offenders and 13 percent by black offenders, while about 91 percent black victims were murdered by black offenders and about 6 percent by white offenders.

The offenders of murders involve both males and females. According to the 2001 Uniform Crime Report, about 87 percent male victims were murdered by male offenders and about 10 percent were murdered by female offenders, while 9 percent of female victims were murdered by female offenders and 90 percent were murdered by male offenders.

Murder victims were killed by both somebody they knew and strangers. A study (Dawson and Lagan 1994) indicated that 64 percent of the victims were killed by friends or acquaintances, 15 percent by family members, and 20 percent by strangers. Statistics indicated that 1.3 percent of all homicides involved husbands murdered by wives, and 3.7 percent involved husbands killing their wives (1996 Uniform Crime Report).

Victim Profile

About 76 percent of murder victims were males and 24 percent were females in 2001. About 49 percent of murder victims were white, 47 percent were black, 3 percent were other races, and 1 percent unknown. Ages of murder victims range from infants to 75-year-olds and above. Among the victims, 17.3 percent were 1–19 years old, 53.1 percent were 20–39, 19.9 percent were 40–59, and 6.4 percent were 60 years old and above.

Hickey (1997) listed strangers sought as victims by serial murders in rank order. The potential victims include young women, especially college students and prostitutes, boys and girls, travelers, people at home, hospital patients, business people including store owners and landlords, people walking on street, older women alone, police officers, employees, people responding to newspaper ads, and people of a race being hated.

Offender Profile

About 90 percent of murders were committed by male offenders, among them, 33 percent were white, 36 percent were black, 2 percent were other races, and 29 percent unknown. The ages of murderers ranged from 5 to 73 years old. Among them, 17.6 percent were 5–19 years old, 42.9 percent were 20–39 years old, 10.8 percent were 40–59 years old, and 2 percent were 60 years old and above.

About 10 percent of murders were committed by females. According to Mann (1996), 75 percent of female murderers were black, 13 percent were white, and 10 percent were Latino. The ages of female killers ranged from 12 to 65 years old, with an average of 31 years old. About 60 percent of female killers were married, 70 percent were mothers, most of them received education less than 11 years, many were unemployed, and 50 percent were arrested for violent crimes before the murder.

Snow (1995) provided warning signs of murder and assaults. These clues include gradually accumulated feelings of hatred and people who react to little things with sudden, violent, and irrational outbursts.

Causes of Murder

According to the 2001 Uniform Crime Report, the following circumstances indicated related causes and reasons for murder in the United States.

27.2%	argument
7.6%	robbery
7.0%	gangland and juvenile gang killing
4.9%	drugs
1.1%	alcohol brawl
0.9%	romantic triangle
0.9%	narcotics brawl
0.5%	burglary
0.4%	rape and other sexual offenses
0.5%	arson
0.3%	baby sitting
0.1%	theft
0.1%	auto theft
0.09%	institutional killing
0.06%	prostitution
0.03%	sniper attack
32.0%	unknown but possibly including all above reasons and other possible reasons:

Victims will be a witness for a trial.

Attackers are in need of victim's place or I.D.

Victims are in the way for competitions.

Victims are just scapegoats.

Attackers kill for life insurance payment.
Attackers want to be famous and attract attention.
Victims are threatened by someone.
Attackers hate the society.

The above statistics indicated several main causes of general murders. Argument is the leading cause, robbery is the second reason, gang-related activities takes third place, and substance related causes are the fourth main reason.

The causes of female killing were 49 percent argument or fight oriented, 19 percent emotionally oriented, and 11 percent economically oriented. On the other hand, these female murderers indicate 39 percent of their murders occurred when they were in self-defense, 15 percent of the time they were innocent, 12 percent of the killing were accidents, and 11 percent were emotional conduct.

Weapons Used in Murder

According to the 2001 Uniform Crime Report, these following weapons were used in murder cases. This also indicated the murders' methods of attack.

63.4%	were using guns
13.1%	by knives
6.7%	by body weapons
16.8%	by other weapons
4.6%	by blunt objects
1.4%	by strangulation
0.9%	by fire
0.6%	by asphyxiation
0.2%	by drowning
0.2%	by narcotics
0.05%	by explosives
0.04%	by poison

Forcible Rape

Facts

Forcible rape mainly means forcing a female into sexual activity against her will. Rapes are committed by both strangers and acquaintances. There were 90,491 forcible rapes reported in the United States in 2001, and this number accounts for 6.3 percent of the violent crimes. However, the actual number of rapes should be three times higher according to a survey (Conklin 1999). In another study (Russell and Bolen 2000), however, only 9.5 percent of the rape victims (64 out of 672) reported to the police. That means the actual number of the rapes could be three to nine times higher.

Forcible rape can also cause severe damages to the victims. It causes pain and injuries, and may transfer diseases—even AIDS—to the victim. Many victims were beaten up and some were even killed during the crime, and about 40 percent of the victims suffered serious injuries. Rape can cause long-term psychological and emotional damages to the victims. Rapes also result in financial loss to victims, and it was estimated that a rape or sexual assault will cost $86,500 per victim.

Characteristics of Different Rapes

Some forcible rapes occur spontaneously, but most (about 75 percent) are planned. Flowers (2001) summarized characteristics of forcible rapes. He indicated that alcohol is the most prominent factor in forcible rapes, offenders and victims generally reside in the same neighborhood, 60 percent of rapes occur in a residence, and 90 percent of the victims and offenders are the same race. About 89 percent of rapes involve in the use of force, and 12 percent involve the use of a gun or knife.

Flowers (2001) also summarized characteristics of date rapes. He indicated that as much as 50 percent of victims are sexually assaulted by the first date, casual date, and romantic acquaintance date. Most victims are single females, 15–25 years old. The scary thing is that most victims do not take measures to protect themselves.

Flowers also provided some information about college date rapes. About 86 percent of college date rapes occur off campus, and 95 percent of rapists were single offenders. Alcohol and drug are two main facilitating factors in date rapes. About 73 percent of offenders used alcohol or drugs in the date rapes, while 55 percent of the victims used alcohol or drugs. About 42 percent of victims never reported, 42 percent of victims will have sex again with the offender, and 41 percent of victims expect to experience similar type of rape. About 20 percent of college students become victims of date rapes.

Acquaintance rapes have a similar pattern. About 50 percent of the rapists are well known by the victims, and casual acquaintances account for 40 percent of the rapes. Almost all rapes are committed by a single offender. Again, acquaintance rape victims are less likely to take self-protection.

Relationship of Offenders and Victims

The percentages of rapes vary from 22 percent to 53 percent by strangers, based on different studies. According to a survey (Skorneck 1992), about 22 percent of rape victims were attacked by strangers, while 29 percent by someone they knew and 46 percent by relatives, ex-husbands, or boyfriends. Girls under 12 are usually raped by family members and acquaintances, and 90 percent of them know their rapists. The chance of being raped by strangers increases as the victim's age increases (*New York Time* June 23, 1994).

Rapists and Their Motives

Why do rape offenders commit this crime? Researchers have identified more than fifty types of rapists, but different researchers summarized them into different categories. Flowers (2001) listed the following types in his book.

Gebhard's 6-type Model

1) Assaulting rapist—the most common type, characterized by sadistic and hostile feelings toward women. 2) Amoral delinquents—second common type. The attackers desire to have sex, regardless of victims' wishes. 3) Drunken Variety—as common as amoral delinquents. 4) Explosive variety—no history of rape but psychotic-oriented. 5) Double standard variety—dividing women into good and bad groups and treat the "bad" women with no respect. 6) Other types—a mixture.

Rata's 5-type Model

1) Psychotic rapists—usually psychotic and violent. 2) Situational stress rapists—rarely violent or have a history of rape; often their actions start with situational stress. 3) Masculine identity conflict rapists—a broad spectrum of rapists due to the lack of masculine roles. These rapists are dangerous and violent, and most time they plan their rapes. 4) Sadistic rapists—small percentage, but have history and plan their rapes. 5) Sociopathic rapists—most common type; they are impulsive and motivated primarily by sex.

Lindquist (2000) 4-Type Model

1) Gentleman Rapist (power reassurance). This type accounts for 70 percent of rapes, and usually this type involves in less violence. 2) Control Break Rapist (power assertive). This type counts for 25 percent of rapes. It is usually more violent, committed by blue-collar workers, and the rapists tend to show quick changes of personality. 3) Revenge Rapist (anger retaliation). It counts for 4 percent of all rapes and usually shows a high level violence. 4) Sexual Sadist Rapist (anger excitative). It counts for 1 percent of all rapes and it happens more in stranger rapes. The rapists are usually thrilled by their crimes. They tend to plan the rapes beforehand and use tricks to get victims, and most of the time they tend to kill their victims.

Groth and Co-Researchers' 3-Component Model

Three factors, including power, anger, and sexuality are present in virtually every forcible rape case. The forcible rape is the sexual expression of an aggression. That means rape becomes a means of expressing nonsexual needs in the psychology of the rapists. Among these three types, the power rapist makes up about 55 percent; these rapists will use whatever force needed to overpower their victims. Their crimes are usually premeditated and repeated. The anger rapists represent 40 percent of all rapes, and they are often impulsive and dangerous. The third type is the rapist murderer, and they often commit multiple rapes. They are usually driven by power, domination, control, and sadism.

The majority of rapists are between 15 and 29 years old, but 40 percent of rapists are over 30 years of age. About 15 percent involved more offenders, and 95 percent were gang rapes which are more violent and cause more damages to victims. Most group rapes involve young male offenders influenced by peer pressure. About 99 percent of rapists are males, and 1 percent of rapists are females.

A study at University of California at Los Angeles indicated that 40 percent of men surveyed said they might force a woman to have sex if they were sure they could get away with it (Snow 1995). This study indicated that what turns regular men into a rapist is the opportunity, and it is impossible to identify potential rapists.

Victims

Most victims of forcible rapes were women and about 9 percent were men, especially male youth in normal circumstances. However, men often become victims of forcible rape in jails. The ages of forcible rape victims range from very young to very old ages. According to the police record in San Jose, California, the youngest victim was 3 months old and the oldest was 86 years old.

Most victims of rapes range from 10 to 29 years old. About 81 percent of the victims are white, but black women are most likely to be raped. Most victims are from low income families, and about 70 percent of victims are unmarried. Victims of rapes are reluctant to report due to the fear of a short prison term for the offender and the insensitivity of the justice system.

Weapons Used in Rapes

Brewer (1994) cited the statistic regarding weapons used against victims of rape. Among rape cases, guns were used in 26.4 percent of the cases, knives were used in 39.7 percent of the cases, sharp objects were used in 6.3 percent of the situations, blunt objects were used 14 percent of the time, and other weapons were used in 13.6 percent of the cases.

Robbery

Facts

Robbery is the taking of property by force or threat of using force (Conklin 1999). The two types of robberies include non-commercial robbery (such as a purse-snatching committed on the street or in a house) and commercial robbery (such as robbing a bank or store). There were 422,921 robberies in the United States in 2001, and these accounted for 29.4 percent of the violent crimes. Although the sole motive of the robbery is for money and other valuables, the consequences of robberies to the victims include not only the loss of the property, but also potential physical injuries and death, and emotional trauma, because robberies are often associated with murders and aggravated assaults. Uniform Crime Report indicated about 8 percent of murders started with a robbery although only 0.3 percent of robberies result in murders. The financial cost per robbery is $19,000 for injuries per victim.

Locations

Robberies may occur anywhere victims are, but they occur more at the following places than other places based on the 2001 Uniform Crime Report. About 44 percent of the robberies occur on streets or highways; 26 percent in banks, gas stations, stores, and commercial establishments, 13 percent at residences; and another 17 percent at miscellaneous places. A new form of robbery is committed when the victims are driving a car and waiting for signals, but no statistics are available yet on this new type of robbery.

Relationship of Robbers and Victims

Robbers and victims rarely know each other because robbers usually feel that if they have to use force to steal, they better deal with strangers who cannot easily identify them (Conklin 1999). They also feel that to get something from the people they know, they can just simply steal instead of using force. More than 75 percent of the robbers are strangers to their victims (Timrot and Rand 1987).

Offenders

Most robberies are committed by men, about 91 percent in both 1999, and about 62 percent of the robbers are under the age of 25. According to Meadows (1998), 36 percent of arrested robbers were white, 62 percent were black, and 2 percent were other races.

Feldman (1993) reported that about 19 percent of robbers worked with co-offenders, 17 percent worked alone, and the rest shifted between the two types. Rand (1997) reported that robbery is more likely to be committed by more than one offender, and about 48 percent of completed robberies involved two or more offenders per robbery. This type of robbery is often committed by loosely organized gangs.

Weapons Used

Robberies very often involve the usage of weapons. The 2001 Uniform Crime Report indicated that 42 percent of victims faced guns, 39 percent of victims were attacked by barehanded robbers, 10 percent faced clubs and similar weapons, and 9 percent faced knives. Physical injuries of the victims are less when they faced robbers with guns and knives, because victims were reluctant to resist against guns or knives. Victims have more chances of injuries when they face barehanded robbers and believe they can overpower an unarmed robber (Conklin 1999).

Characteristics

Many robberies are planned a few minutes before the action, but some robberies are planned well in advance. Robbery detectives agree that being a robbery victim can be life-threatening since any armed robber is a potential killer. Among these robberies, street robbery, residence robbery, and gang robbery are highly dangerous. Street robbery is usually quick and spontaneous, and robbers tend to use any methods they can when they do not know what to expect. Residence robberies usually have no witnesses and robbers can do anything they want, especially when they fail to get valuables they expected. Gang robberies involve more people and more violence, and very often gang robbery is an initiation ritual of new gang members who would do more than just robbery to show that they are qualified to be in the gang (Snow 1995).

Research indicated that more than 75 percent of the robbers are drug addicts who need money for their drug supplies. Since they only can get an average of $80 per robbery, they need to commit more robberies. Furthermore, 40 percent of robbers are under the influence of drugs, and they desperately need the money, otherwise they cannot behave in their normal ways (Snow, 1995). Another dangerous thing is that these addicted robbers hate to go through a painful drug withdrawal in jails if they are identified and caught, and that increases the danger of robbery-related killing.

A Different Form of Robbery—Carjacking

Carjacking is the stealing of a car by force or threat of force, and it accounted for 2 percent of the motor theft in 2001. The common places where carjackings occur include intersections with lights and signs, garages of parking lots for mass transit, shopping centers, grocery stores, self-service gas stations and car wash, automatic teller machines, residential driveways, and places where people get in and out of cars, and highway exits and entry ramps where people have to stop or slow down (Meadows 1998).

About 87 percent of the carjacking offenders were men, including 32 percent white and 49 percent black. In all reported carjacking cases, more than 50 percent of were committed by two or more offenders, and 77 percent of the offenders used weapons. Most carjacking were committed on the street during evenings and nights (Rand 1994).

Meadows (1998) analyzed 28 cases of carjacking which occurred in the Los Angeles area in 1996. The results indicated that most offenders were offenders were teenagers in their early 20s using handguns. All attackers were strangers, and the scary thing is that many attackers were armed teenagers who showed no remorse for the victims. Most victims were lone women at parking lots or street, and were battered or assaulted. Most attacks occurred in evening near victims' homes.

The consequences of robberies to the victims are very unpredictable. Some were released without serious injury, and some were kidnapped, robbed, assaulted, raped, or killed. Meadows reported that out of 28 carjacking cases, 6 victims escaped, and 8 were murdered or seriously wounded. Victims of carjacking were targeted by their vulnerability and the car they were driving. A real-life case is the carjacking and killing of the famous TV comedian Bill Cosby's son, who was carjacked and murdered by Freeway 5 near San Diego in California. Another real-life case is that a female professor and scientist in New Jersey in 1992 was carjacked while she was putting her two-year-old daughter in the car seat. Two men came behind, dragged her out, then jumped into the car and drove away. Since the baby was still inside, the professor hung onto the door while the car was moving. After two miles, the robbers stopped the car. They threw the professor and her daughter by the road and drove on. Soon they ran into a cornfield and were later caught by police. But the professor was already dead. Carjacking is getting popular and bloody in China. It was reported that one carjacking gang only robs good cars, and they kill all victims and feed them to dogs they have raised in the backyard. They killed many people, and the last two were a police officer and a retired army officer. Killing taxi drivers is very often reported in newspapers there.

One strategy used by the offenders is to cause a fender-bender called Bump and Rob. When the victim steps out of the car to deal with the damage and insurance issues, they are vulnerable and easily become victims. Another strategy to jack a car is to thumb a ride. People's sympathy gives carjackers a good opportunity to commit the crime. While I was writing this section, the TV news just reported a perfect real-life case. On April 30th, 2002 in Oakland, California, a man of 29 years old picked up a hitchhiker who was a woman about 19 years old. When they arrived at the destination the woman wanted, the woman took out a knife and stabbed the driver many times on his neck, stomach, and limbs. Then she drove the car away. The man was rescued and is in the hospital, and the chase for the carjacker is still going on as I finish this paragraph.

Aggravated Assault

Facts

Aggravated assault is the illegal attack of one person by another, and attackers usually use weapons and try to cause severe bodily injuries (Conklin 1999). There were 907,219 aggravated assaults in the United States in 2001, which accounted for 63 percent of the violent crimes (1999 Uniform Crime Report). But due to the fear of retaliation, embarrassment, and protection of family members, many people did not report their cases. Therefore the actual number should be much higher. Victims of aggravated assaults suffer pain, injuries, permanent disability, emotional trauma, and financial loss, averaged at $9,350 per assault.

Weapons Used

Most of the assaults involved the usage of weapons. The 1999 crime report indicated that in 18 percent of the aggravated assaults the offenders used guns, 18 percent used knives, 36 percent used clubs or similar weapons, and 27 percent used body parts.

Offenders

Male offenders accounted for 80 percent of the aggravated assaults in 2001, and female offenders accounted for 20 percent. About 20 percent of the aggravated assaults were committed by strangers; 33 percent by lovers, friends, acquaintances, or neighbors; 14 percent by family members, 10 percent between police and a criminal, and 25 percent unknown (Conklin 1999).

Causes

The reasons for aggravated assaults are not indicated in the crime report, but experts believe that the causes of assaults are similar to murders, vandalism, arson, and rape. The causes and reasons which trigger the aggressive assaults may include the following aspects:

1. Argument oriented. Nowadays, due the fast life pace and lack of traditional morals, people tend to get involved more often in arguments and fights over small things. When people start the argument, nobody likes to back off, since they feel that backing off means the loss of dignity and being a chicken, therefore both sides tend to upgrade the argument, very often from oral argument to physical violence.

2. Gang related. Aggravated assault is an activity used often in gang related activities. It may start that new gang members need to beat up someone to be qualified for the organization. It may start with a street fight between the gangs. Bullies in schools or on the street very often use physical force against their victims.

3. Other crime oriented. Assault is very often related to other crimes. In the process of rape, robbery, burglary, and theft, victims often are beaten up because the criminals are afraid the victim will fight back, or attackers use force to warn the victims, or make victims lose their fighting-back ability. A new assault occurred in pocket-lifting in China in recent years. In the old time, when a thief was caught, he or she would be beaten up by spectators. But nowadays, thieves most of the time work together to make the process safer for them. When one of the thieves is caught by the victim, the rest of the thieves all rush up to beat up the victim and claim the victim is the thief. The victim often is helpless because other people do not really know what happened, and sometimes they do not want to help because of the fear of the gang.

4. Behavior oriented: Many victims of assaults precipitated the crimes due to their personality and behavior. Some people have a bad temper and always exhibit a hostile attitude toward other people. About 20 percent of people in the United States have angry personality, and 60 percent show this kind of personality sometimes. This kind of personality often is demonstrated through bad manners and nasty or rude behavior, therefore they insult people either intentionally, or they are not aware of it. This kind of behavior is stressful for others and makes people hate them. When people cannot tolerate their bad temper or behavior, assault which uses physical language certainly becomes a natural way of expressing the anger. Bad tempers and behavior make enemies, and assault is the common way of revenge and retaliation or giving the person who starts the trouble a lesson. For example, getting involved in a romantic triangle creates enemies immediately, and assault seems the most proper way to give the intruder a lesson.

5. Drug and alcohol related: When people use alcohol and drugs, their mind is not clear, their courage is increasing, and their self-control ability is low. Under these conditions, any small things such as an argument or even a glance or a word may trigger the assault.

6. Conflicts related. Conflicts are everywhere in everyday life and can be triggered by anything. Misunderstanding is one source of conflict, and it causes disagreement, bias, and hate. Conflicts also occur in racial and other ethnic issue. Bias and discrimination will result in mistreatment and unfairness. All of these conflicts can make people use assault as a way to express their anger as a revenge and retaliation.

Cross-Board Crimes

Hate Crime

Facts

Hate crime is a new form of crime and the Uniform Crime Report has already started displaying data on this crime. This crime spreads in the whole society and impacts many people in the country. This crime starts with a single motive—hate toward different groups of people—and ends with using violence against victims or their property. The offenders commit all different kinds of violent crimes and property crimes against victim but the targets are narrower. Aggravated assaults are more common in this kind of crime. Other crimes committed also include arson or rape.

Offenders

The offenders of hate crime can be a single person or a group. There are such groups scattered in the United States (Meadows 1998). According to the 2001 Uniform Crime Report, 66 percent of known offenders were white, and 20 percent were black.

Victims

The hate crime usually includes hate against immigrants and foreigners, gays and lesbians, against a certain religion, or against white, black, Asian, or Hispanics. The targeting groups of hate crime change over time. Before the 1980s, black people were the major targets, but since the

1990s, the Mexican and Asian groups very often become the victims, while gays and lesbians also face the same problem. Immediately after the hijacking and bombing event on September 11, 2001, people from the Middle East became victims.

Causes

The FBI report in 1996 indicated that 45 percent of the hate crimes were race oriented, 19 percent were religion oriented, 14 percent were sexual oriented, and 22 percent were ethnicity oriented. Although the government tried to call a stop to hate crime in the United States, it is not an easy task to complete in a short time because of the conflicts of interests and beliefs of different groups. Another important reason is that people do not know which person from this race is the bad guy, and they tend to treat them as the same or stereotype them. Misunderstanding is also a triggering factor in hate crimes.

Methods

2001 Uniform Crime Report indicated that in 63 percent of the hate crimes, the offenders attacked the victims physically, in 36 percent the victims' property became the targets, and in 1 percent the society became the victim. Among the victims of hate crime, 36 percent were facing intimidation, 17 percent became victims of simple assaults, 9 percent became victims of aggravated assaults, 30 percent faced property destruction and damage, and 5 percent became victims of robbery, burglary, and theft.

To reduce hate crimes, people suggest enforcing personal responsibility, some focus on community effort, and some focus on legislations.

Family and Intimate Violence

Facts

This type of crime occurs between intimates such as family members or relatives, ex-spouses and boy/girl friends, and friends or acquaintances. The violence can range from stalking, abuse, and battery to rape, robbery, assault, and murder. Intimate violence represents 13 percent of all violent victimizations. Family violence impacts many families in the United States and destroys people's lives not only during the family time but also during work and school time.

Victims

The victims of this type of crime are mainly women, elderly, and children but can include other populations too. Becoming victims of this type of crime is very unfortunate and dangerous because victims may have to suffer for a long time. About 50 percent of women who leave violent relationships were followed and threatened by their abusers, and more women who left their batterers than those who stayed were killed (Meadows 1998). Young black and Hispanic women living in inner cities, poor single women with low education levels, and separated and divorced women are more vulnerable.

Causes

The reasons for intimates and family violence can be different. Among these are the amount of time spent together, conflicting interests, tension of family interactions, age gaps, finances and lack of privacy (Gelles 1993). Lack of communication and understanding, lack of love, bad personalities, and lack of control of temper can be potential reasons as well.

Warning signals

Meadows (1998) also provided the criteria to evaluate if the abuser is likely to kill the partner. Meadows' criteria include threats of homicide or suicide, fantasies of homicide or suicide, weapons, being obsessive about partner or family, pet abuse, and rage.

Gelles & Cornell (1990) listed features of families which have a higher potential to abuse a child:

➤ Both parents orally attacked child.
➤ More arguments between parents.
➤ Husband orally or physically attacked wife.
➤ Husband is a blue-collar worker.
➤ Husband is not happy with his life now.
➤ Wife is a blue-collar worker or a housewife.
➤ Wife is under 30, and both parents experienced physical punishment in youth.
➤ There are two or more children in the family.
➤ Parents married less than ten years.
➤ Moved to this house less than two years.
➤ Husband does not go to church.

Gelles and Cornell (1990) also listed indicators of wife-abusers:

➤ Husband has a temporary job or jobless.
➤ Income is below $6,000.
➤ Husband is a blue-collar worker.
➤ Both worry about their economy problems in the house.
➤ Wife is not happy with the living level.
➤ Two or more children.
➤ Dispute on children issues.
➤ Both lived in a family where their father battered moms.
➤ Less than ten years of marriage.
➤ Both under 30.
➤ Non-white race.
➤ More marriage related conflicts.
➤ Under huge stress.
➤ One controls the family.
➤ One side or other orally attacked other side.
➤ Drunk often.
➤ Live there less than two years.
➤ Both not going to church.
➤ Wife is a housewife.

Workplace Crimes

Facts

Workplace crimes include all other crimes and the expression of anger through assault in a working environment. The workplace crime impacts a major part of the population, since most people belong to the work force for most of their lives. There are 3.2 million violent crimes in the workplace each year, with 500,000 victims losing 1.8 million workdays and $55 million in lost wages (Bachman 1994).

Bureau of Justice Statistics indicated that 50 percent incidents were not reported to police. These workplace crimes can cause all physical and emotional injuries occurring in all other violent crime to victims. Workplace crime is the leading cause of job-related death and the leading health-threatening factor. About 60 percent cases of workplace violence result in serious injury in victims. A study in 1993 (Meadows 1998) indicated that violence and harassment affect health and productivity of employees, and job stress, violence, and harassment are strongly connected.

Victims

Victims of workplace violence can include anyone. Existing cases include school teachers, doctors, post office clerks, managers, and more. Most victims of workplace homicide were women working in retail trade by robberies. Studies summarized by Meadows (1998) reported that 33 percent managers experienced violence, 43 percent of 1500 human resource managers experienced violence in the last three years but 64 percent indicated that they had no training to handle the crimes! Two studies indicated that 67 percent of the emergency department nurses experienced assaults and 60% hospital staff from 103 hospitals suffered injuries from visitors and patients.

Types and Methods

Blow (1994) indicated several types of violence in the workplace. Included are: 1) robbery, 2) domestic or misdirected violence (taking personal problems to work), 3) employer-directed violence (unfair, layoff), 4) terrorism and hate crimes (1995 Oklahoma Federal Building bombing, and 911 hijacking and bombing). California Office of Occupational Safety and Health Administration divided workplace crimes into three categories: 1) no relationship such as robbery (60 percent); 2) service such as police officers, hospital workers, correctional workers, teachers (30 percent); and 3) employment related, such as layoff, or unfair treatment (10 percent).

A 1995 study of managers indicated that 33 percent managers experienced violence. Among these people, 75 percent were fist-fighting, 17 percent shooting, 9 percent stabbing, and 6 percent sexual harassment. Another 1995 study of 1500 human resource managers indicated that 43% experienced violence in the last three years, and the common incidents were threatening call/bomb threat/fights. A study of 103 hospitals indicated that 60 percent of staff suffered injuries from visitors and patients, and guns and knives are the most commonly used weapons. Bureau of Justice Statistics indicated that 62 percent cases used no arms and 30 percent were armed with guns.

Causes

Johnson (1994) indicated that in a study that about 50 percent workplace homicides were committed by layoff employees. Other research found out that factors contributing to the workplace violence also include job stress (cause and effect), feeling of lack of control, less support, adversarial relationships, unfair policies and procedures, and pressure to please customers. Meadows reported that the major reason was personality conflicts.

Offenders

Bachman (1994) reported that among women victims in the workplace, 40 percent were attacked by strangers, 35 percent were attacked by casual acquaintances, 19 percent were attacked by well-known acquaintances, 5 percent were attacked by a husband, boyfriends or former boyfriends, and 1 percent were attacked by relatives. Among the male victims, 58 percent were attacked by strangers, 30 percent by casual people, 10 percent by well known people, and 2 percent by intimates and relatives. Harassment usually came from bosses and colleagues while attackers are usually customers. About 54 percent were attacked by another employee and more than 80 percent attackers were males (Meadows 1998),

Locations

23 percent of workplace crimes occurred at commercial establishment, 14 percent factory/office/warehouse, 13 percent at restaurant/bar/night club, 11 percent at parking lot/garage, and 9 percent in schools. Bureau of Justice Statistics indicated that 60 percent occurred at private companies, 30 percent in government agencies, and 8 percent at self-employment places. Government offices and post offices are the worst places for workplace.

Warning Signals

Baron (1993) provided a list of clues that serve as warning signals of violence. He stated that the possibility of violence is 90% if one or more of the following warning signals shows up in the potential attackers:

➤ Violent history
➤ Evidence of psychosis
➤ Chemical or alcohol dependence
➤ Depression
➤ Blaming all the time
➤ Elevated frustration level
➤ Interest in weapons
➤ Personality disorder
➤ Strange behavior

Other warning signals were also suggested by experts:

➤ A loner
➤ Angry without an outlet
➤ Socially withdrawn
➤ Frequent verbal complaints
➤ Self-destructive behavior
➤ Excessive tardiness, increased supervision, reduced productivity
➤ Strained relationships
➤ Conflict
➤ Feeling of being victimized by other people
➤ Unwanted anger or sudden outburst
➤ Unable to take criticism
➤ Talks about personal problems with boss for a long time
➤ No concern for other people's safety or the company's property
➤ Complaints by co-workers

Factors Increasing the Risks

Meadows (1998) provided a list of factors which increase the chances of workplace crimes. The list includes the following situations employees may be in:

➤ Contact with the public
➤ Exchange of money
➤ Delivering passengers, goods, or services

- ➤ Working with unstable people and criminals
- ➤ Working alone
- ➤ Working late and very early
- ➤ Working in high crime areas
- ➤ Guarding valuables or possessions

Meadows also presented a list of risk predictors for businesses. The more these predictors present in the business, the more chances workplace crimes will occur in these businesses.

- ➤ Previous intrusions
- ➤ Operating in the evenings
- ➤ Public access
- ➤ Alcohol served
- ➤ Several uncontrolled entries
- ➤ Dealing with cash
- ➤ Experienced assaults
- ➤ Having female employees
- ➤ Offering public entertainment
- ➤ Crimes occurred nearby
- ➤ Near freeway
- ➤ Near metropolitan area
- ➤ Weapons seen on the premises
- ➤ Drug use by employees or nearby
- ➤ Street fights
- ➤ Threat by discharged or disgruntled employees
- ➤ Drugs or prostitutes in neighborhood

Crimes in Schools

Facts

Violent crimes are spreading in the schools, and students are mugged, harassed, abused, and threatened daily. Kids are bullied for their lunch money, teenagers are afraid of drive-by shootings and massacre shooting, youths brag about their guns and violent behaviors, drugs are brought to schools, gangs rule the school corners and corridors, weapons are carried in schools, and teachers and principles face violent students and violent behaviors (Bosch 1997).

About 12 percent of all violent crimes are committed inside a school or on school property. About 3 million crimes occur at schools every year, and about one million youths become victims of violent crimes each year. Four thousand rapes and sexual batteries and 11,000 school fights with weapons were reported in public schools in the 1996-97 academic years. There were 98,490 cases of vandalism, 4,170 rapes or sexual batteries, 7,150 robberies, 115,500 thefts and larceny, and 11,000 incidents in which weapons were used in schools.

Victims

The victims of school violence are students, teachers, and staff. Meadows (1998) indicated that 29 percent of teachers are threatened with physical harm each month, 28 percent of teachers hesitated in the month preceding the study to confront misbehaving students because they were afraid of their own safety. About 33 percent of students were threatened, 24 percent students were afraid of being hurt, and 20 percent reported being kicked, hit, or slapped. The 1999 Columbine High

School shooting killed 13 students and one teacher, and similar shootings and attempted shootings occurred at several schools. Meadows indicated that 9th graders are more likely to be victim in high schools.

Weapons

About 33 percent of students carried a pistol daily and 8 percent of carried a knife to schools either for self-protection or attacks. The weapons they carried included guns, knives, BB guns, stun guns, brass knuckles, darts, clubs, martial art weapons, mace, explosives, pepper spray, and clubs. Miller (1999) reported that 20 percent of high school students said they had carried weapons sometimes in 1998, and it was estimated that 270,000 guns are taken to school every day. Miller also indicated that 43 percent of youths carried a weapon because they feel the need for self-protection, 35 percent held a weapon for someone, 18 percent used their weapons to scare someone, 10 percent said most of their friends carry weapons, 10 percent felt carrying weapons makes them feel important, and 10 percent used weapons in crimes. How many people can feel safe when they are surrounded by students carrying these weapons?

Danger

Violent crimes have severe consequences to school children. Physically, crimes can cause death, physical injuries and pain, permanent disability, a distorted sense of time and thoughts or perception, and nightmares. Psychologically and emotionally, crimes spread the fear of becoming a victim and cause prolonged fear after becoming a victim. Crimes also cause stress and psychological pressure which have a negative influence on everyday life. Financially, crimes cause problems for the victim's family. These problems include loss of property, unpaid wages, hospitalization expenses, therapeutic services, loss of social security, loss of survivor's benefits, funeral costs, and replacement costs of stolen property, often well beyond the original prices. Socially, crimes cause a variety of problems which include: the inability to trust others, fear of public places and streets, disruption of your home or school or office atmosphere, a sense of less choice and freedom, low self-esteem and less confidence, hostility toward other children, more fights, and a greater tendency to carry weapons.

School students are very vulnerable in protecting themselves from crime and violence, simply because of the following reasons: 1) Mentally these students are not mature enough and they do not have enough experience to handle these threatening situations. 2) Physically most of them are not strong enough to resist physical attacks of adult attackers. 3) Increasing youth crimes and violence make these students potential victims of not only adult criminals but also youth criminals.

Preparation

The author has conducted four studies on self-defense education in elementary, high schools, and universities. According to these studies, self-defense education in elementary schools is basically blank. Few students received formal self-defense education, and what they have so far is simple basic advice from the teachers and parents who do not have formal self-defense education either. In California, self-defense and martial arts are listed as subjects in 7th and 10th grades, but only a small percentage of middle and high schools tried self-defense education. Most of them have not started yet due to the lack of qualified instructors or equipment. Although another researcher in 1994 reported that 19 percent of urban youth had learned self-defense, the quality of their education is not a comprehensive. At the college level, self-defense has become an elective course, but still more than 80 percent of the college students never received any self-defense education; less than 1 percent of students actually took a university self-defense course, even though in a recent survey students indicated that self-defense was considered the most useful class.

Self-defense education beyond the college level depends on community classes that are usually short and only cover a small part of self-defense.

Dealing with School Violence

To fight against school violence, schools have tried many strategies. Miller (1999) summarized the following strategies which are considered effective at preventing school violence:

- ➤ Safe school hotline
- ➤ Safety committee
- ➤ Speakers on safety issues
- ➤ Student court to solve conflicts
- ➤ Student code of conduct
- ➤ Workshops and conferences on safety
- ➤ Student representatives in school administration
- ➤ Peer mediation
- ➤ Student support groups
- ➤ Student tutoring groups
- ➤ Issues forums
- ➤ Cultural events
- ➤ School checklist
- ➤ After school programs
- ➤ Miller (1999) also reported that schools with the following characteristics have less violence.
- ➤ Small school
- ➤ Strong principal
- ➤ Fair but firm discipline
- ➤ Teachers hold high expectations for all students
- ➤ More parent participation
- ➤ Real learning atmosphere

Organized Crimes

Organized crime is the criminal activity committed by a formal organization developed and devoted primarily to the pursuit of profits through illegal means (Conklin 1999). The types of organized crime include gangs, smuggling of drugs/firearms/immigrants, and terrorism. Organized crimes involve formal or informal organizations from the local (most of them) to the international level. The organized crimes self-defense concerns include gangs and terrorism.

Gangs

Facts

Gangs are collectives in which the interaction of individuals—both leadership and rank and file—is organized and governed by a set of rules and roles (Jankowski 1991). They are willing to use deadly force to defend territory, attack other gangs, steal money, or engage in other group-related activities (Sanders 1994). Survival is a major concern of gangs. They must deal with the external environment and gain support or avoid conflicts with local residents and establish connections with government and law enforcement systems. It is important for gangs to meet the needs of their members in terms of entertainment, protection, and well-being. Gangs recruit new members through in three ways: 1) college fraternity pattern, 2) persuade residents to join them for their community, and 3) coercion (Conklin 1999). Gang members usually start at early ages, about 50 percent under 14 and 10 percent under 10 (Snow 1995). The age of gang members ranges from 10 through 45 years old.

Characteristics

Gangs tend to express their identity through having a name, wearing colors or dress, and spraying their turf with graffiti (Conklin 1999). Usually local police departments have the information about gang activities in their areas. Gangs have different forms; some are less organized and some are strictly organized. Miller (1999) classified gangs into three types: the scavenger gang, which is least organized; territorial gang, which is highly organized; and the corporate gangs, which is highly structured.

Some gangs are engaged in street fighting; some are engaged in illegal business. Some gangs are not violent gangs, while some use violence and commit all kinds of crimes, such as murder, robbery, assault, rape, burglary, and smuggling. The victims of these kinds of gang activities usually include gang members they are associated with and they fight against; people who are targeted for robbery, rape, assault, burglary, and bullying; people who are associated with them (such as in drug selling); people who are in their way or used as scapegoats; or people who own a business and are ideal for extortion.

Danger of Gangs

Gangs poses a serious problem for American society because gangs go hand in hand with crimes. Gang members committed 5 times more crimes than non-gang people with similar backgrounds (Miller 1999). The major threats of gang activities to the public are usually murders, assault, rape, robbery, burglary, arson, vandalism, street fighting, drug sales, bullying in schools, and extortion. Gang members usually are fearless about the law and the possibility of losing their life, and they tend to be hard-hearted and have no sympathy toward victims at all. They are more dangerous and brutal when they commit crimes. Gangs are hard to crack and to sentence due to the lack of evidence and witnesses and the potential retaliation from the at-large gang members. Gangs thus create fears of becoming victims of violent crimes in communities. These gangs create a dangerous problem for cities and towns in the United States (Margolis 1997).

Scary Situation

Gangs and gang activities are getting more popular in the United States. While other crimes are decreasing, gangs are increasing, and it is getting worse in 50 percent of the communities. For the last two decades, gang members increased from 100,000 to 600,000 and violent street gangs are operating in 94 percent of medium and large cities (Wolff 2000). The city of Los Angeles is believed to have six hundred gangs with over 75 thousand members (Margolis 1997). The worst part is that gangs are spreading from large cities to small cities and towns (Miller 1999).

Reasons for Joining Gangs

Although gangs are a danger to the society, they provide attractive benefits to their members in many ways. The attraction to join gangs is so high that their members can not resist. That is why gangs are growing even though the law enforcement system is trying to crack them.

People join gangs for different reasons. Wolff (2000) stated that factors that make gangs so popular in society include media influence, peer pressure, family traditions, gangs as a substitute family, brotherhood and the sense of community, rules and rituals, the appeal of the organization, the rewards of gang membership, the promise of respect, and the seeking of protection. Gang members usually come from families which have divorce, violence, fights and constant argument, drugs, and alcohol. The families who exhibit a lack of love, lack of attention to children, lack of proper family education, poor role modeling of parent, and lack of a bright future and hope in the family have more danger of pushing their youth to join gangs.

Major Gangs and Their Activities

There are many gangs in the United States, and most of gangs are developed based on racial groups. These gangs have focuses on different kinds of activities and commit different kinds of crimes. Kenney and Finckenauer (1995) compared activities of ethnic gangs in the United States. From the self-defense standpoint, their activities include mainly the following. Chinese gangs are involved in extortion, robbery, murder, smuggling of weapons and immigrants, and prostitution. Japanese gangs conduct murder and extortion. Colombian gangs deal with cocaine smuggling. Vietnamese gangs commit extortion, prostitution, auto theft, arson, and armed robbery. Jamaican gangs engage in cocaine and firearms, robbery, murder, kidnapping, and auto theft. Russian gangs market illegal goods and commit extortion as well as kidnapping. As reported by the World Journal on the kidnapping and murder in Los Angeles in March 2002, the Russian Mafias kidnapped and killed six rich people who immigrated from Europe.

Conklin (1999) also described other types of gangs. White gangs usually commit race-related crimes which are based on discrimination or anti-government activities. Black gangs are usually involved in rape, street fights, and money related crimes, such as robbery, burglary, and drug smuggling. Hispanic gangs commonly commit crimes related to their territories, such as fighting against other gangs which invade their areas. Youth gangs often target students by robbing, bullying, and attacking them on the way home or in isolated areas in schools. Outlaw motorcycle gangs mainly are involved in drug manufacturing and distribution, prostitution, and contract killing (Ellis and Walsh 2000).

White gangs usually target colored populations. Black gangs mainly target the same race, but also target whites for hate and rape, and at other races for robbery and burglary. Hispanic gangs target their own race in territory fight but also other populations for burglary and auto theft. The Asian gangs tend to target at Asian populations.

Gangs in China

The rapid developing of gang crimes in China deserves our attention since it has demonstrated much more severe consequences to the civilians and the society. Since China is a huge market for American business, and so many American companies and Americans go to and work in China, understanding these gang-related crimes will help American business, workers in China, and travelers to China. The organized crimes in China have several features (Gong 2001). First, criminals use extreme violence against victims in murders, robberies, kidnapping, forcible rapes, street-fighting for territory, extortions, attacking people in public, and smuggling. Secondly, they tend to commit crimes in groups to outnumber the victims (including police) to make self-defense or the law-enforcement system useless. One example is the aggravated assaults on a train in 2002. A gang of more than thirty attacked passengers and police officers with kitchen chopping knives without any reason. Third, gangs bully everywhere in some cities and they often associate with some people in the law-enforcement system and use group force so that no one dares to fight against them or to crack down on them. Fourth, their activities include almost everything besides the above violent crimes, forced prostitution, kidnapping and selling children and women, extortion, setting up their territory, and smuggling firearms and drugs.

Societal Prevention of Gangs

Solving gang problems is a huge undertaking, and no single solution works. Society first needs to dig into the root of gang problems: poverty, discrimination, poor education, and broken families. At the same time, there are various strategies to reduce gangs and their activities. The following strategies have been used to deal with gangs:

- ➤ Curfew
- ➤ Prohibit gang clothing, signs, loitering, cellular phones
- ➤ Provide more recreational activities for youth
- ➤ Establish community organizations
- ➤ Police, court, school, and community join hands to prevent gangs
- ➤ Education as a key element in keeping kids from joining a gang
- ➤ Former gang members talk to kids from their perspectives
- ➤ Gang Resistance And Education Training
- ➤ Mentor for kids
- ➤ Change the peer pressure from negative to positive aspects
- ➤ Rehabilitate gang members
- ➤ Keep kids off the streets
- ➤ Enforce uniforms in schools
- ➤ Install metal detectors
- ➤ More structured education, discipline, and homework

Terrorism

Facts

Defined by Kushner (1998), terrorism is the use of force against governments or civilian populations to create fear in order to create political or social change. Terrorism may come from the inside of a country, such as the 1995 Oklahoma bombing of the federal building; or outside, such as the 1998 Pan Am Flight 103 bombing from Frankfurt to New York; or outside terrorists committing crimes in the country, such as the 911 hijacking and bombing which killed thousands of people in New York. Since 911 hijacking and bombing, terrorism has been considered as the top threat to the safety of people in the United States. Although the American army has been making progress with the military actions to eliminate potential terrorists and their bases, the terrorists are still there and plan to commit more terrorism attacks. The American Government has issued several warnings regarding potential attacks on bridges, oil pipelines, and most recently, the financial centers and even supermarkets. In May 2002, the Vice President warned that the retaliation for the terrorism attacks will come sooner or later. The government has also established a warning system which uses different colors to indicate different levels of danger. These terrorism organizations threat to attack again soon.

Types and Activities

Based on Miller and File (2001), terrorism has several types. They are: single issue terrorism, extremist political terrorism, separatist terrorism, religious terrorism, and pathological terrorism. Most terrorism has clear political, social, or financial purposes for causing fears in people, retaliating, or holding hostages in exchange of money or release of their members in jails. Terrorists usually try to get people's attention, and they usually target at the notable victims in notable places. The activities of terrorism include kidnapping, assassination, bombing, poisoning, hijacking, et cetera. Although victims may include famous people, most of them are civilians.

Another type of terrorism is pirate activities. In recent years, the cases of pirate attacks are increasing. In the year 2000, 309 cases were reported in the world. The experts classify pirates into three types. The first type is the amateur pirates. Their mission is to rob materials, and they often will not kill victims. They tend to use regular weapons such as knives or sticks. The second type is professional pirates. These pirates are armed with modern weapons, and they target not only on valuables but also the ship, which they sell for big money. These pirates are dangerous and tend to kill all witnesses and victims. The third type is the teamwork between corrupted law enforcement officers and the pirates. The corrupted officers often stop the ships under the guise of a regular checkup. They inform the pirates when they find stuff they want; then the pirates commit the robbery.

Danger

Terrorism presents tremendous dangers to people and society in many ways. From the consequence standpoint, the terrorism can massacre hundreds to thousands of lives with one attack. A good example is the 911 hijacking and bombing of the World Trade Center buildings and the Pentagon, as well as the Oklahoma Federal Building. These acts caused loss of lives, huge materials damages, and severe fear and psychological impact.

From the self-defense perspective, the terrorism attacks are very difficult to prevent for many reasons. One reason is that terrorists plot everything in secret, and it is almost impossible to know where, when, and how they will attack. Another reason is that they can use any methods to attack. Their methods can range from kidnapping, bombing, and mass shooting to using chemical, biological, and nuclear weapons. The third reason is that they always target places that are extremely vulnerable and are almost impossible to guard. Among these are business centers, shopping centers, schools, bridges, railways, hospitals, and large gatherings.

Property Crimes

Burglary

Facts

Burglary is the illegal breaking into of a building in order to steal valuables. The sole purpose of burglary is to steal the valuables while the residents are not in. Burglary targets private residences and commercial houses but about two/thirds occurs at residences. There were 2,109,767 burglaries reported to the police in 2001 according the Uniform Crime Report.

About 40 percent of burglaries are committed by relatives, acquaintances, or someone victims know. About 53 percent of burglaries occur during the daytime and 47% during the evening and nights. About 64 percent of burglars forced their way in, and 29 percent made unlawful entry through unlocked doors or windows.

Danger

Burglary may turn into robbery if confronted with people inside, and sometimes burglary is associated with murder, assaults and rape; however most burglaries do not have confrontations. About 60 percent of all rapes and robbery in the home were committed by burglars, and 13 percent of burglaries were committed when someone is in the house (Snow 1995). Burglary makes victims feel scared and insecure in their houses since burglars may kill, rape, or assault residents. They make victims lose property at the rate of $1,100 per burglary (Conklin 1999).

Targets

Target suitability is the basic consideration of burglary from the criminological perspective (Conklin 1999). Target suitability includes form and value of the property, visibility and accessibility of targets, vulnerability of property and people, and guardianship.

Burglars usually try to avoid confrontations with the residents, and therefore they are very careful when choosing their targets. Burglaries are usually planned, and the burglars look for several clues when they plan on burglarizing a house. These clues include unlocked doors or windows for easy entry, and no sign of alarm systems, occupants, or nearby witnesses (Conklin 1999). In recent years in the Asian communities, burglars look for shoes as a clue since Asians tend to leave their shoes beside the house entrance when they are home. The clues also include that houses that look rich, are easy to get in and escape, have no security system or a dog, and the owner is careless. Other dangerous clues which invite burglars include hollow-core doors, wide gaps, outward opening doors, windows close to doors, sliding doors, sightless doors, AC, skylights, and window glass which is easy to break.

Reppetto (1974) indicated reasons for burglary targets. The reasons include ease of access (44 percent), appearance of affluence (41 percent), inconspicuous location (21 percent), isolation of neighborhood (19 percent), absence of police patrol (19 percent), and lack of surveillance by neighbors (12 percent). Burglars also want to have the following information before their actions. Among the information they need: whether occupants are present is their first consideration (70 percent of burglars agreed), alarm is another important factor (36 percent), what valuables are location there (34 percent), available escape routes (20 percent), location of entrance (15 percent), and police or security patrols (14 percent).

Deterrence

Another researcher (Mantice, 1992) interviewed 589 burglars in jails about the effectiveness of deterrents. The results listed these deterrents from more to less effective as follows: alarms, sensors, cameras, private security patrol, dogs, weapons, random police patrol, exterior lights, neighborhood watch, safety boxes, and timers for interior. However, burglars are also scared of something else when they break into a house. A researcher of a study interviewed several hundreds of burglars in jails and asked them what would scare them off when they try to burglarize a house. Four things were identified to effectively prevent these burglars, including a dog, security alarm system, police officer, and shooting by the owner.

Arson

Facts

Arson is the purposeful burning of other people's property. It mainly causes property damage but may also cause physical injury. There were 76,760 cases of arson in the United States in 2001 at a cost of about $900 millions.

There are several motives for arson. Sometimes the purpose is to claim the loss from the insurance company. This is the case when the offender burns his/her own property. Sometimes arson is the result of gang activities while revenge is another motive (Conklin, 1999). In 1995 and 1996 there were many arsons to black churches, and the obvious motive was racial discrimination (FBI report, 1996).

Larceny-Theft

Facts:

Larceny is the illegal taking away of other people's belongings. In 2001, 7,076,171 larceny and 1,226,456 auto theft cases happened in the United States. There are several types of larceny including shoplifting, bike theft (half a million a year), pickpocketing, purse snatching, and necklace snatching, and theft from a vending machine. Some acts of larceny are planned, and some are done on the spur of the moment. About 90 percent of the victims of larceny are complete strangers (Conklin 1999).

People who are too trusting and unaware give thieves more opportunities. Often offenders target predictable habits. Pickpocketers often work in teams. A typical scheme is one thief distracts the victim, and the second thief steals and passes the money to a third person. In recent years in China, this is the common way of pickpocketing, and very often the thieves hit the victim and claim the victim is the thief.

Vandalism

Facts:

Vandalism is the purposeful destruction, injury, or disfigurement of property without consent of the owner (Conklin 1999). These acts are typically committed by gangs, teenagers, or other people found on the streets. The vandalism may start with retaliation, antisocial behavior, or for fun. It usually does not cause physical injuries to the victim, but will cause loss of money on repairing the damage and emotional stress and fear. It usually involves no confrontations with the owner, but when there is a confrontation, it may become other crimes such as murder, aggravated assault, or rape.

Other Crimes

White-Collar Crime

Facts

White-collar crime is the illegal taking of property which belongs to other people, organizations, or the government. This is an intelligent crime which is usually money-oriented. The white-collar crime is often planned and may involve other crimes. Some types of white-collar crime include deceptive advertisements, tax fraud, bribery, unsafe working conditions, the production of dangerous products, and environmental law violations (Conklin 1999).

Victimless Crime

Facts

Victimless crime is the offense that lacks a victim, except sometimes the criminal himself. The types of victimless crimes include drug use (which often turns to other crimes to support the expense), gambling (with cheating and violence often involved), prostitution (with robbery and beating sometimes involved along with the risk of having HIV passed to clients), and pornography (Conklin 1999).

REFERENCES

Bachman, R. *Violence Against Women: A National Crime Victimization Survey Report.* Washington DC: US Department of Justice Bureau of Justice Statistics, 1994.

Bartol, C. T., and A. M Bartol. *Criminal Behavior* 2nd ed. New Jersey: Prentice-Hall, 1986.

Bosch, C. *Schools Under Siege.* Springfield: Enslow Publisher, 1997.

Brewer, J.D. *The Dander from Strangers: Confronting the Threat of Assault.* New York: Insight Book, 1994.

Conklin, J. E. *Criminology.* New York: Macmillan Publishing Company, 1999.

Dawson, J. M., and P. A Langan. *Murder in Families.* Washington D.C.: U.S. Department of Justice, July 1994.

Donziger S. R. The Real War on Crime. New York: HarperCollin Publishers, 1996.

Ellis, L. *Theories of Rape.* New York: Hemisphere Publishing Corporation, 1989.

Ellis, L., and A. Walsh. *Criminology: A Global Perspective.* MA: Needham Hights. Allyn and Bacon, 2000.

Fieldman, P. *The Psychology of Crime.* New York: Cambridge University Press, 1993.

Flowers, R.B. *Sex Crimes, Predators, Perpetrators, Prostitutes, and Victims.* Springfield: Charles Thomas Publisher, 2001.

Gelles, R. *Through a Sociological Lens: Social Structure and Family Violence.* Newbury Park: Sage, 1993.

Gong, A.X. *Underground Society in China.* Changchu China: v302, pp6. Shenhua Publisher, 2001.

Grossman, D. Trained to Kill. *Christianity Today* August 10, 1998.

Hickey, E.W. *Serial Murders and Their Victims.* CA: Wadsworth, 1997.

Jankowski, M. S. *Islands in the Street: Gangs and American Urban Society.* Berkeley: University of California Press, 1991.

Johnson, P. R., and J. Indvik. *"Workplace Violence: An issue of the Nineties."* Public Personnel Management 23(4), 515-523, 1994.

Kenney, D.J., and J. O. Finckenauer. *Organized Crime in America.* Belmont: Wadsworth, 1995.

Kushner, H.W. *Terrorism in America.* Springfield: Charles Thomas Publisher, 1998.

Levin, J., and J McDevitt. *Hate Crimes.* New York: Plenum Press, 1993.

Lindquist, S. *The Date Rape Prevention Book.* Naperville: Sourcebook, 2000.

Mann, C. R. How Women Kill. Albany: State University of New York Press, New York 1996

Mantice, J. *Bug Off!* Evanston: Walnut Grove Publishers, 1992.

Margolis, J. A. Teen Crime Wave: A Growing Problem. Springfield: Enslow Publishers, 1997.

Meadows, R.J. *Understanding Violence and Victimization.* Upper Saddle River: Simon & Schuste /A Viacom Company, 1998.

Miller, M. *Coping with Weapons and Violence at School and on Your Streets.* New York: The Rosen Publishing Group, 1999.

Miller, M., and J. File. *Terrorism Factbook.* Peoria: Bollix Books, 2000.

Rand, M. *Carjacking: A National Victimization Study.* Washington D.C.: Bureau of Justice Statistics, Department of Justice, 1994.

Rand, M. *Criminal Victimization in the United States.* Washington D.C.: Bureau of Justice Statistics, Department of Justice. 1997.

Reppetto, T. A. *Residential Crime*. Cambridge: Ballinger, 1974.

Russell, D.E., and R. M. Bolen. The Epidemic of Rape and Child Sexual Abuse in the United States. Thousand Oaks: Sage Publishing Inc, 2000.

Sanders, W.B. *Gangbangs and Drive-bys:* Grounded Culture and Juvenile Gang Violence. New York: Adline de Gruyter, 1994.

Skorneck, C "683,000 Women Raped in 1990, New Government Study Finds." Boston Globe, April 24, 1992.

Snow, R. L. *Protecting Your Life, Home, and Property: A Cop Shows You How*. New York: Plenum Press, 1995.

Timrod, A.D., and M. R Rand. *Violent Crimes by Strangers and Nonstrangers*. Washington D.C: U.S. Department of Justice, 1987.

Wang, Y.D. "Photographer Caught Pocket-Lifters on Photos." Youth Generation, November, 2001.

Wolff, L. *Gangs*. San Diego: Lucent Book, 2000.

Chapter 5
Legal Aspects and Services

This chapter focuses on legal concerns relevant to self-defense. Among the discussions are the defender's legal right to protect themselves, their limits in using physical skills, justification of self-defense actions, and other issues.

Concerns

Self-defense often involves the use of force from both sides: the attacker usually uses force first, and the defender uses force to counter back. Body injuries and death may occur during the attack and fighting-back. The law prohibits the use of force to attack other people. However, criminals do not care about the law. They will use any necessary force to achieve their objectives with no thought of harm to the potential victims. When the attacker breaks the law, very often there is no way for the defender to escape, except by using force to fight back. The law, however, has some limits on the degree of force a defender can use. Failure to follow the law may result in a lawsuit against the defender, even when the defender is simply using self-defense to protect herself or himself. Sometimes the defender ends up in jail or paying for damages to the attacker. This may sound ridiculous, but it is true. A typical example was a case that occurred in San Francisco, California several years ago. A robber robbed a lady's purse and tried to run away. A taxi driver saw what was happening and drove after the robber. He finally caught the robber by pinning his knees against a wall using the front bumper of the cab. Was the cab driver a hero? Yes, in the eyes of the community, but not in the judgment of the court. The robber sued the driver and won! The court ordered the driver to pay the criminal for the bodily injuries due to the use of excessive force. This is a ridiculous and unbelievable, but true story. Sometimes the rights of the criminals get more attention than the victim's rights in this country. There are many cases where defenders have been sued by the attacker.

Defenders may run into the following tough problems that they should know how to deal with 1) Your boss harasses you in the office. Can you fight back and break his arm, or should you remain silent? He will continue to harass you if you do not do anything, but he may sue you if you injure him. 2) You are cornered by a man in an isolated area, and you know he is going to attack you for sure. You will lose for sure if he starts attacking you first. Can you attack him first and get away? Will you become the attacker and be sued? 3) A man gets into your house, and you point your handgun at him and ask him to leave. Instead of leaving the house, he walks toward you peacefully and tries to take your gun away. Should you shoot him or let him take your weapon away? You will become a killer if you shoot him, but he will shoot you when he gets the gun. Most states, however, take a dim view of the homeowner shooting a burglar just to protect his home or possessions. This is especially true when the burglar is about to enter or leave a house. The burglar has the right to sue if injured. In many jurisdictions, shooting is justified only when proof can be established that your life is threatened. It is very difficult to have the proof (Mantice 1992). 4) A man gives you a bear-hug attack in an isolated area when you are jogging alone. You give him an elbow strike and knock him down. Can you give him more kicks before you run away or just walk away? It is illegal to use more force against him when he has lost the ability to attack you again, but how can you be sure he cannot attack anymore? If you do not know how to deal with a situation, then you may not have a chance to defend yourself successfully.

The defender may run into following issues when using self-defense techniques. 1) How much force can a defender safely use? 2) Can a defender keep using force when the attacker is down on the ground? 3) How do you justify your self-defense actions when you are attacked, the criminal is injured, and then sues you? 4) How does the defender bring the attacker to justice? To successfully defend him/herself and avoid legal problems, a defender should have a good understanding of the issues involved.

Impacts of Legal Issues on Self-Defense

Legal issues have important psychological impacts on self-defenders and have direct impacts on their self-defense actions. Most defenders are good people, and they have high life goals and bright futures. Therefore, they do not want to ruin their life goals and future because they do something wrong to break the law. When they have to use physical force to defend themselves in self-defense, they tend to worry too much about the legal problems that result from their actions and not enough about their life and death issues, such as "will I be locked in jail if I injure or kill the attacker", or "I know I can defend myself but how can I prove I was doing self-defense?" When defenders think too much about the legal issues, they tend to hesitate, and the hesitation limits their skills and applications. They tend not to use their best effort to fight back at the life-threatening situations or at the right timing. On the other hand, however, the criminals do not care about the law or the consequence of their crimes, and they tend to use any violent force against the victims. Defenders will lose their fighting-back easily due to the hesitation and worries in a life-threatening situation. This is not a fair fight between the defender and attacker, since practically the law gives attackers more freedom and at the same time reduces defenders' freedom. This kind of situation usually puts the defenders at a great disadvantage.

What a Defender Can Do in Self-Defense: These Are Your Rights

The law provides three guidelines for self-defense. 1) Everybody should try to avoid physical confrontations. 2) Defenders can use reasonable and necessary force to protect themselves when they cannot avoid a physical fight. A defender has the right to use physical force to keep the attacker away or disable the attacker for safety reasons. 3) The defender can not use more force than necessary for his/her own safety in order to teach the attacker a lesson or to cause further damage after the attacker loses the ability to further hurt or threaten the victim. That means that the defender has to look at the situation and control precisely how much force he/she uses. If the attacker just makes some harassing remarks, and does not actually threaten the defender's life, then the defender should not try to break his nose or strike his groin.

Although the law gives defenders some right to use physical skills, there are also some limitations. Self-defense situations vary, and it is impossible to exactly follow the law in such complicated self-defense situations. Defenders have to make necessary adjustments and apply the law creatively based on the situation. There are several practical guidelines to use in a fighting back situation.

Experts suggest that when the defender gets into a life-threatening situation, the first concern should be safety, not a lawsuit. It is better that the defender remain alive, even with the risk of being sued, than if the defender dies-even if the attacker ends up in jail. The defender should use enough force, even sometimes a little excessive force, because in life-threatening situations, it is impossible to precisely control the level of force. The defender should focus on fighting and winning, and then think about the legal issues later.

In a life threatening situation where the attacker has not started the attack yet, the defender may have to use physical force first instead of waiting for the attacker to strike first. This gives the defender a greater chance to get out safely and avoid additional injuries. The defender should give the attacker a warning to ask him to back up and at the same time try to get out. If the attacker keeps coming toward you and invading your private space, the defender should not hesitate to use physical skills first to fight their way out or to disable the attacker.

When your attacker is injured or looks injured but you are not sure yet, you should continue your self-defense until you are sure the attacker does not have the ability to come back anymore. During the fighting-back situation, you should try your best and use any skills to save your life. It is practically impossible to control your force precisely when fighting in life or death situations. You will not feel sorry if your use the maximum effort.

Justify Your Self-Defense Actions

After defeating the attacker and winning the battle, the defender should consider how to win another potential battle in court if the attacker files a law-suit. The court and jury look for several kinds of evidence that are the keys to winning the case. This evidence includes witnesses, proof of injuries, contrast between the appearance of the attacker and defender, any available physical evidence, words used, and other materials.

First, the court considers the witnesses. If the defender has a witness to support him/her, it is much easier to win the case. Sometimes it is very difficult because some witnesses do not want to come forward due to the fear that the criminal may seek revenge or they think they do not have a clear view of what really happened. The defenders should do their best to get the witness to support their cases.

The second factor is bodily injuries. Injuries to the attacker provide them with an advantage, because juries tend to believe that the person injured is the victim even though very often this is not true. The defenders should also show their injuries to the court and jury, and state firmly that they were using reasonable self-defense. The attacker deserves whatever consequences occur because they initiated the crime.

The third factor is the look of the attacker and the defender. It is common that most victims are women and attackers are men, and most attackers are stronger than the defenders. The jury and judge tend to believe that, and this is one of their major criteria for court decisions. This factor gives most defenders an advantage in winning the case. If it is the opposite, the defender should use other evidence.

The fourth factor is the other evidence, such as the attacker's weapon, clothes, blood, and the scene of the crime (like in the defender's home). You may have to consult with a lawyer regarding how to use this evidence. Such evidence may give you the needed advantage to win the case and protect your rights to fight back.

The fifth factor is the use of words. Very often, there is no witness or evidence to support either you or the attacker. It is a case of one person's words against another. The attacker may show the court his/her injuries which he/she claims were caused by the defender using excessive force. However, because there is no witness or evidence, it is impossible to determine who caused the injury. Maybe the attacker fell or a car hit him in a completely unrelated incident. Defenders should not be responsible for such injuries.

It is very important that defenders develop the basic knowledge of how to justify their self-defense actions because with this knowledge, defenders will not worry too much about a potential lawsuit, thus they can concentrate more on fighting back effectively to protect their life.

According to the Supreme Court opinion (Madden 1981), a proper self-defense instruction to a jury considering a homicide committed by a woman defending herself against assault by a male should include the following:

1. Events prior to the assault that resulted in the killing should be admitted as evidence, and it is important in understanding the defendant's point of view at the time.

2. The woman's subjective evaluation of the danger in the situation should be given priority consideration.

3. Relevant factors including the woman's inexperience in defending herself, inability to defend, and actual inequalities of size and strength compared to the attacker.

4. The use of a weapon may be necessary for a woman to defend herself equally against an unarmed male attacker.

Bringing Criminals to Justice

Another important issue related to legal concerns in self-defense is to bring the attacker to justice. Every defender has the responsibility to help the police and court in their efforts to put criminals in jail. This way, there will be less criminals on the street, society will be much safer, and the defender will also benefit from the safe environment. On the other hand, however, if we do not bring these criminals to justice, they will still be on the street committing more crimes since they have not been punished. They won't stop when they benefit from their crimes and are not being caught. Thus, criminals who attack a victim will have a chance to then attack other victims.

Bringing the attackers to justice is not easy. It takes a great deal of courage to do so because to be a witness may result in the revenge of the criminals. The basic criteria for bringing the attacker to justice are to do it without risking the defender's life. In other words, the defender's safety should be the first priority, and bringing attackers to justice is the second. Defenders should make this decision in consultation with their family and lawyer.

To bring the attacker to justice the defender will need evidence and the defender should try to provide these facts to the police and court. This evidence may include witnesses, injuries, weapons, etc. The defender should try to grab anything which is useful for this purpose without getting the attention of the attacker. Defenders should not inform the attacker that they want to bring them to justice, or stare at the attacker in order to remember the appearance of their face, or say, "I will remember you and I'll report this to the police". The reason is obvious. The attacker will try to wipe out any evidence when they find out that the defender will report them to police. In addition, this could further agitate the attacker and lead to greater violence against the defender.

If You Are Attacked (Medical and Social Support)

In case you become the victim of a crime, there are several things you should do to recover from the nightmare and reduce further risks. 1) Find someone to help you to a safe place, and then go to the doctor for a physical examination in order to avoid any serious medical consequences from the injuries. 2) Report the crime to the police in an effort to bring the attacker to justice. 3) Find a support group to help you go through the emotional shock. This group may include family members, teachers, counselors, and friends. This is a difficult time for you, and support is important to most victims. 4) Take precautions and try to prevent this kind of attack from happening again. It is not uncommon for the victims to be attacked again because they may belong to a high-risk group. The victim needs to sit down and analyze how this happened and how they can prevent it the next time. Self-defense teachers and police officers may give you more advice on this.

REFERENCES

Brown, S. L. *Counseling Victims of Violence.* American Association for Counseling and Development, Virginia, 1991.

Fike, R. A. *Staying Alive.* Washington, D. C: Acropolis Books, Ltd., 1994.

Quigley, P. *Not an Easy Target.* New York: Fireside Book, 1995.

Mantice, J. *Bug off!* Evanston: Walnut Grove Publishers, 1992.

Madden, S. "Fighting Back with Deadly Force: Women Who Kill in Self-defense". In *Fight Back* edited by F. Delacoste and F. Newman. MN: Minneapolis: Cleis Press, 1982.

PART TWO

Prevention in Self-Defense

➤ Prevention at Different Locations

➤ Prevention of Different Types of Crimes

➤ Crime Prevention for Different Populations

Chapter 6
Prevention at Different Locations

This chapter covers prevention principles and prevention strategies in self-defense at different locations. Practically everywhere you are, there are chances you may become a victim, even though some places are safer than other places. Therefore, anywhere you are or you go, you should be alert about the potential danger and take precautions. Since most of time the victims do not know exactly what kinds of attacks they will face, it is practical that they know how to prevent all possible crimes at any locations they might be in. These strategies are developed based on research, principles of crime prevention, real-life cases, and recommendations from experts.

Students should not only understand these principles and strategies, but also apply them to everyday life. None of these strategies will work for you unless you actually apply them in your everyday life. Students are encouraged to look through these strategies and skills, write down those they can do, and then put them into action. Also, students should not just limit their minds into these skills only. They always can and should creatively use these skills and learn more new skills.

Implications of Prevention

Prevention is the first and the most important step in self-defense. The main purpose is to keep you away from any life-threatening situations in order to reduce the chance of becoming a victim of crimes. The old saying in medicine, "One ounce of prevention is worth a pound of cure" also fits into self-defense perfectly. We can say one act of prevention is worth a hundred fighting skills. It is much easier to stay away from the trouble than to fight in a life-threatening situation.

No single strategy works well alone in prevention of crimes; what we can do is to eliminate the risk factors one-by-one to reduce the chance of becoming victims of crimes.

As discussed earlier, crimes are committed based on several elements: the motivation of the criminals, the right place, the right time, and the right victim. In another words, the criminals look for good opportunities. The best prevention is to reduce these elements in order to limit their opportunities. There are several important principles in prevention, and based on these principles, specific strategies and skills are developed for and applied to different situations. These principles and strategies can be applied to most self-defense and crime prevention situations.

Principles of Prevention

The basic principles of prevention in self-defense are based on the analysis of the crime process. Taking one or more rings away from the crime ring will dramatically reduce the chance of becoming victims.

1. Believe you may become a victim of crimes. Believing anyone may become a victim of crimes can make people aware of the importance of crime prevention and self-defense and take it seriously. Therefore, they are more likely to put safety as the top priority in everyday life and to initiate actions for better preparation.

2. Establish a safe lifestyle. A safe lifestyle plays an important role in crime prevention and self-defense. A safe lifestyle, such as always thinking of safety first before going anywhere, can reduce the risk of becoming a victim of crimes. On the other hand, an unsafe lifestyle, such as regularly going to bars at night or jogging in the dark alone in an unsafe area, exposes you to dangerous situations. People should eliminate these unsafe lifestyles. Avoiding drinking and drugs will certainly reduce the facilitating factor of the crime process.

3. Do not create enemies (a good fellow model). Creating enemies puts victims in the worst situation. It triggers the crimes and makes you the victim of hate oriented crime easily. Remember, hate is one of the two major motivations of criminals, and many cases are initiated by the victims. There is little you can do to prevent this kind of crime because your enemy is highly motivated to attack you, while you cannot predict when, where, and how you are going to be attacked. You may have to live in fear and under stress everyday. Making an enemy is very easy, sometimes before you know it. Examples include getting involved in an argument which has tension, treating people in a nasty way, trashing people, making nasty remarks, tailgating while driving, insulting other people's feelings, tricking people, and taking away another person's property.

4. Avoid dangerous places (the beaver model—beavers build their homes in a safe place only). Location is an essential factor which may facilitate or impair the criminal's decision to attack or not. You can avoid many bad situations by not going to the scenes where criminals can attack you easily. The dangerous places include isolated areas, dark areas, gang-active areas, drug-related areas, and areas involving a lot of money.

5. Avoid dangerous times. Time is another factor which may facilitate or impair the criminal's decision to attack or not. You can avoid many bad situations by not going to dangerous scenes at dangerous times. These dangerous times include when it is dark, you are alone, you are not prepared or alert, you are concentrating on something else (distracted), and anytime when you are in dangerous places.

6. Be a tough target (the porcupine model—few animals dare to attack a porcupine). Vulnerability is the most essential factor which influences the criminal's decisions and actions. Most criminals select weak victims because either they have more confidence to put the victim under control, or they can finish the crimes very quickly, thus with less risk of being found and caught; or they feel safe because the vulnerable victims will not fight back. Tough targets warn the attackers to stay away and have less chance to be selected by criminals. Becoming a tough target can be carried out in many ways. For example, having a big dog in the house or installing an alarm system will make your house tough or look tough. Walking with a mace in your hand also makes you look tough. Being assertive is also recommended by experts.

7. Become an invisible target (the chameleon model). The main idea of this principle is that you behave the same way as other people in your environment so that the criminals have no particular reason to pick you as the target among so many people. On the other hand, showing off your richness or making someone hate you will make you a visible target and that can trigger the crimes easily. Being an invisible target may be done in many ways. For example, hiding your valuables instead of showing off your richness will not attract criminals to rob you, and being nice to other people will reduce the chance of becoming a target of revenge which may result in assaults or murders.

8. Take actions now. Most people know the danger of crimes, but many of them are reluctant to take any actions to prevent and prepare for it. No strategies or skills can make you safe, no matter how good they are unless you really want to apply them and actually carry out these principles, strategies, and skills in your life.

Prevention at Residence

Prevention at Home

Most people spend more time at home, and they tend to be relaxed there since the home is your harbor after a whole day's work or school. However, murders, assaults, rapes, and robberies and burglaries all occur in homes across this nation. People should do their best to make their home a safe place to be. The following strategies may help you prevent crimes in your home.

1. Find a safe place as your home. Maybe a safe place is more expensive or farther away from your school or work, but nothing is more important than your safety. Of course, people need to make this kind of decision based on their priorities. Would you rather live in a house which is close to school but in a bad neighborhood or would you rather live in a house farther away from your school or work where you can have greater safety?

2. Make your house a tough place for crimes. There are many specific skills you can use to make the potential crimes extremely difficult and risky, and make the criminals feel it is not worth trying. You may like to have a dog which scares most criminals because a dog can bite and bark. Even putting a dog bowl out as well as a sign "BEWARE OF KILLER DOG" will inform people you have a dog (Bittenbinder 1992). You can install an alarm system connected to police and put a sign out so that people can see you have an alarm hooked up. You also can put up fences and clear the bushes so that there is no place for the criminal to hide. You can install lights around the house to make the night seem like daylight or use floodlights which turn on automatically when someone walks into your yard. And you can put up chains to make your doors stronger and a peephole on the front door to screen your guests. Have solid doors and dead-bolt locks. Have a very safe room with strong doors and windows for emergencies. Engrave your initials or identification marks on your property.

3. Make your home an invisible target. Many skills can be used to reduce the attention of criminals so that they do not select your house as a target. You should not identify your gender in the phone book or on the mailbox, since some criminals use this clue to track you. You should not identify your status on a telephone answering machine recording (such as saying no one is home, or this is Wendy). Forward your message or turn off your answering machine when you are out for a long time, or state that this phone can indicate the caller's phone number when dealing with harassment calls. Do not advertise your travel. You should leave lights and a radio or TV on (of course a timer can do the same thing) and have mail picked up by neighbors when you are not home so that potential criminals do not have this clue. You also can leave an opened soda can and chips on the table. You should not show off your wealth so that the criminals will not pick you as a target. You should lock doors and windows, and close the curtains even when you are home. Even when you are just leaving for laundry or garbage, do not leave the door open. Remove all burglar invitations: computer, unprotected windows, bushes, climbable trees, any note on the door for deliveryman, and uncut lawn. Lock up your ladder, poles, axes, and other things burglars can use. Secure basement windows and garage windows. Close your garage door all the time.

4. Do not put yourself in a bad situation. Necessary skills include being alert and observing anything suspicious in your neighborhood, having a good relationship with your neighbors, avoid getting home too late or if this cannot be avoided, then asking someone to come with you, and avoid entering a home that may have been burglarized—let the police handle it. Beware of the possibility that attackers may shove you in when you enter your house. Do not intentionally confront burglars, but if unintentionally confronted with armed burglars, let them have what they want (Snow 1995).

5. Do not invite potential attackers into your house. Do not give your address or phone number to anyone if you are not sure they are good or bad people, and do not invite a salesperson into your home no matter how attractive his offer sounds. Have someone with you when you are expecting a repairman, and check with his company to confirm what he looks like. Do not let anyone use your telephone, even if it looks like they are in trouble—you can make the call for them. The reason is simple—many criminals pretend they are good people to fool you. Do not leave your keys under the door mat and do not tie a nametag on your keychain. Watch people your children bring home.

6. Form a neighborhood watch connection. Get together with your neighbors to start it and exchange phone numbers and connect with the local police department to get official signs for doors and windows. Discuss with your neighbors the focuses of the program. Pay attention to the following signs as suggested by police:

   ➤ Anyone coming to your door,
   ➤ Anyone hanging around your house when you are not home,
   ➤ Uninvited service people,
   ➤ Anyone parking in front of your house and won't come out,
   ➤ Anyone looking into your windows or car, and
   ➤ Strangers loading computers into their pickups.

7. After you have done all appropriate security actions discussed above, check your house from the burglar's view and fix the problems.

Prevention at Apartments

1. Find a safe apartment in a safe area. You will have less trouble, less fear, and less worry about crimes when living in a good apartment in a good area, even though you may have some trouble in terms of parking convenience or other problems. For example, apartments in downtown areas in big cities are close to schools or campuses, but they may have more robberies, gangs, and drug activities.

2. Investigate the location, the neighborhood, and the inside of the apartment complex to see if it is safe to live. You can see clearly from the environment, the condition of the building, car parking nearby, and people around the complex and in the complex. You can also check with the local police department for the crime status of the apartment.

3. Check the inside design of the room or unit you want to rent. Make sure the doors and windows are strong with secure locks, and that there are no previous lost keys. It is safer for you to change the locks first, add a dead-bolt lock inside, and install a security alarm.

4. Rent the apartment with friends but avoid strangers. Know your neighbors well. If your neighbors are good people, set up communication with them or a small neighborhood watch program. Find a better unit if your neighborhood is not safe.

5. Watch people in the apartment. A person with a key in his hand does not mean he lives in that apartment. Put up a sign to reject any solicitations at your door. Do not open the buzzer for strangers.

6. Always lock your doors and windows, and secure balcony sliding doors to avoid balcony hoppers. Never leave your key under the doormat or a wall hole by your door.

7. There are more strategies and guidelines for residence safety in the section on home safety. Those strategies also apply to apartment safety.

Prevention at Dorms

1. Find a safe dorm in a safe area. Investigate the location, the neighborhood, the rules and traditions, and the design to see if it is safe to live. You can check with the campus police department for the current crime status and history of the dorm. You can also get information from the residents who lived there.

2. Check the inside design of the room or unit you want live in. Make sure the doors and windows are strong with secure locks. You may like to change the locks if this unit has previous lost keys. Add dead-bolt lock inside, and install a security alarm.

3. Live with friends and avoid strangers. Know your neighbors well. If your neighbors are good people, set up communication with them or a small neighborhood watch program.

4. Watch people and their behavior in the dorm. Be cautious when dealing with people. Make friends carefully and do not invite strangers to your room. Do not give out your personal information to others since you do not really know them well.

5. Always lock your door and windows, and secure balcony sliding doors to avoid balcony hoppers. Never leave your key under the doormat or above the door.

6. Be cautious when attending dorm activities. Avoid drinks and drugs or other provocative behavior. Be assertive and dare to resist peer pressure on all these kinds of activities.

7. Make yourself look tough. You can hang a picture on the wall of yourself taking a self-defense class or sparring with a man, or display a martial arts trophy on the self.

8. There are more strategies and guidelines for residence safety in the section on home safety. Those strategies also apply to dorm safety.

Prevention at Hotels/Motels

1. Always stay in a good hotel in a safe area when traveling. The famous chain hotels usually are much safer than a local small hotel, and hotels are usually much safer than motels. Know the surrounding environment well for walking and driving safety.

2. Check if doors and windows are safe and make sure there is no door connecting to the neighbor's room. Choose the second floor if living in a motel to reduce the chance of break-ins. Use personal alarms on doors and windows if living in a motel.

3. Hide your valuables well and never display your cash or wealth openly. Watch people in surroundings but do not flirt with them or give out your personal information.

4. There are more strategies and guidelines for residence safety in the section on home safety. Those strategies also apply to hotel safety.

Prevention When Driving and Parking

Prevention When Driving

There have been many crimes directly related to the car: murders, assaults, rapes, and robberies all occur when drivers are getting in or out of their car at a parking lot, when waiting for signals at a junction or stop sign, while picking up strangers, while having a car problem down the road, or when stepping out of the car when bumped by someone, etcetera. Some strategies need to be considered seriously when you use your car.

1. Keep your car reliable. A car out of gas or broken down at midnight in an unsafe area is a nightmare and creates great dangers for the driver. Therefore, always keep your car in good condition and full of gas. Install a car alarm or use a steering wheel club to keep the crooks away (losing a car is not that serious, but when you are left in the dark alone because your car is gone, you are in a bad situation). You should have some weapons such

as mace, pepper spray, a stick, and a flashlight in the car in case you are in trouble. Have a second key in your wallet for emergencies.

2. If the car breaks down, put up the hood and lock the door, and put help signs in the front and back window while waiting for help. Do not accept stranger's help if you are isolated. Learn how to fix the small problems such as changing tires. A cellular phone can give you a great advantage in getting help quickly in bad situations.

3. Do not drive through a bad area, since you may run into gang or street fighting, your car may break down there, people may jump in front of you to make you stop, or cause a fender-bender to stop you. Avoid looking at your map in a bad place. When you drive a rental car on trips, know the direction and areas first.

4. Careful driving. Do not pick up hitchhikers because you have no idea who they really are. Do not step out to help other people when you feel unsafe, but send help to them. Do not blame yourself for being selfish, since this is really risky when many criminals abuse people's kindness to commit crimes. Roll down the window just one inch when asking directions or answering other people. Do not get mad at other people when they tailgate, honk at you in a nasty way, cut in without using turn signals, shout dirty remarks, or make bad gestures. On the other hand, do not do any of these things to other people. Remember that all people feel strong and more empowered in their cars, and they can get angry and seek revenge easily.

5. Do not step out of the car in isolated areas when someone bumps your car because that might be a trick to get you out of the car (Bittenbinder 1992). In small accidents, you can signal to the other side to follow you to a nearby station to exchange the insurance. Do not stop and get out when someone blocks your way. If other people follow you, go to the police station, or flash your emergency lights or turn on the alarm.

6. If you have to drive in the dark, think about taking a carpool, or drive with someone or use a rubber dummy on the passenger side. When entering your garage with an automatic door, look around first to check if anyone is hiding there.

7. When driving in especially unsafe areas, roll up and lock windows and sunroof, keep your convertible top up, and be aware of people standing by. Do not leave valuables in sight.

8. If you have to accept a ride from stranger in a bad area, or you are in danger, or there is no help around when your car breaks down, you may have to take a risk to forgo a greater risk. You have to use your intuition and judge if you can trust him/her. Inform your family or friend about his/her car plate and leave the information in your car. It is better to ride with a woman than a man, and it is better to ride with one than two or more people. You should check the handle of the door, and sit in the back with a weapon ready, but without looking like a kidnapper or a carjacker. Make the trip short. You should avoid telling him your personal information or talking too much. If you talk, you may disclose that you are a martial arts expert.

Prevention at Parking Lot and Garage

1. Find a safe place for the car. Avoid parking your car in unsafe places. These places include unfamiliar areas, dark areas, isolated areas, and high crime areas such as gang-occupied or drug activity areas.

2. Be careful getting into your vehicle. Approach the car carefully and check to see if there is anything suspicious nearby. Check the back, underneath, and the other side when approaching your car. Get your key ready when approaching the car, look around when opening the door and putting things in, and keep both processes short and fast. Lock the doors and windows when going inside.

3. Do not talk too much to people without paying attention to the outside environment. Move away when you see people loitering and suspicious people staring at you. Look around when leaving the car and lock all doors and windows. Never leave valuables in the car.

4. Park close to your destination and keep the walking short. Do not get out unless you feel safe. Ask people to meet you or take you to the parking area if you do not feel safe. Get your weapon ready for any potential attacks when getting in or out your car, and prepare some money to give out in case of robberies. Pay attention to pillars and cars where bad guys may hide.

5. When you bring a child and you have to put him/her in the safety seat, check the environment constantly during the process, or get in and lock the door when you do this. Get familiar with the process and make it short and fast.

6. Avoid arguments for a parking space. At some places where parking is tight, people tend to fight for a parking space. Since few people want to give up their right or privilege, such arguments can easily be upgraded into confrontations that often result in violence.

Prevention on Public Transportation

Public transportation is a place where there are many murders and robberies. The crimes may happen in a taxi, bus, subway, or elevator, and victims are very vulnerable in these places. The following strategies can help you reduce the risk.

Prevention on the Bus

1. Wait for the bus and get out of the bus in a safe area, and be aware of the surroundings when stepping off. Have an open view and know the stores around that area.

2. Look at your watch and look around to show people that you are waiting for someone. Do not fall asleep at the bus station and avoid using restroom there, especially in a bad area. Avoid talking to others and disclosing your personal information, and never flirt with strangers since you do really know who they are. Be polite but assertive and ignore provocative language and actions.

3. Take the bus when there are no suspicious people present. Sit behind the driver on the bus and keep your valuables invisible. Do not talk to strangers and be aware what is going on inside and outside of the bus.

4. Avoid taking the bus late at night or going into unsafe areas, even when traveling with someone else. Ask someone to meet you at the bus station if arriving late.

5. Be on guard all time and be ready to react to any potential attacks. Never be ashamed of overreacting since it is safer to apologize later when you find it is a mistake than to be a victim. Always keep some cash (for example, $100) handy to save your life when being robbed.

Prevention in Subways

The subway is always the battleground and playground for the city crooks. Gang robberies and murders are common in subways.

1. Choose a safe station to get in and a safe place to get out. Know your subway lines and stops and where police station or stores are.

2. Check the tunnel before you go through. Do not enter when someone is loitering. Avoid young gangs and do not let yourself be surrounded by gang members. Pull emergency cord if surrounded or threatened by gangs or strangers.

3. Stay close to the token booth and move when you hear the train coming. Walk defensively, stand against pillar. Watch and be alert. Avoid the last car since it is easy to block the exit and walk too long. Stay away from the punks in the car, and move to other car if do not feel comfortable.

4. Do not drink before using the subway. Do not wear or show off jewelry. Hide your wallet or purse, but do not make it look like you are carrying a lot of cash.

5. Avoid talking to others and disclosing personal information, and never flirt with strangers since you do really know who they are. Be polite but assertive and ignore provocative language and actions.

6. Be on guard at all times and be ready to react to any potential attacks. Never be ashamed of overreacting, since it is safer to apologize later when you find it is a mistake than to be a victim. Always keep some cash (for example, $100) handy to save your life when being robbed.

Prevention When Taking a Taxi

Even though only a small percentage of taxi drivers are bad guys and most taxi drivers are good people and can be trusted, we do not know which are the bad ones. Furthermore, good people sometimes can commit crimes when opportunities present themselves. The good part of taking a taxi compared to public transportation is that you do not have to wait in the dark, and you can go to your destination directly. The bad part is that when taking the taxi, people stay alone with a driver who may be a potential offender, or a robber may have just robbed the taxi and become the driver. Therefore, we would be better off to treat all drivers as potentially bad people and to act accordingly.

1. Whenever you can, ask friends, family members, or relatives to give you a ride instead of taking a taxi. It is worth the trouble for them to make sure you are safe.

2. When you have to take a taxi, let the driver know that your friends and other people know you are taking this taxi, so that he will not take the risk of attacking you. One easy way to do this is to use a cellular phone to call people and tell them the license plate number and the driver's name or I.D. number. Taking the taxi in front of people seeing you off is another good prevention idea.

3. Avoid talking too much and especially avoid giving out your personal information. Send information to the driver that you are an expert in martial arts, if you have to talk.

4. Beware where the taxi is going and what is happening outside and inside. Get the fee ready ahead of time so that you do not have to open your wallet in front of other people. Get out at a safe place and make sure no one follows you.

Prevention in Elevators and Stairwells

There are potential dangers when taking an elevator or walking in a stairwell. You may be isolated with a stranger, and face a rape, assault, or robbery.

1. Always choose a safe elevator or stairwell in a safe place. Wait for other people to go together if possible.

2. Never get in an elevator or stairwell when something or someone seems to be suspicious. Get out immediately if a suspicious person comes into the elevator or stairwell with you in there only.

3. Stand by the control panel in the elevator and face the whole elevator so that you can see what is going on. Press all of the buttons when threatened or attacked because the elevator will stop at every level and you will have more chances to get out or get help. Do not press the emergency button, because that will give the attacker more time with you (Bittenbinder 1992).

4. Show assertive attitudes and do not flirt with strangers. Be ready to fight back anytime.

Prevention in Public Areas

Prevention on Street

Walking or hiking can be fun, but can also be dangerous too, depending on the situation. Murders, assaults, rapes, and robberies all occur on the street or other places where you walk around. Victims are very vulnerable on the street, simply because they can be approached very easily without warning, and victims usually have no shelter to avoid the crimes. There are several street safety strategies you may use.

1. Safe areas. No matter what your purpose is, you should always avoid walking in unsafe areas which may include isolated areas, dark areas, drug areas, and areas with gangs and high rates of crimes. If you have to go to such regions (remember, you are putting yourself in a risky situation), go during the daytime and with someone, and keep the walking as short as possible.
2. Be alert and be ready. You should dress properly for potential running. Obviously, spiked heals and skirts are not ideal in terms of self-defense. Keep your valuables invisible but keep some change available as "buying the road" money which you are ready to give up in exchange for your safety in a robbery situation. Walking with confidence is also recommended by many experts because you look tough and you look like you are going to meet someone. Hold your mace, pepper spray, or stun gun in your hand for a quick reaction if something happens. Avoid walking near doors, trees, or other objects where someone may hide and you will have no time to react if something happens.
3. No flirting. There is no way one can make friends on the street, so do not flirt with strangers. Keep a safe distance when you have to talk to people you do not know. Ignore any rude remarks from other people because any response from you may trigger trouble. Do not accept a ride from someone you do not know.
4. Beware of your surroundings and do not use a walkman or thumb a ride. If a car pulls over beside you, quickly turn and go back in the other direction. When you walk or ride your bike along the road, beware if a car is coming close and might hit you on purpose.

Prevention in Restrooms

Dangers in public restrooms include potential robberies, rapes, and purse snatches. Sometimes, the offenders are the same gender, but sometimes can be a different gender. The sign "Men" or "Women" are just for good citizens only, and have no impact on criminals. In other words, a man may sneak into a women's restroom or dress up like a woman in the lady's room to commit crimes, especially rapes and robberies. There are many real-life cases already.

1. Avoid using isolated public restrooms and restrooms nobody else is using at the time you are. If you have to use it, go in with someone or at least have that person stay outside and keep communication with you.
2. Check the inside of the restroom for suspicious people when going in there. Be alert when using it and get out when something or someone suspicious happens.
3. Do not carry your purse in or hold it tight. Do not leave your luggage outside or ask strangers to watch it for you. Do not be too trusting.
4. Never let little children use the restroom alone. Go in there with him/her if possible, or at least stay outside and keep conversation going with him/her.

Prevention at Telephone Booths

1. Since robbery is the most possible crime at the telephone booth, it is critical that you should avoid using a phone booth, especially at a bad area and dark time. If you have to, use a phone at a public place where other people are around.
2. Do not keep your back to the door and only concentrate on your talking. Face the door and look around when making the call and keep the conversation short.
3. Remember to keep your valuables out of sight. Prepare some changes for the call before getting in the booth. Get out and walk away when suspicious people loiter around or approach you.

Prevention at Banks

The major danger at a bank is bank robbery. You may be robbed, shot or stabbed, or held as a hostage during a bank robbery.

1. Go to banks as little as possible. Banks are the favorite places for robbers. Although bank robberies do not occur everyday, it is unpredictable when and where they may occur. Using direct deposit is one way to reduce your need for going to the bank. Getting cash from supermarkets also reduce your trips to the bank.
2. Go to a bank where their safety record is good. Check the surroundings for suspicious things or people before going into the bank. Get everything ready for your task and keep the time short in the bank.
3. Cover your cash when taking it from the bank teller, and do not let people inside or outside the bank see your money. Be alert when stepping out.
4. Try not to use the ATM machine. If you have to, find a safe one or go with someone, and do it fast.

Prevention at Parks

A park is a good place to commit crimes, since some places in the park are isolated, offenders can approach the victims easily and get away easily. People at parks are usually relaxed and tend to forget the potential attacks.

1. Never go to a park which is unfamiliar, has woods and is isolated, and has drugs and gangs. Check with the police department about the frequency of crimes at local parks where you like to go.
2. Never explore the unknown part of a park. Jogging, hiking, or biking alone through hills and trees are not safe practices. Do these activities with other people in daylight in populated areas.
3. Avoid sleeping in the park alone or meditating alone without other people around. Dating lovers also need to be aware of surroundings and the people around. Parents should watch and follow their children.

Prevention at Shopping Malls

Shopping malls are generally safe, but potential dangers also exist. These risks include robberies, pickpockets, terrorism bombings and shootings, and gang-related assaults.

1. Shop at a safe mall in a good area. Avoid low income areas and gang or drug areas. Be sure the parking lot is close and safe too.

2. Avoid isolated pathways or stairwells. Never go into the backroom of a store for any reason. Use the restroom with caution as guided in the Restroom Safety section.

3. Do not flirt with strangers. Stay away from people showing provocative behaviors or language. Be polite to people, but assertive.

4. Beware of potential shooting and bombing in the crowded areas. Avoid places where a bomb may be hidden such as trashcan. Be alert about people around and suspicious actions.

5. Follow the Parking Lot Safety guidelines listed in that section.

Prevention at Stores

Dangers at stores, especially convenience stores, include becoming a victim of parking lot robbery and being a scapegoat of store robbery. The following strategies can help you reduce the risk.

1. Plan your shopping so that you do not have to shop at a convenience store in a bad area and bad time in a hurry. Choose a safe store in a good area for your regular shopping.

2. When you have to go to a convenience store for quick shopping, check the environment first, then park close to the store to reduce the walking distance. Get what you want and leave quickly.

3. Beware of people or things around you. Do not leave your purse on the counter or shopping cart, and beware of distractions from other people.

4. Follow the Parking Lot Safety guidelines listed in that section.

Prevention at Events (Arenas, Stadiums)

Potential dangers at crowded events include terrorism bombing and shooting, parking lot robbery, riots, and pickpocket. The following strategies can help you reduce the risk:

1. Know what event it is and where and when it is held. Avoid events held at a bad location and/or at a bad time. Avoid events where the fans are crazy about winning or losing a game and thus riots start easily, for example, a soccer game in Europe, South America, and Asian countries. Events where important people will show up and there might be a terrorism attack are also bad. Locate the escape route and sit close to the exits.

2. Stay away from the garbage cans where a bomb may be hidden. Check and find a hiding place in case of shooting or riot. Look around and be alert all time.

3. Avoid drinking before the event. Be polite and do not make enemies. Avoid arguments or conflicts due to small things and back away from the bad confrontations.

4. Hide your money and valuables. Follow the Parking Lot safety guidelines listed in that section.

Prevention at the Beach

Potential dangers at a beach include rape or sexual harassment, and fight or assault. The following strategies can help you reduce the risk:

1. Avoid isolated beaches where gangs and drug dealers are active. Avoid isolated areas of a beach, such as old trails and old buildings.

2. Know where the lifeguard or helper is, and know the environment well. Go with a group instead of alone.

3. Do not flirt with people. Ignore people using provocative language and behaviors. Be assertive but polite.

4. Avoid arguments or conflicts with other people over small things. These arguments can be easily upgraded into confrontations which often result in violence, especially when you get into argument with gang members.

Prevention at Recreation and Leisure Places

Recreation and entertainment places involve some danger too, but many people do not want to think about it. People become victims easily since they tend to relax at these places and be off guard, and that gives the criminal better chances to commit a crime. The entertainment and recreation places include restaurants, movies, parties, shows, clubs, sport fields, gyms, and shopping centers. The following are general safety strategies for these places:

1. A safe place and time. Always choose a safe place and a safe time for entertainment or exercise. It is not worth having a little fun at the price of your safety.
2. Be alert. Even at a safe place, one also should be on guard and watch the environment, since something may happen unexpectedly. Keep your valuables invisible and keep the children close to you (not just in sight). Watch the parking lot and the restrooms, some criminals may hide in these places.
3. Do not trigger crimes. Do not make any enemies when out in these places, by talking to, pointing to, directly looking at, or insulting other people. Do not get into an argument for a seat or a parking place. Back up when involved in a potential fight. Do not try to make friends with strangers. Be aware if someone is observing or following you.

Prevention at Arcades

1. Choose a decent arcade in a good area. Never go to an arcade where gang members are present. Places with nasty and drunk people around should be avoided as well.
2. Check who is playing in that place. Always get out when suspicious people or gang members get in. Be alert what is going on around you.
3. Be polite to people there, wait for your turn, and avoid showing inappropriate language or behaviors which make people hate you. Do not flirt with strangers or start trouble.
4. Do not bring a large amount of cash and always hide your wallet. If you bring your children there, you should monitor them at all times.

Prevention at Bars

A bar is a place for some kind of socializing and leisure. But from the self-defense perspective, it is not a safe place to go since you will be socializing with drunken people, and these people have no ability to control their own behaviors. Furthermore, some criminals are taking advantage of this situation to commit crimes. Potential dangers in a bar include follow-up rapes and robberies, confrontations and fights, and assaults from drunken people, gang members, or real criminals.

1. Avoid going to the bar. If you have to, choose one that you are familiar with, that is located in a good area, has only decent people, and no gang members or drug activities.
2. Check the bar when getting in. Find a safe seat where you can see the whole room and you can duck from potential shooting or fighting. Walk away if suspicious people walk in or sit near you. You should also know where exits are and how to get out fast.
3. Go with a group of people. Show appropriate behaviors. Do not make trouble or make enemies. Do not bring a large amount of cash and do not flash your cash openly. Avoid any arguments or conflicts over little things. If an argument or confrontation bursts out, back up and leave. Do not show your courage or upgrade the confrontation.
4. Do not associate or flirt with strange people in the bar. Never accept escorts or rides by strangers to go home. Do not go out on date immediately, until you investigate his background. Do not give out your personal information.

5. Take less drink than you can handle. Know your limit and do not get yourself drunk. Watch your drink all time. If you leave your drink unattended when going to the restroom, then you should throw it away and get a new drink. Do not take drinks from strangers.
6. Take extreme cautions in the parking lot following the guidelines in this chapter.

Prevention at Movies

Movies are usually safe, but sometimes they can be a place for crimes. Potential dangers include gang fights, assault, dirty tricks such a putting a needle on the seat, or pickpocket.

1. Choose a decent theater in a good area free of gangs and drugs inside and outside of the theater. Go with a group of people. Do not associate with gangs or drugs.
2. Be careful of your seat. Check it for needles or packages before you sit down. Sit by the aisles for quick exit if something happens.
3. Be alert about what is going on around you. Watch out for suspicious people and gang members. Walk way from these people.
4. Take precautions in the parking lot as suggested at that section in the book.

Prevention at Bowling Alleys

Potential dangers at the bowling alley involve robbery in the parking lot, assault and fights from confrontations with gangs.

1. Choose a safe bowling alley without gangs and other bad people. Know the alley and the surrounding area well. Know the exits of the alley in case of emergency.
2. Use good manners at the alley. Do not insult other people for any reason. Do not make trouble that you cannot handle. Avoid any conflicts or confrontations with people, especially youth. Do not take drinks or food from strangers. Back up when there are potential confrontations.
3. Avoid playing there when it is dark. Play with a group or friends.

Prevention When Camping

Camping out can be fun, but can be dangerous as well. It is easy to become a victim since people are vulnerable when they sleep out in the tents. No matter whether you camp out with school teams, with church participants, or by your family or friends, there are potential risks. An American tourist who camped out near Beijing was murdered in 2003.

1. Make sure the campsite is a safe place. It is better that a campground has patrol and security guards on duty—either police or self-organized security guards.
2. Stay in groups for activities. Never walk in or explore isolated areas alone or with one person. Know the surrounding areas well and let people know where you are.
3. If sleeping in the cabin, you should lock all doors and windows in the night. If sleeping in the tent, then secure the entrance of the tent and have some weapons ready (such as flashlight, and sticks). Sleeping in a sleeping bag has no shelter to protect yourself, except if you have a dog or sensor-activated alarm around you.
4. Go to the restroom with a group, especially during the night, with flashlight and weapons in the hand. Report any suspicious people or things to the security or chaperons.

Prevention When Hiking, Walking, Jogging, and Biking

Rapes and murders are common threats to hikers, joggers, walkers, and bikers. These people are often alone in isolated areas, and that puts them in dangerous situation.

1. Avoid hiking/biking in the dark and in isolated areas. Hills with trees give the attackers the best circumstances to attack you without much risk. They can approach you without signals and attack you before you can react. There will not be witnesses or help around. They can get out easily. No matter how pretty these areas are, it is not worth risking your life for it. Choose places where there are many people around in public, and where there are no gangs or drugs. Do not go to unfamiliar areas.

2. Hike/bike with a large group of people. Hiking with one partner is better than going alone and most people feel safe. But two ladies hiking alone are not much better than one. In isolate areas, even a male attacker can disable one of the victims easily and catch the second one. Going with a large group significantly reduces the danger.

3. When you take your children on a hike, be sure to have several adults with the group. A large group does not mean only an adult with several children. In emergency circumstances, children usually do not have the ability to handle it.

4. Always be alert when hiking. Dress up in sportswear and shoes, dress up in male clothing, have male partners, and have some weapons in your hand. Do not flirt with strangers, especially single males. If someone walks behind you, stop and let them stay in front so you can see what is going on.

5. Keep your bike in good shape so that it does not give you trouble in isolated and dark areas. Have the repair kit ready and know how to use it.

Prevention When Fishing

Fishing is great recreation for some people. But like hiking, fishers often choose isolated areas and that provides chances for criminals to commit rapes, robberies, and murders. The attackers include wanted criminals or escaped prisoners, criminals with special purposes, or regular people who see the opportunity then commit crimes.

The safety guidelines for fishing are similar to the hiking guidelines, but there are additional tips. One tip is to avoid taking a nap without a partner or partners around. The second is to watch where you are going when you are on the boat.

Prevention When Skiing

Robbery and murders are the two potential crimes to skiers, even though they do not occur often. The guidelines for safety include: 1) Avoid isolated unfamiliar areas. 2) Avoid dark times. 3) Stay with a group and avoid hanging out with strangers. The guidelines for hiking and biking are also useful to skiers.

Prevention When Exercising

Exercise includes indoor exercise and outdoor exercise. Potential dangers in gyms and fields as well as the parking lot and restroom include murders, rapes, assaults and fights, and robberies. The safety guidelines for jogging, walking, hiking, or biking in the wild have been discussed in the previous sections. The safety guidelines for the gym and sport field are different.

1. Choose a gym or field where it is safe inside and outside. There should be no gangs, no drugs, no prostitutes, and no bad people.

2. Follow the rules and respect other people. Do not argue over little things such as a space or opening or a better seat. People in the gym and field are often active and strong, and therefore they tend to have hotter tempers.

3. Do not flirt with people and watch the suspicious people around you. Do not accept a ride from a strange male if you are female. Do not give out personal information and never let other people figure out your routine and follow you.

4. Avoid the dark time schedule. However, many people have to work all day and their only time to exercise is the evening. In these cases, go there with more people or let your family members pick you up.

Prevention in the Locker Room

Danger in locker rooms includes potential robberies, rapes, and purse snatches. Sometimes, the offenders are the same gender, but sometime can be a different gender. The sign "Men" or "Women" are just for good citizens only, and have no impact on criminals. In another word, a man may sneak into a women's locker room or dress up like a woman in the lady's locker room to commit crimes especially rapes and robberies.

1. Avoid using public locker rooms. Taking a shower at home is much safer than in the public locker room unless there are a lot of people there. If you have to, go in with someone or at least ask that person to stay outside and keep communication with you.
2. Check the inside of the locker room. If nobody is inside, do not use it. Check out the locker-room for any suspicious people or behaviors when getting in there. Be alert when using it and get out when something or someone suspicious happens.
3. Avoid getting into the locker room with gang members, bullies, or bad people. Locker rooms are relatively isolated and provide good opportunities for these people to attack you. If you find them inside, walk out immediately.

Prevention on Tours and Travels

Taking a tour can be great fun, but sometimes it can also be risky because people on tours are usually not familiar with the area, they carry a lot of cash, and they are off guard most of the time. Therefore, these people easily become the targets of crime. Statistics indicated that 39 percent of violent crimes and 25 percent of burglaries occurred when the victim was in activities away from home. The following strategies can be used for your safety on tours and travels:

1. Know the places you are going. Avoid going to areas full of gangs, drugs, riots, or terrorism. Study your trip and plan with cautions. When you arrive, investigate the safety situation from the hotel information center or friends living there.
2. Find a safe place to stay and follow the hotel safety guidelines. When you take public transportation or a taxi, follow the general guidelines and the special tips in that area.
3. Inform friends, family, or business partners about your traveling plans, and ask for their assistance on hotels, transportation, sightseeing, and leisure.
4. If you travel to foreign countries, exchange money in the bank. Never do this on the street with strangers. Hide your valuables and do not flash cash.
5. Avoid loitering people and be careful when people surround you say good things about you. In European countries, that is a trick for purse snatches.
6. Know where the police are and how you can get help fast in case of emergency. Do not hang out with strangers or accept rides from them.
7. Watch your food and drinks all time in case people put sleeping pills in it.

Prevention in Special Circumstances

Prevention at Parties

Dangers when going to parties include rapes, assaults, and fights with gang members. Drinking and using drugs facilitate and trigger these crimes at parties. The following guidelines can be used to help reduce the risk:

1. After receiving the invitation, you should investigate who is organizing it and who will participate. If you do not feel comfortable with the organizers or participants, do not go.
2. Find where the party is held and when. Do not go to parties held in bad places and late at night.
3. Let family members or friends know the phone number and location of the party and how to communicate with you. Let the organizers know your family knows where you are and who they are.
4. Go with someone instead of alone. Stay with the group and avoid going to isolated rooms with a single man or men. Do not flirt with strangers and give out your number to them. Get out if you do not feel comfortable or you feel the danger.
5. Try not to drink alcohol at the party and definitely do not use any drugs. If you feel the pressure to do this, walk out.
6. Drink from the common bowl, only after seeing other people do it. Do not accept drinks from other people. Watch your food and drinks all time, and dump it and get a different plate when coming back from restroom. The best way is to finish your meal before going to the restroom.
7. Do not take a ride with strangers at the party. Drive your own car or ask a male friend or family member to pick you up.

Prevention When Dating

Dangers of dating include stranger and date rapes, robberies, assaults, and even murders. The following strategies can help you reduce the risks:

1. Make sure your date is a good person and safe to stay with. Set and communicate limits on behaviors and be assertive on self-respect and respect. Do not stimulate his desire through body language, eye contact, tone of voice, verbal responses, and dress. No alcohol and drugs on the date. Pour your own drink and watch your drink.
2. Avoid isolated and bad places and really late times. Be alert to the potential dangers and be on guard. Dating couples tend to go to isolated areas where criminals like to catch victims.
3. When having conflicts with other people, try to solve the problem peacefully and avoid upgrading the argument. The man should not show off in front of the date by out-powering the other party. Back away and enjoy your time with your date. Do not let small things ruin your good time or endanger your life.

Prevention in the Workplace

The workplace is another location where most people spend an average of about eight hours each day for about 40-50 years. The workplace is also a place which is becoming more and more dangerous. Murders, assaults, rapes, and robberies all occur in the workplace. There are several strategies which may help you stay safe at work.

1. Work at good locations and at daylight time without gangs, drugs, prostitutions, riots, and street fights. Travel with people at good locations and at good times only. Find out security information on places you are going.
2. Work with extremely more caution if you have a job which deals with cash or with criminals, such as working at convenience stores or bank, or working as a law enforcement officer to deal with drugs and gangs. Put your safety as a priority, try all strategies available, and be on guard all the time. You can ask your boss to take your safety into serious consideration and provide necessary protections.
3. Treat people with a good attitude and manners, no matter whether they are your boss, co-workers, or customers. Be polite, considerate, helpful, and have a smiling face as much as you can. Handle difficult people with kid's gloves and avoid direct conflicts or confrontations

with them. Solve any conflicts peacefully. Have a good working and personal relationship with people so that they will not pick you as the target or scapegoat when something happens, such as layoffs. Treat people the way you like to be treated. Respect other people and also demand respect and take a stand.

Prevention in Schools

1. Find a good school with good students at a good location. Avoid schools with gangs, and drugs or a bad neighborhood with gangs or drugs or prostitution. Find a school with more discipline and learning atmosphere, and with friendly students.
2. Set up high life goals, and join a supporting group made of good students and engage in healthy activities only. Stay away from gangs, drugs, alcohol, smoking, and other unhealthy activities. Do not compete and offend gangs and violent people, or make comments on them. Just avoid any contact with these people.
3. Learn how to get along with people in school. Be nice, polite, considerate, and helpful. Treat people with respect and good manners. Do not insult or bully other students.
4. Handle the romantic relationship with caution. Date good people and do a little investigation on your dates or girl/boy friend. Follow the guidelines for date safety and party safety. When finding your date is not your type, break up with caution by using polite strategies to avoid creating hate from the other party.

Prevention on Campus

Safety on university campuses varies from school to school. Universities located in downtown areas within a bad neighborhood in large cities obviously have more risks than universities located in small towns and good neighborhoods. Murders, assaults, rapes (especially date rape and acquaintance rape), and robberies all occur on university campuses. The following strategies may increase your safety on campus.

1. Know where you are. It is smart to know what environment you are in, how safe it is, and what kinds of problems the campus has experienced. Know how to locate the campus police and how to use campus escort services. Try to avoid isolated areas, and don't take late classes or study late by yourself. Use the escort service provided by the campus police department.
2. Beware of whom you deal with. University students usually have an active social life and deal with many kinds of people. It is also a time for dating and establishing serious relationships. Students need to know whom they are dealing with, especially the background of the person, instead of only considering how good that person looks. And keep this in mind, when someone tries to take advantage of you, they will try to make you believe that they are really a nice person when actually they are planning a crime.
3. Control your temper. University students are young and have less self-control. They can easily become angry and lose their temper, and that is a major way to trigger fights and revenges. You should try to control your emotion and respect other people's feelings. Try not to create enemies. Backing away from conflicts and confrontations is very small than upgrading.

REFERENCES

Bart, P. B. and P. H. O'Brien. *Stopping Rape.* New York: Pergagamon Press, 1985.

Bittenbinder, J. J. *Street Smart.* Illinois: Video Publishing House, Inc., 1992.

Fike, R. A. *Staying Alive.* Washington, D.C.: Acropolis Books, Ltd., 1994.

Quigley, P. *Not an Easy Target.* New York: A Fireside Book, 1995.

McClure, L. F. *Risky Business.* New York: The Hawworth Press, 1996.

Measows, R.J. *Understanding Violence and Victimization.* Upper Saddle River: Simon & Schuster/A Viacom Company, 1998.

Smith, S. *Fear or Freedom.* Wisconsin: Mother Courage Press,1985.

Snow, R. L. *Protecting Your Life, Home, and Property: A Cop Shows You How.* New York: Plenum Press, 1995.

Strong, S. *Strong on Defense.* New York: Pocket Book, 1996.

Chapter 7
Prevention of Different Types of Crime

This chapter will discuss warning signals in each crime and provide basic principles and strategies to prevent each crime. These principles and strategies are applications of basic prevention principles on different crimes.

Murder Prevention

The following behaviors are considered dangerous behavior of victims. These behaviors are more like a magnet which attract criminals to commit murders. Therefore, these behaviors should be avoided to reduce the chance of becoming victims of murder.

Warning Signals

Check to see if you have the following behavior. If you have one or more, you will have more chance of becoming victims of murder. Therefore you should try your best to terminate that behavior.

1. Join gangs or associate with gangs in any way, such as your friends or family members are gang members or have any relationship with gangs.
2. Live nearby or often walk by gang territories, drug areas, or low income areas.
3. Involved in argument and conflicts with other people often and never back up.
4. Start troubles often, such as insulting other people.
5. Make people hate you easily.
6. Use or sell drugs or associate with drug dealers.
7. Drink heavily or associate with drunken people often.
8. Abuse or bully other people.
9. Involved in romantic triangles.
10. Involved in work handling cash, dealing with criminals, working as prostitutes.
11. You are rich or you have a lot of insurance which benefit others when you die.

Prevention

The following principles are suggested to reduce your chances of becoming a victim of murders.

1. Never join gangs or associate with gangs and their activities. Convince your family members and friends to stay away from gangs and gang-related activities. Stay away from gang members and people who associate with them. Do not get in their way and do not challenge or offend gangs.
2. Never try drugs or associate with drug-related activities or people who use or sell drugs. Never try to make money from selling drugs.
3. Avoid arguments with people over small things. Solve the problems peacefully. Avoid upgrading the argument and learn to back up from argument which seems like it is leading to violence. Do not let ego or dignity block your way of withdrawing from argument. Nothing is worth of your life.
4. Never bully or try to out-power other people so they will not hate you and want revenge. Do not insult or mistreat other people. They might be vulnerable when facing you. But when you are asleep, you are the vulnerable one.

5. Never flash your cash or advertise your wealth so criminals do not have to go after you for money. Avoid buying big insurance policies to benefit other people in case you die.

6. Be very careful when engaging in romantic relationships. Do not hurt other side's feeling and make him/her hate you, especially at the break-up period. Avoid triangle romance.

7. Be very careful when your position or what you do gets into other people's way. Equally important, beware of other people who want your job, but you are still in good health.

8. Take great cautions when you want to be a witness to a crime, especially to a crime committed by gangs. Talk to your lawyer or police about how to eliminate the potential dangers.

9. Try your best to avoid potential rapes. In case of you become a victim of rape, do not threaten to report to the police to avoid further danger of murder when the rapist tries to wipe out the witness.

10. Do well on robbery and burglary prevention. These preventions will reduce the chance of associated murders.

Robbery Prevention

Warning Signals

Check yourself to see if you have the following behavior(s). If you do have one or more, you will have more chance of becoming a victim of robberies. Therefore you should try your best to eliminate those behaviors.

1. Use ATM machine often, especially at bad places or time.
2. Walk alone in darkness or in bad areas.
3. Show off your wealth or flash your money openly.
4. Work at convenience stores, and at bad place and late time.
5. Deliver cash to banks and stores.
6. Careless about your belongings and they are loosely guarded.
7. Wear expensive jewelry.

Prevention. The following principles are suggested to reduce your chances of becoming a victim of robberies.

1. Reduce your chance of handling cash. That includes using direct deposit, getting cash inside the bank, or using ATM at daylight at secured places and with other people. Otherwise avoid using ATMs. Try to avoid working at convenient stores in a bad area and late time.

2. Hide your valuables. That includes never flashing money openly, never advertising expensive jewelry and fashion clothing, and hiding your wallet and purse when you are walking and driving.

3. Avoid walking or shopping in bad places or at a late time. Walking with a large group of people can reduce the chance, since robbers do not like to attack people outnumbering him. Avoid shopping at convenience stores and parking lots, since these are common places for robberies.

4. Beware of people and environment. Watch behaviors of strangers carefully and be ready to avoid potential attacks by moving away from them or into a crowd or stores, ahead of their actions.

5. Be very careful at driving and parking. Robberies and carjackings always occur at these places. You can follow prevention guidelines introduced in the previous chapter.

Rape Prevention

Warning Signals

Check yourself to see if you have the following behavior(s). If you do have one or more, you will have more chance of becoming victims of rape. Therefore you should try your best to avoid those behaviors.

Stranger Rapes

1. Dress up provocatively.
2. Flirt with people and make yourself look like a target.
3. Give out phone number or address to people.
4. Drink or walk with strangers.
5. Stay or walk alone often, especially at bad places and bad times.
6. Carelessness about the danger and off-guard.

Acquaintance or Date Rapes

1. Unawareness of the danger and off-guard.
2. Too trusting of people.
3. Do not know the past behaviors of the person you are hanging with.
4. Your boss hits on you and you cannot change your job.
5. Provocative dress or talk or behavior.
6. Drink too much at dates or parties.
7. Use drugs or alcohol at dates or parties.

Prevention

The following principles are suggested to reduce your chances of becoming a victim of date or acquaintance rape.

Stranger Rape Prevention

1. Keep in mind that all men are potential rapists, since you do not know who they really are and which one is the real rapist. Be aware of the danger when associating with male strangers.
2. Do not trust male strangers at bars, on buses, or in parks. Do not stay alone with them, and do not accept their invitations to any private places.
3. Do not give out your address, phone number, or personal information to male strangers. Do not be fooled by handsome guys since you do not know who they really are. If you really like him and want to start a relationship, do a thorough investigation on him first, but stay on-guard all time.
4. Do not stay alone or let people know you are alone at home or at work. Avoid walking in bad areas at bad time by yourself. Instead always go with someone if you have to go to these places at a late time and keep your trip as short as possible.
5. Inform family members or friends who you are dealing with and where you are going.

Date or Acquaintance Rape Prevention

1. Investigate your date first.
2. Insist on equal rights, self-respect, and respect.
3. Set and communicate limits on behaviors and be assertive.
4. Do not stimulate his desire by using improper body language, eye contact, tone of voice, verbal responses, and dress.
5. No alcohol and drugs on the date. Pour your own drink and watch your drink.
6. Avoid isolated places and late times.
7. Be alert of the potential dangers and be on guard.
8. Use double dates.
9. Do not give your dorm key out.
10. Use your own car and have a good control of the date environment.

Aggravated Assault Prevention

Warning Signals

Check yourself to see if you have the following behavior(s). If you do have one or more, you will have more chance of becoming victims of assaults. Therefore you should try your best to avoid those behaviors.

1. Join gangs or associate with gangs in any way, such as your friends or family members are gang members or have any relationship with gangs.
2. Live nearby or often walk by gang territories or low income areas.
3. Have a bad temper and are involved in arguments often for small things.
4. Be nasty to others and start troubles often.
5. Insult, abuse, and make people angry easily.
6. Involved in drinking and drug activities.
7. Live in a neighborhood where you are a minority.

Prevention

The following principles are suggested to reduce your chances of becoming a victim of assault.

1. Never join gangs or associate with gangs and their activities. Convince your family members and friends stay away from gangs and gang-related activities. Stay away from gang members and people who associate with them. Do not stay in their way, and do not challenge or offend gangs.
2. Never try drugs, drinking, gambling, or associate with people involved in these activities
3. Avoid arguments with people over small things. Solve the problems peacefully. Avoid upgrading the argument and learn to back up from arguments or conflicts which seem to be leading to violence. Do not let ego or dignity block your way of withdrawing from argument. Nothing is worth your life.
4. Never bully or try to out-power other people so they will not hate you and want revenge. Do not insult or mistreat other people. They might be vulnerable when facing you. But when you are asleep, you are the vulnerable one. Be friendly with people, then you will get the same treatment back. Treat people the way you like to be treated.

Terrorism Crime Prevention

Warning Signals

Check yourself to see if you have the following behavior(s). If you do have one or more, you will have more of a chance of becoming a victim of terrorism attacks. Therefore you should try your best to avoid those behaviors.

1. You or your family members are considered as a political leader who has conflicts with terrorism groups.
2. You or your family members are wealthy and worth kidnapping by terrorism.
3. You go to large gatherings or events that may be the target of the terrorism.
4. You travel a lot by airplanes or take ship trips.
5. You travel to foreign countries where terrorism is active.
6. You travel to foreign countries where Americans are hated.
7. You live or work in a crowded place or near important buildings where terrorism targets.

Prevention

The following principles are suggested to reduce your chances of becoming a victim of terrorism attacks.

1. Take a low-key attitude and stay away from the spotlight if you or your family members are political leaders or wealthy. Do not let people know you are part of it, and that it is worth to do something to you as revenge or hostage.
2. Avoid flights as much as you can. Avoid traveling to countries where terrorism is active and where Americans are hated. Avoid taking ship travel.
3. Avoid working or living in crowded or famous places or near any important buildings such as military bases, banks, or government buildings.

Gang Crime Prevention

Warning Signals

Check yourself to see if you have the following behavior(s). If you do have one or more, you will have more of a chance of becoming a victim of gang-related crimes. Therefore you should try your best to avoid those behaviors.

1. You or your family member or your friends are part of a gang.
2. You or your family members or friends do business with gangs.
3. You or your family members or friends associate with gangs on drugs, firearms, and smuggling of other things.
4. You live or work and pass by gang-occupied areas or low-income areas or drug areas.
5. You have a business in gang-occupied areas.
6. Your business has competitions with these of gangs.
7. You are in the way of gangs due to your work as law enforcement officer or witness.
8. You or your family members or friends have arguments or conflicts with gang members.
9. You or your family members are wealthy and are considered as good targets for kidnapping, robbery, or burglary by gangs.

Prevention

The following principles are suggested to reduce your chances of becoming a victim of gang-related crimes.

1. Convince yourself, your family members, as well as friends never to join gangs. If they are in there, you should advise them to leave as soon as possible in a way not to provoke gangs to hate you.
2. Have a thorough background investigation when doing business with suspicious gangs. Do not associate with gangs on business.
3. Do not live or work in gang territory or areas. Do not open your business in these areas either.
4. Do not compete with gangs on business. Remember they are not bound by laws, and this kind of competition will not be a fair one for you, but it will be a dangerous.
5. Control your temper and be polite to other people. Do not argue with people for small things, since you do not know if the other party is a gang member.
6. Do a little research on gangs in the areas where you live, work, do business, or do recreation. You will have a good idea about their organizations and territories which have impacts on you and your family or business. You can find information from local police departments and gang prevention organizations.

Burglary Prevention

Warning Signals

Check yourself to see if you have the following behavior(s). If you do have one or more, you will have more chance of becoming victims of burglaries. Therefore you should try your best to avoid those behaviors.

1. You live in an area with low income houses, gangs, or drug traffic.
2. Your house looks wealthy and worth a burglary.
3. Your house is located in an area where it is easy to approach, hard to be seen by neighbors, and close to an escape exit such as freeway.
4. Your house looks vulnerable since there is no security alarm, dog, video camera, or neighborhood watch. The lighting is poor and bushes block doors and windows. Doors, windows, the garage, and basement are easy to break into.
5. Doors, windows, garage, or basement are left open with carelessness.
6. Signs of nobody at home are obvious. These include piled up mail, darkness during evenings, or lack of shoes by the door in Asian families.

Prevention

Principles and specific strategies for burglary are provided in the previous chapter of Prevention at Different Locations.

Auto Theft Prevention

Warning Signals

Check yourself to see if you have the following behavior(s). If you do have one or more, you will have more chance of becoming a victim of auto theft. Becoming a victim of auto theft does not have direct physical injuries, but the loss of your transportation may leave you in the dark alone and that makes you a potential victim of murder, rape, and robbery. Furthermore, it may cost you a fortune to buy another car. Therefore you should try your best to avoid those behaviors.

1. You have a popular car which thieves like.
2. You live in a bad area or park your car at isolated areas.
3. Your car protection is poor. There is no alarm, club, or other protections.
4. You leave doors open, windows down, or key in the ignition while you are not there.

Prevention

The following principles are suggested to reduce your chances of becoming a victim of auto theft.

1. Check with police, insurance, and auto dealers for information about cars thieves like, and avoid buying these cars.
2. Install all possible anti-theft equipment, such as alarm, club, or identification system.
3. Etch the VIN on every window for easy identification.
4. Do not display or leave your valuables in the car.
5. Lock the car and roll up windows all time.
6. Park the car in a safe place.
7. Do not leave personal information in the glove apartment.

Pickpocket and Larceny Prevention

Warning signals

Check yourself to see if you have the following behavior(s). If you do have one or more, you will have more of a chance of becoming a victim of larceny. Becoming a victim of larceny does not have direct physical injuries, but the loss of your wallet may leave you in a helpless status and that makes you a potential victim of murder, rape, and robbery. If you travel or live in China, you may become victims of assault when confronted with thefts. Therefore you should try your best to avoid those behaviors.

1. You carry a lot of money, or you flash your money in public.
2. You are in crowded places such as in subways, shopping malls, or shows.
3. You wear expensive jewelry.
4. Your wallet is in a pocket which is easy to steal.
5. You are distracted and careless about the environment.

Prevention

The following principles are suggested to reduce your chances of becoming a victim of larceny and pickpocket.

1. Do not carry a lot of cash.
2. Do not flash money in public and do not leave valuables visible.
3. When working in the business, do not leave your valuables where outside people can see them.
4. Hold your purse and wallet in your hand when in crowded areas.
5. Use velcro pocket for wallet or attach with a strap.
6. Separate your money in different pockets.

Family Violence Prevention

Warning Signals

Check yourself to see if you have the following behaviors. If you do have one or more, you will have more of a chance of becoming a victim of family violence including abuses and fights. Therefore you should try your best to avoid those behaviors.

1. Lack of love, respect, understanding, tolerance, and communication in the house.
2. Tension in the house and no peacefully channel of release.
3. Lots of argument and conflicts.
4. Orally attack, insult each other often among family members.
5. One person dominates the house and is bossy, even a bully.
6. Not happy with the existing life and spouse but see no way to change it.
7. Worry about economy problems in the house.
8. Drunk often or use drugs.
9. Temporary job, blue-collar job, or jobless.
10. Low education, low income.
11. Too many family problems and too much stress.
12. Previous influence of family battery and abuse and fight.
13. Many children, non-white, young, and short marriage history.
14. Lack of healthy activities or church activity.

Prevention

The following principles are suggested to reduce your chances of becoming a victim of family violence.

1. Build strong family ties. Initiate and establish love, kindness, consideration, respect, tolerance, trust, encouragement, understanding, and good manners in the house through various healthy activities.
2. Enhance good communication in the house. Exchange opinions about the family and talk about problems in the family promptly and openly. Try to take more responsibilities, promote understanding of the family issues and everyone's problems, and try to help each other instead of blaming each other.
3. Solve conflicts and problems in a peaceful way. Back up from any argument temporarily to avoid upgrading the tension while both sides are mad. Learn to say "sorry" and apologize and take the responsibility.
4. Set up reasonable goals for the family and enjoy the life at hand while trying together to achieve higher goals. Put family union as a higher goal than the higher material life.
5. Spend time together with family members in various healthy activities. Reduce the chance of heavy drink and drug problems. Avoid gangs and unhealthy activities.

6. Do not bring problems from work or school back to the house. Instead, leave them outside of the house. Talk to family members to help you deal with the problems. That will strengthen the family ties and generate better solutions, since two heads are better than one.

Workplace Violence Prevention

Warning Signals

Check yourself to see if you have the following behaviors. If you do have one or more, you will have more of a chance of becoming a victim of workplace violence. Therefore you should try your best to avoid those behaviors.

1. Your work deals with cash and valuables.
2. Your job deals with criminals and law enforcement.
3. Your job deals with tough personnel decisions such as layoffs.
4. Your job deals with difficult outside customers.
5. You worksite is located in or near bad areas where there are gangs, drugs, and prostitution.
6. You have to work at late hours.
7. Your job offends people easily.
8. Your work competes with that of gangs.
9. You travel too much to unfamiliar or dangerous areas.
10. You have a bad temper and treat people in nasty ways.

Prevention

The following principles are suggested to reduce your chances of becoming a victim of workplace violence.

1. Work at good locations and at daylight time, in an area without gangs, drugs, prostitutions, riots, and street fights. Travel with people at good locations and good time only. Find out security information on places you are going.
2. Work with extremely more caution if you have a job which deals with cash or criminals, such as working at convenience stores or banks, or working as a law enforcement officer to deal with drug and gangs. Put your safety as the highest priority, try all strategies available, and be on guard at all times. You can ask your boss to take your safety into serious consideration and provide necessary protections.
3. Treat people with a good attitude and manners, no matter who they are: your boss, co-workers, or customers. Be polite, considerate, helpful, and have smiling face as much as you can. Handle difficult people with kid gloves and avoid direct conflicts or confrontations with them. Have a good working and personal relationship with people.

School Violence Prevention

Warning Signals

Check yourself to see if you have the following behavior(s). If you do have one or more, you will have more of a chance of becoming a victim of school violence. Therefore you should try your best to avoid those behaviors.

1. Your school is located in a bad area, or the school is bad.
2. The school has too many students from low income or blue-collar families.
3. The school has bad and violent students in the class or school.
4. The school has gangs, drugs, firearms, and bullies in school.
5. School lacks discipline, healthy activities, and strong principles and faculty.
6. Outside bad influence is too strong in school.
7. You have a bad temper and have conflicts with people often.
8. You compete with gangs or you are en enemy of gangs.

Prevention

The following principles are suggested to reduce your chances of becoming a victim of school violence.

1. Find a good school with good students at a good location. It is better to attend a school with more discipline, learning atmosphere, and friendly students.
2. Set high life goals, and join a supporting group made of good students and engage in healthy activities only. Stay away from gangs, drugs, smoke, and sexual activities. Do not compete and offend gangs and violent people, or make comments about them. Just avoid any contact.
3. Learn how to get along with people in school. Be nice, polite, considerate, and helpful. Treat people with respect and good manners. Do not insult or bully other students.
4. Handle any romantic relationship with caution. Date good people and do a little investigation on your dates or girl/boy friend. Follow the guidelines for date safety and party safety. When finding your date is not your type, break up with caution by using polite strategies to avoid creating hate from the other party.

Hate Crime Prevention

Warning Signals

Check yourself to see if you have the following behavior(s). If you do have one or more, you will have more of a chance of becoming a victim of hate crime. Therefore you should try your best to avoid those behaviors.

1. You are a minority.
2. You display inappropriate behavior or manners.
3. Other people have misunderstandings about you or your group.
4. Conflicts of values and political opinions.
5. Conflicts of benefits.
6. Competitions of business or jobs.
7. People from your race or group did something bad, and you became the scapegoat.

Prevention

The following principles are suggested to reduce your chances of becoming a victim of hate crime.

1. Merge yourself into the mainstream of society, make more friends from other races, and increase communication and understanding about your cultural or ethnic values.
2. Follow the rules and traditions of the mainstream society, even though it sometimes has little conflicts with your tradition. Show appropriate manners and behaviors accepted in the main society.
3. Treat yourself as a part of the society you live in, take care of the public property, make your contributions, and help people and the community.
4. Do not make enemies, and avoid unnecessary competitions and confrontation over little things. Learn how to back up and apologize when you are outnumbered.

REFERENCES

Kicks, J. *Dating Violence.* Brookfield: The Millbrook Press, 1996.

Chapter 8
Crime Prevention for Different Populations

In this chapter, we will discuss potential dangers of different populations and the basic principles and strategies of prevention. The first purpose of this chapter is to provide information on major potential dangers of different jobs to help students make decisions on their career choices from the self-defense perspective. The second purpose is to provide information on unique dangers of different populations so that college students can use these to protect their families. Each group or population will be discussed regarding the unique risks for that group besides the general risks that everyone can encounter, discussed in the two previous chapters and tips on prevention.

Children and School Students

Children are very vulnerable in protecting themselves from crime and violence. The reasons include, but are not limited to, the following: 1) Mentally these students are not mature enough to handle any kinds of life threatening situations. 2) Physically they are not strong enough to resist physical attacks from adult attackers. 3) Increasing youth crime and violence make these students potential victims of not only adult criminals but also youth criminals. These students often become the targets of criminals due to their vulnerability, and crime and violence have become a major factor threatening the health and life of these students. A report indicated that 20 percent of victims developed long term serious psychological problems. Therefore, the safety of school students should be the top priority to parents, teachers, school administrators, the community, and the government. The responsibility of crime self-defense for children should be mainly on the parents when the children are at a very early age, then gradually transfer to children themselves as they grow up.

Preschool Children

Potential risks

The unique risks for preschool children include kidnapping, abuse, and molestation. Kidnapping mainly is done by strangers, but may be committed by one parent after divorce. These children have no psychological or physical ability to protect themselves at all, so the parent should take full responsibility for the safety on these young children.

Prevention

Safety tips parents can follow to prevent kidnapping and abuse include the following:

1. Never leave children alone at home, in the park, in the car, or other places. Always keep your eyes on them wherever they go and whatever they do.
2. Never let strangers have the chance to stay with children alone, no matter where you are. Avoid going to isolated places. Hold children tight when in a big crowd such as in a sport event.
3. Follow the safety guidelines on all crimes for your safety. Your children become victims too, when you become a victim.
4. Create a peaceful family environment. Do not allow any substance abuses or any violent behavior.

Most child molesters are family members, relatives, friends, people they know, even people with reputations of being good to children (Snow 1995). Several tips were presented by Snow on the prevention and handling of child molestation.

1. Listen to your child.
2. Watch abrupt, radical, changes in behavior.
3. Do not show horror, shock, anger, or judgment.
4. Never say it is impossible.
5. Notify the police.
6. Watch people who insist on spending time with your children.
7. Be suspicious of any houses children like hanging around.
8. Teach children they have the right to say no.

Elementary School Students

Self-defense is not a part of the elementary school curriculum. There are no classes for this school level, except sometime police officers go to schools and give short lectures on self-defense together with riding safety. The following prevention strategies were designed for elementary school students in self-defense, based on theoretical analysis and practical applications of self-defense.

Aware of the Specific Risks

The unique risks of elementary school students include, but are not limited to, the following. Students in this period can become victims of real criminals and regular people, including family members.

1. Be bullied or to bully other people then suffer from the retaliation.
2. Participate in street fights, drug activity, and burglary.
3. Become victims of gang activities or become gang members and suffer from the gang-oriented crimes in schools or connected with gangs outside schools.
4. Involved in more everyday arguments, conflicts, assaults, and fights while lack of tolerance, self-control, and handling ability.
5. Run away from home to suffer from consequences such as rape, drugs, gangs, murder, or assault.
7. Hang out with bad people and commit crimes under peer pressure and suffer from the consequences, such as street fights and retaliation.
8. Become victims of kidnapping and rapes.
9. Become victims of school shooting or any types of terrorism attacks.
10. Become victims of family violence.
11. Become victims of Internet related crimes.

General Prevention Strategies

1. Understanding the common risks in their daily lives.
2. Analyze their personal risks and how to eliminate these risks.
3. Prevent crimes at school, home, street, and entertainment places.
4. Know about criminals' tricks and how to deal with them.
5. Develop safe lifestyle, personality, and habits.

6. Understand their rights and responsibilities in self-defense.
7. Handle small conflicts and avoid confrontations.
8. Develop family crime prevention plans.

Prevention of School Oriented Crimes

1. Set up high life expectations and prepare a plan to go for it. Have a supporting group of good students to achieve your goals.
2. Engage in healthy activities such as sports, art, music, invention, et cetera. Completely stay away from gangs, drugs, smoking, and sexual and destructive activities. All these activities can either make you a victim of relevant activities or make you a criminal that will suffer from consequences of being expelled or spending time in the prison.
3. Do not join gangs, and do not compete and offend gangs and violent people, or make comments about them. Just avoid any contact with them.
4. Learn how to get along with people in the school. Be nice, polite, considerate, and helpful. Treat people with respect and good manners. Do not get involved in arguments or confrontations over small things and resolve the conflicts peacefully.
5. Do not insult or bully other students. Do not challenge or precipitate any violent activities. Do not commit any crimes or destructive activities.
6. Never run away from home. Talk to your family members, communicate with each other, and solve problems peacefully. There is nobody who can give you more love than your family. Running away can put you in an extremely dangerous position of becoming victims of murder, rape, robbery, assault, and prostitution.
7. Be alert to any suspicious activities in school. School shooting or terrorism attack is the main focus of this tip.
8. Learn how to protect yourself on the way to school and home, and learn how to stay safely at home and at friend's home.
9. Report to parent if someone touches your privates or abuses you. Always tell parents the truth.
10. Know where to call for help in emergency.
11. Follow prevention guidelines on other crimes.

Parent Involvement

1. Discuss with children all potential risks in school, and plan with children how to prevent and handle these crimes.
2. Keep good communication with children, encourage them to speak out, and help them solve problems.
3. Create a peaceful, warm, and supportive family environment. Encourage and help children to set up life goals and plan steps to achieve them. Love your children and make the home the safest place for them.
4. Watch whom children hang with. Set limits and encourage children to avoid gangs, drugs, drinking, smoking, sexual activity, or destructive activities.
5. Create connections and relationships with good students and their families, and encourage children engage in healthy activities.
6. Monitor your children's Internet activities and prevent potential problems. Warn your children about the potential dangers of the Internet, since not all they see is true, and they do not really know people on the Internet. Tell your children never to provide personal information to net people.

7. Never leave your children alone at home, and choose a trusted babysitter-someone you know well. Be a bodyguard when selling cookies, follow them to the restroom in public, do not allow them to play alone, especially the bad areas. Do not let them go to a movie alone.

8. Secure your house and keep eyes on the children at a party at home, especially in the evening and night. Avoid letting children going to school alone through isolated or bad areas. Do not let them go to other people's house by themselves.

9. Teach your children to avoid talking to strangers, to not answer questions from a stranger, to not accept things from strangers, and never go with a stranger even if he says your mom wants you or she is sick.

10. Do not let them answer the phone, or do not let them answer the door.

Middle School Students

California Physical Education Standard requires self-defense courses to be offered at 7th grade, but not many schools are actually offering it due to the lack of a standard curriculum and instructor training. The following prevention strategies were designed for middle school students in self-defense, based on theoretical analysis and practical applications of self-defense.

Aware of the Specific Risks

The unique risks of middle school students include, but are not limited to, the following. A large portion of the crimes may be committed by regular people instead of real criminals.

1. Be bullied or bully other people then suffer from the retaliation.
2. Participate in street fighting, drug activity, robbery, and burglary.
3. Become victims of gang activities or be gang members and suffer from the gang-oriented crimes in schools or connected with gangs outside schools.
4. Involved in more everyday arguments, conflicts, assaults, and fights while lack of tolerance, self-control, and handling ability.
5. Run away from home to suffer from consequences such as rape, drug, gang, murder, or assault.
6. Hang out with bad people and commit crimes under peer pressure and suffer from the consequences, such as street fighting and retaliation.
7. Become victims of kidnapping and rapes.
8. Become victims of school shooting or any types of terrorism attacks.
9. Become victims of family violence.

General Prevention Strategies

1. Understanding the common risks in their daily lives.
2. Analyze their personal risks and how to eliminate these risks.
3. Prevent crimes at school, home, street, and entertainment places.
4. Know about criminals' tricks.
5. Develop safe lifestyle, personality, and habits.
6. Understand their rights and responsibilities in self-defense.
7. Handle small conflicts and avoid confrontations.
8. Avoid getting into trouble.
9. Take a self-defense class

Prevention of School Oriented Crimes

1. Set up high life expectations and prepare a plan to go for it. Have a supporting group of good students to achieve your goals. Do not let other things ruin your life goals.
2. Engage in healthy activities such as sports, art, music, invention, et cetera. Completely stay away from gangs, drugs, smoke, and sexual and destructive activities. All these activities can either make you a victim of relevant activities or make you a criminal that will suffer from the consequences of being expelled or spending time in the prison.
3. Do not join gangs, and do not compete and offend gangs and violent people, or make comments about them. Just avoid any contact with them.
4. Hang out only with good friends in and out of school. If your friends or classmates do any unhealthy activities, break out with them.
5. Learn how to get along with people in the school. Be nice, polite, considerate, and helpful. Treat people with respect and good manners. Do not get involved in arguments or confrontations over small things and resolve the conflicts peacefully.
6. Do not insult or bully other students. Do not challenge or precipitate any violent activities. Do not commit any crimes or destructive activities.
7. Never run away from home. Talk to your family members, communicate with each other, and solve the problems peacefully. There is nobody who can give you more love than your family. Running away can put you in an extremely dangerous position of becoming victims of murder, rape, robbery, assault, and prostitution.
8. Be alert to any suspicious activities in school. School shooting or terrorism attack is the main focus of this tip.
9. Learn how to protect yourself on the way to school and home, and learn how to stay safely at home and at friend's home.
10. Follow prevention guidelines on other crimes.

Parent Involvement

1. Create a peaceful, warm, and supportive family environment. Encourage and help children to set up life goals and plan steps to achieve them.
2. Keep good communication with children and help them solve problems.
3. Watch whom children hang with. Set limits and encourage children to avoid gangs, drug, drinking, smoking, sexual activity, or destructive activities.
4. Create connections and relationship with good students and their families and encourage children engage in healthy activities.
5. Discuss with children all potential risks in school and plan with children to prevent and handle these crimes.
6. Discuss with children all crimes of violence and how to deal with.
7. Love children and always stay behind them.

High School Students

California Physical Education Standard also requires self-defense courses to be offered at 10th grade, but not many schools are actually offering these due to the lack of a standard curriculum and instructor training. The following prevention strategies were designed for high school students in self-defense, based on theoretical analysis and practical applications of self-defense.

Potential Risks for High School Students

The unique risks of high school students include, but are not limited to, the following. A large portion of the crimes may be committed by regular people instead of real criminals.

1. Be bullied or bully other people then suffer from the retaliation.
2. Drop out of school and join gangs and suffer the consequences.
3. Be victims of gang activities or be gang members and suffer from the gang-oriented crimes in schools or connected with gangs outside schools.
4. Use drugs and be victims of drug related crimes.
5. Involved in more everyday arguments, conflicts, assaults, and fights while lack of tolerance, self-control, and handling ability.
6. Experience more sport-oriented conflicts and continuous impacts outside of school sites.
7. Run away from home to suffer from consequences such as rape, drugs, gangs, murder, or assault.
8. Suffer from rape or abuse in dating, at a party, and driving.
9. Hang out with bad people and commit crimes under peer pressure and suffer from the consequences, such as street fighting.
10. Become victims of kidnapping and rapes on the way to school.
11. Become victims of school shooting or any types of terrorism attacks.
12. Become victims of family violence.
13. Driving anger and other related crimes such as carjacking or robbery.
14. Become victims at part-time job and other community works.

Student Guidelines for Preventing and Handling High School-Oriented Crimes

1. Set up high life expectations and prepare a plan to go for it. Have a supporting group of good students to achieve your goals. Do not let other things ruin your life goals.
2. Engage in healthy activities only, such as sports, art, music, invention, et cetera. Completely stay away from gangs, drugs, smoking, and sexual and destructive activities. All of these activities can either make you a victim of relevant activities or make you a criminal that still suffers from consequences of being expelled or spending time in the prison.
3. Do not join gangs, and not compete and offend gangs and violent people, or make comments on them. Just avoid any contact with them.
4. Hang out only with good friends in and out of school. If your friends or classmates do any unhealthy activities, break out with them.
5. Learn how to get along with people in school. Be nice, polite, considerate, and helpful. Treat people with respect and good manners. Do not get involved in arguments or confrontations.
6. Do not insult or bully other students. Do not challenge or precipitate any violent activities. Do not commit any crimes or destructive activities.
7. Handle romantic relationships with caution. Date good people and do a little investigation on your dates or girl/boy friend. Follow the guidelines for date safety and party safety. When finding your date is not your type, break up with caution by using polite strategies to avoid creating hate from the other side.
8. Never run away from home. Talk to your family members, communicate each other, and solve problems peacefully. There is nobody who can give you more love than your family. Running away can put you in an extremely dangerous position of becoming victims of murder, rape, robbery, assault, and prostitution.

9. Be alert to any suspicious activities in school. School shooting or terrorism attack is the main focus of this tip.
10. Follow prevention guidelines on other crimes.

Parent Guidelines for High School Safety

Self-defense at the high school level is not just the responsibility of the students. Parents also have an important role in advising and directing their high school students for their safety. The following strategies are suggested by experts for the parent:

1. Create a peaceful, warm, and supportive family environment. Encourage and help children to set up life goals and plan steps to achieve them. Build strong family ties. Initiate and establish love, kindness, consideration, respect, tolerance, trust, encouragement, understanding, and good manners in the house through various healthy activities.
2. Keep good communication with children and help them solve problems. Exchange opinions about the family and talk about problems in the family promptly and openly. Try to take more responsibilities, promote understanding of the family issues and everyone's problems, and try to help each other instead of blaming each other.
3. Watch whom children hang with. Set limits and encourage children to avoid gangs, drugs, smoking, sexual activity, or destructive activities.
4. Create connections and relationships with good students and their families and encourage children to engage in healthy activities.
5. Discuss with children all potential risks in school and plan with children to prevent and handle these crimes.
6. Discuss with children all crimes of violence and how to deal with them.
7. Solve conflicts and problems in a peaceful way. Back up from the argument temporarily to avoid upgrading the tension while both sides are mad and there is no understanding. Learn to say sorry and apologize and take the responsibility.
8. Spend time together with family members on various healthy activities. Reduce the chance of heavy drinking and drug problems. Avoid gangs and unhealthy activities.

Student Guidelines for General Prevention in Self-Defense

1. Understand your rights and responsibilities in self-defense.
2. Know about criminals their tricks.
3. Understand the common risks in daily life and prevention.
4. Analyze specific risks for high school male and female students and develop prevention strategies respectively.
5. Analyze personal risks and how to eliminate these risks.
6. Prevent different crimes at places (home, street, drive, date, party, sport, and entertainment places, et cetera.).
7. Develop safe lifestyle, personality, and habits.
8. Know about the applications in life and continuous learning.
9. Know the law and avoid becoming criminals.
10. Know how to apply self-defense in daily life.
11. Take a self-defense class.

University Students

Potential Risks for University Students

The unique risks for students include, but are not limited to the following. University students are adults and are most times away from home. Therefore, safety is their own responsibility, even though parents may have some influence.

1. Have a bad temper and angry personality; lack of tolerance, self-control, and handling ability; and get into conflicts or arguments for small things but never want to back. It is easy for them to become victims of aggravated assaults and fights.
2. Drink alcohol or use drugs and have lost control of themselves. Female students tend to become victims of rapes and aggravated assaults.
3. Travel too much to dangerous places and become victims of robbery, rape, murder, or terrorism crimes.
4. Have more problems from romantic activities: dating, party, romantic triangle, and marriage violence.
5. Become victims in the workplace.
6. Become victims of all different types of crimes.

Prevention Strategies

1. Take a comprehensive self-defense class and become well prepared to deal with all crimes independently. Become smart and tough in self-defense.
2. Establish a safe lifestyle. Wherever you are and whatever you are, you should always consider your safety first.
3. Develop a good personality and learn how to get along with other people well. Always make more friends and no enemies.
4. Avoid dangerous places, bad times, and bad works (dealing with money or dangerous people).
5. Do not attract attention of the criminals. Be an invisible target.
6. Take dating and marriage issues very seriously. Never hang with potential dangerous people. The most important thing is to handle breaking-up very carefully and avoid becoming a victim.

Workplace Crime Prevention

This section will mainly discuss the potential risks of different jobs. There are hundreds of different jobs, and it is impossible to cover every job in this section. Instead, this section divides jobs/work into several major categories related to crimes and prevention, and provides typical examples to reflect the potential dangers of these types of jobs and basic prevention strategies. These jobs are divided two types: dealing with money and dealing with dangerous people. Jobs not covered here also can refer to similar jobs and apply similar prevention principles and strategies.

Bank Tellers

Risk

Banks handle big cash and therefore are always the main target of bank robbery. Shooting during robberies and becoming hostages are the major threat to bank workers.

Prevention

1. Choose a bank at a good location away from the highway.
2. Choose a bank with good security.
3. Become aware of the suspicious people or behaviors. Watch the environment closely.

Convenience Store Workers

Risks

Robbery is always the major threat to workers at convenience stores. Other crimes such as follow-up murder, rape, and assaults are common in robberies at these stores.

Prevention

1. Avoid working late hours, in bad areas, and places without protection.
2. Set up silent alarm, security camera, and bulletproof windows and doors.
3. Receive proper training on recognizing potential robbers, deterrence, and safety.
4. Work with more people at late hours, and have someone go home with you.

Teachers

Risks

1. Work at bad school and bad area.
2. Work with bad students or students as gang members.
3. Treat students unfairly and retaliate, or become a scapegoat.
4. Do not handle conflicts effectively.
5. Grading oriented confrontation.
6. Terrorism attacks or gang fights in or near schools.

Prevention

1. Choose a good school to work in with good students.
2. Treat students fairly and well, like they are your own family members.
3. Handle conflicts carefully or get the school involved.
4. Beware of any warning signals of gang or terrorism crimes.
5. Avoid working late and alone.
6. Take a self-defense class.

Taxi Driver

Risks

Robbery for money or for the car is the main threat to taxi drivers. Potential murder or rape is possible with robberies. In China, taxi drivers have become a high risk group for robberies.

Prevention

1. Avoid driving potentially dangerous people.
2. Pay attention to the passenger's moves.
3. Use cellular phones to inform people where you are going.
4. Crash into a parked car in crowded area if carjacked.

Nurses and Doctors

Risks

The major threats to doctors and nurses include working in the evenings, working with mad patients, dealing with gang patients, being retaliated upon by patients who did not heal, and abortion-oriented issues.

Prevention

1. Work at a good location.
2. Be alert to the surroundings.
3. Request safety guards on duty or an escort if you need to travel far in the hospital.
4. Avoid coming and going during evenings and at night.
5. Take a self-defense class and prepare for potential attacks.
6. Carry mace and pepper spray.
7. Handle patients with bad tempers carefully.
8. Deal with gangs with caution, and do not agitate them.

Flight Attendants

Risks

The risks to flight attendants include dealing with hijackers, bad passengers, and drunk passengers. Taking the night shift and traveling in strange places or bad areas can also cause problems.

Prevention

1. Beware of the danger and stay alert at all time.
2. Treat people politely and avoid direct conflicts.
3. Handle the bad tempered passengers carefully without stimulating them.
4. Avoid giving personal information to strangers.
5. Know where you are going and the traditions and habits of people there.

Real Estate Agents

Risks

The major risks for these people include the following: 1) They go anywhere for business and often to bad areas and bad locations. 2) They go out any time, including in the dark. 3) They deal with strangers most of the time, and very often stay with strangers alone in private places.

Prevention

1. Inform colleagues or family members where you are going in front of the client so that he knows other people know you are with him.
2. Use a cellular phone to keep other people informed of your activity.
3. Avoid going to bad areas at bad times of the day.
4. Brag about your martial arts background to make you sound tough.
5. Try not to drive a strange client around.
6. Beware of the danger when you stay with a stranger alone in a house.
7. Do not carry valuables.

Engineers

Risks

The major threats to engineers are layoff related crimes, everyday conflicts with colleagues, competition related crimes, and working late oriented crimes.

Prevention

1. Establish good relationships with other people and do not become a trouble maker.
2. Do not show off often and make other people hate you or be jealous.
3. Handle conflicts with care and learn to back up when necessary.
4. Keep secrets about what you do in your company, especially so as not to get the attention of the competitor of your company.
5. Avoid working late and at bad times.

Administrators

Risks

The major threats to administrators come from different sources. They very often have to do the dirty jobs, such as lay off people, and make people hate them. Whenever people think they are not treated fairly, they hate the administrators and sometimes they will look for revenge. When there is a violent person in the department, the administrator will have more trouble handling that. That person hangs around everyday and makes you feel nervous, but he will retaliate when he is fired.

Prevention

1. Treat people fairly without personal preference.
2. Get your boss involved in the tasks such as layoffs, and get the monkey off your back.
3. Treat people equally, like you treat your boss, and never boss around people or create negative feelings.
4. When there is a violent person in the department, try not to stimulate him, and plan a strategy to make him quit the job by himself.

Business Owners

Risks

The major threats to business (especially small business) owners include extortion from gangs, competition with gang-owned businesses, robbery, burglary, and kidnapping of the owner or family members.

Prevention

1. Avoid opening a business in gang-occupied areas. Find a good neighborhood and safe location for your business.
2. Avoid direct competitions with gang-owned business.
3. Take a low-key attitude and never brag up your wealth.
4. Train yourself and your employees about robbery and burglary prevention and handling. Install security equipment and a monitoring system.
5. Treat people well and never make enemies.

Police

Risks

Police officers usually face two risks on their jobs. The first is that they deal with dangerous people most of the time and have confrontations with criminals often. The second major threat to police officers is that they catch criminals and regular people violating the law. Their job often results in revenge from these people.

Prevention

Prevention of crimes against police is very difficult because the nature of their jobs puts them at high risk. The first thing they can do is to be very careful when they deal with criminals. The second is that they can treat regular people fairly to reduce the chance of retaliation.

Special Population

Elderly

Risks

Elderly people are usually weak physically and slow mentally. They often depend on others in their everyday life. They are not sensitive to potential dangers outside. Criminals can easily get elderly into robberies and burglaries, and very often murder and assaults are associated with robberies and burglaries.

Prevention

1. Focus on safety on the street, the home, social, and while parking and driving.
2. Try to stay with a group and never venture out alone at night.
3. Live with family and walk to your car with other people.
4. Avoid carrying too much cash, and try to hide your wallet.

5. Lock windows and hide your purse when driving.
6. Reject soliciting calls.
7. Learn some self-defense skills and strategies, have a mace or pepper spray, and exercise to keep fit.

Disabled

Risks

People with disabilities usually have some physical limits and are usually vulnerable, and therefore become easy targets of crimes such as robbery, rape, and burglary.

Prevention

1. Avoid situations and locations that invite crime.
2. Learn how to prevent crimes at major places you stay. Have a plan to deal with confrontation beforehand.
3. Mentally rehearse your plan.
4. Hide your condition from other people and do not advertise.
5. Stay with someone or a group. Do not flash your money.
6. Inform your family where you are going and avoid bad places and times.

REFERENCES

Hunter, R.D. and C.R. Jeffrey. "Preventing Convenience Store Robbery through Environmental design." In *Situational Crime Prevention*, edited by R. Clarke. New York: Harrow and Heston, 1992.

Snow, R. L. *Protecting Your Life, Home, and Property: A Cop Shows You How*. New York: Plenum Press, 1995.

PART THREE

On-Site Responses—Non-Fighting Strategies

➤ Handling Dangerous Situations with Back-Away Skills

➤ Handling Everyday Arguments and Confrontations

Chapter 9
Handling Dangerous Situations with Back-Away Skills

This chapter provides students with basic knowledge about how to recognize dangerous situations and how to back away from the attacks or potential attacks. However, although these strategies and skills are recommended by experts, they cannot guarantee that you will be 100 percent safe when using them, because each attack is different and depends upon the particular situation.

Recognize Situations

Sense the Danger

With the alarm of self-defense in mind all times, people can sense an uncomfortable situation and the potential danger signals. Consistently sensing the surroundings for potential danger can give the defender time and space to avoid being caught in a bad situation. Defenders will become aware of danger through the place, the time, and the appearance or behaviors of people around them, such as someone staring at them or approaching them when no one else is around. When sensing danger, it is better to get away as soon as possible or get ready to deal with it if you cannot get away.

Meadows (1998) gave advice on how to recognize high crime areas. Meadows felt that the areas with the following characteristics are more dangerous: areas with fewer residential properties and more vacant land, areas with more blocks with major thoroughfares, areas with mixed land use, and areas of low social economic status. From a practical perspective, potential dangerous situations include being in bad areas (gang, drug, poverty, isolated, dark) or at a bad time, dealing with cash (bank, convenience stores), or dealing with potentially dangerous people.

Recognize and Assess the Situation

Before something happens or before the attacker takes the initial action, the defender should quickly recognize and assess the situation for quick decision-making. Making a perfect decision in this kind of situation is difficult because it is hard to know what the attacker's real intention is. Usually the attacker will say something or do something which can give the defender a clue as to what the attacker is after and how dangerous the situation is.

The common ways the attackers behave include: staring at you, following you, approaching you, touching or grabbing you, pointing a gun or knife at you, throwing you to the ground, or dragging you to another place or into a car. The common things attackers will say may include: "do not move or I'll kill you," "give me your money (or other valuables)," "get into the car," "strip," and the use of foul expressions (swearing, racial remarks, etcetera.).

From what the attacker says or does, the defender can guess what the attacker wants and respond accordingly. For example, if he just wants money, the defender may give him the money in the hope that he will not hurt the victim. If the attacker wants you to take off your clothes, then it is likely that he will attempt to rape you. The defender has to make the decision either to be raped in exchange for their life or to fight back. If the attacker wants you to get into his car, he is more likely to take you to a private place where he can do anything to you. And if the attacker uses words such as "damn Asians (or whites, blacks, Hispanics)," he is more likely to beat you, but murder or rape are also among the possibilities.

Decision Making

The decision-making process when attacked usually has to be very short, ranging from a split second to several seconds. Your brain has to perform like a high speed computer which quickly assesses all of the available information: the attacker's intention (murder, rape, assault, or robbery), your priority (life, physical injury, dignity, or valuables), comparison of you and the attacker (weapons, size, or skills), chance of survival (win, get away, or lose), and strategies or skills to be used (fight, run, talk). The hope of survival is very unpredictable when caught in bad situations where the defenders have to take chances. Usually the defenders will use the strategies or skills they have practiced before, and very often these strategies or skills will occur automatically. Therefore, it is essential for the defenders to prepare in the use of these strategies and skills beforehand and to a degree that they can use them without thinking about it.

Brewer's (1994) philosophy for making decisions on-site is stated as:

1. Avoid rather than check.
2. Check rather than hurt.
3. Hurt rather than maim.
4. Maim rather than kill.
5. Kill rather than be killed.

Brewer (1994) also cited how people resist actual attacks. The common tactics victims used against rape included: 16 percent fought back, 14 percent persuaded, 13 percent attacked with a weapon, 11 percent ran or hid, 10 percent scared or warned, 10 percent screamed, and 9 percent got help or gave alarm. It looks like more people try to use back away strategies rather than fighting back. However, the results of these actions were not reported. Ways to deal with aggravated assaults included: 21 percent ran or hid, 19 percent fought back, 13 percent persuaded, 12 percent got help or gave alarm, 8 percent attacked with a weapon, and 8 percent threatened and warned. Ferguson (1994) also reported how people resisted rapes. The actions included: 21 percent physically, 20 percent screamed, 19 percent appeased, 13 percent hit/ran, 13 percent scared off attackers, and 8 percent threatened or attacked with weapons. Again, the effectiveness of these strategies was not reported unfortunately.

Brewer (1994, 101-02) gave his rule of thumb on on-site self-defense response:

1. Talk if you can.
2. Apologize if necessary.
3. Attract attention.
4. Yell or run.
5. If cornered by an attacker, fight only when there is an actual attack.
6. When facing an armed robbery, give up.
7. Whenever you feel you will be seriously injured or killed regardless of your response, attack immediately.

From the author's standpoint, Brewer's rule #5 is questionable because the victim will lose the battle for sure if he or she waits for the attacker to start first.

Back-Away Strategies

The following strategies are introduced to help potential victims reduce the chance of severe consequences or get away without fighting. Students can look through these strategies and select their favorite ones in order to develop a personal back-away style. However, students should keep in mind that although these strategies are recommended by some experts and used by other people, no back-away strategy works 100 percent effectively, since the situations vary from case to case. Many new terms which represent different models of back-away strategies were created by the author in this section to help students get a clear image.

Run Away—The Rabbit Model

The run-away model is probably the best self-defense back-away strategy just prior to or during the attack. The purpose is simply to get out of the scene and leave the trouble behind.

The pros of running away include the following: 1) It is easy and does not require any special skills. 2) It is safe since the defender simply avoids the confrontation. 3) Usually the attacker is reluctant to chase the defender in public since it is easier to be seen. It may take a long time to catch the defender, and they usually prefer victims who are easier to get.

The cons of running away include the following. 1) Sometimes the defender is cornered or held, therefore has no room or time to run. 2) Proper clothing and proper body conditioning for speed and endurance is required for effective running.

Running away can be used in many situations: 1) when the defender is at a great disadvantage, such as the attacker has a knife or gun, or there are multiple-attackers, or the attacker is too strong to handle; 2) when the attacker wants to take the defender to a different place, such as to his car or to an isolated area; 3) before the attacker gets too close, such as seeing that potential trouble is coming or before the attacker grabs or starts the attack; and 4) anytime during the fighting or negotiation, such as after releasing from any holds or when the attacker is forced to back up.

The running techniques and timing have different variations. 1) The defender can simply turn and run when they see trouble coming or when they have a chance. 2) The defender can run in one direction and call "Roger, I'm here" to make it sound like you are with someone to delay the attack. 3) Throw money or valuables in one direction and run the opposite way (Bittenbinder 1992). It is possible that the attacker will just pick up the money and go away instead of chasing the victim. This model is called the "Lizard model" because lizards will leave a piece of their tail for the attacker when they run away. 4) Look over the attacker's shoulder and yell "officer, help," then run away; or disable the opponent and then run when the attacker is looking back. This strategy is called the "Octopus model" since the defender sets up a screen before running away. There are many more choices and the defender should use his/her creativity to find a running pattern that is best for them.

Talk—The Salesperson Model

The talking strategy is preferred by many people, especially when they are at gunpoint or knife-point, or when they have no chance to get away or fight back. People who are not strong physically and have less confidence to run or fight also like this strategy. The purpose of this strategy is to change the criminal's mind or delay the attack. Some instructors believe that women should use more talking strategies instead of physical skills, since they feel that women do not have enough body strength.

The pros of the talking model include the following: 1) It will reduce the chance to agitate some attackers who might use more violence when victims fight back or run. 2) It might convince some attackers to give up the action or use less violence. 3) It may delay the attack so that the defender can find other opportunities to get away.

The cons of the talking model include the following: 1) The defender may not have a chance to talk. 2) The defender's mind is blank due to the scary situation. 3) It depends on the attacker to make the decision. The criminal may let the defender go if they believe what is said, but most of the time they will not. Criminals usually have no sympathy, and the victim is just another statistic to them. The defender cannot control the situation, and the chance of survival using this strategy is very unpredictable.

The talking strategy includes many variations. 1) Negotiation—the consumer model. The defender tries to sacrifice something to save his/her life, for example, give up money in exchange of their physical safety. 2) Reasoning—the counselor model. The defender tries to awaken the attacker's internal morals in the hope that the attacker will realize that what they are doing is wrong and stop the attack. It seems that this model works when the victim knows the attacker, or if the attacker is committing the crime on impulse. Actually, the author had a female student who used this model to successfully get away from a very difficult situation in which she did not have any chance to fight back or run away. 3) Making excuses—the liar model. The defender tries to use any excuse, such as having an infectious disease like AIDS, to delay the attack. For example, a would-be rapist may become scared and have to decide if what the defender says is true. Some attackers may change their mind, but most of them probably will not. Some people are reluctant to use this strategy because they think telling a lie is not right. The defender needs to keep in mind that it is not a matter of honesty or dishonesty when facing attackers. This is a battle concerning life or death, and life is more important than anything else. Defenders have the right to use any strategy to get away, since any actions used for self-defense purposes are moral. The talking model can be used in many situations: 1) when the defender has no chance to run or fight; 2) the defender tries to use talk to delay the attack and look for other opportunities; and 3) the attacker seems to be receptive to talking.

Cooperate—The Patient Model

Cooperation means the defender cooperates with the attacker's demands and does exactly what the attacker wants in the hope that the attacker will be satisfied and not hurt the victim, or the attacker will become relaxed and off-guard. The cooperation strategy is often used to avoid the immediate danger of agitating the attacker and to look for chances to get away.

The pros of this strategy include the following: 1) It reduces the chance of agitating the attacker and thus reduces the level of violence. 2) It makes the attacker feel in control of the situation and may place him off guard. 3) The defender has more time and space to think and look for other chances to deal with the situation.

The major con of the cooperation model is that the attacker may trick the defender into a trap step-by-step, and the defender may lose the chance to get away or fight back. For example, the attacker convinces the defender that she will not get hurt if she allows the attacker to tie her to a chair. But the defender may find the attacker was lying, and the cooperation caused her to lose the last chance to act since she is now tied up. The 911 highjacking is a perfect example. The second con is that the defender has no control over the situation and has to take whatever the attacker offers.

The applications of this strategy include offensive and defensive applications. The defensive application is used when the defender has no other options but cooperation, otherwise their life is in danger. For example, the defender is at gunpoint or loses the chance to get away or fight back. The offensive application is used when the defender tries to calm the attacker down in order to reduce the immediate danger, and then watches what the attacker will do next. The defender can also use cooperation to trick the attacker, catch him off guard, and then look for other opportunities such as fighting or running away.

Defenders should set up a bottom line where they should stop the cooperation, since they might be in a worse situation if the cooperation continues. Some recommended limits include the defender being taken to an isolated area or being tied up.

Bluff—The Barking Dog Model

Bluffing strategies are used in self-defense to warn or scare the attacker by showing the attacker that the defender is not a weak target and is ready to fight back. It also sends information to the attacker that the attack might be a long battle, and the attacker may not have an easy chance to win. The attacker might back up and look for an easier victim and for a quick attack elsewhere.

There are some pros of this strategy. 1) Bluffing can increase the defender's spirit and courage to handle the situation. 2) It surprises the attacker because the bluffing is not expected and the attacker may not be ready to deal with a hard victim. 3) It scares the attacker because they do not know how good the defender really is at fighting back, and the attacker does not want to get hurt. 4) The attacker may not want to start the attack since this might become a long lasting attack which could be seen by other people, including the police.

There are also some cons of bluffing. 1) The attacker may not be stopped by the bluffing, and fighting may be unavoidable. 2) The attacker may become agitated and use more violence than intended at the beginning. It may not work if the attacker is ready or has more advantage.

The common bluffing skills may include the following: 1) Use verbal threatening, such as "back up," or "go away or you will get hurt," or "you want to fight a Karate black-belt?" 2) Use physical posture, such as a fighting stance used in martial arts, or utilize some real movements. 3) Use a combination of verbal and physical threats. The applications of bluffing in self-defense may include the following situations: 1) when the defender is facing an attacker who has no obvious advantage; 2) the defender has more confidence; and 3) before the start of the attack.

Make Yourself Unattractive—The Skunk Model

This strategy is used to make the defender seem so dirty or gross that the attacker does not want to touch the defender and leaves them alone. This strategy works better when used to avoid rapes, especially date rapes or acquaintance rapes.

There are many ways the defender can make themselves into a skunk. Vomiting or wetting their pants is a common method recommended by many instructors. Putting on paint or ketchup can serve the same purpose. Messing the hair and rolling in the mud also can have similar functions.

The defender may apply this strategy in several situations. 1) The defender is confronted in date rape or acquaintance rape. Since this kind of attacker usually will not get very agitated and will have less chance of becoming more violence. 2) The defender is in an attempted rape by a stranger and has to use this strategy to delay the attack.

Becoming a skunk has some pros in self-defense. 1) It changes the image of the defender in the attacker's mind, from an attractive woman to a dirty and gross person, thus reducing the attacker's desire to rape. 2) It may surprise the attacker since this kind of behavior is not expected, and he is not ready for this. 3) It delays the attack and allows the defender more time to think of other strategies.

But there are problems with the skunk model in self-defense. 1) It is up to the attacker to make the final decision on attacking the victim or not, no matter how gross a victim can be. 2) The defender may not have the chance to become a skunk. 3) The attacker may recognize that the defender is playing tricks. Since this strategy is taught in common self-defense courses and in many books, it has become well known and it will not stop the attack. 4) The attacker may get very mad and agitated and therefore use more violence against the defender. 5) This strategy does not work well in other crimes such as robbery, assault, and murder.

Acting Crazy—The Clown Model

Acting crazy is also a strategy which has been taught in some self-defense books. The purpose of this strategy is to surprise the attacker who psychologically is not prepared to attack this kind of victim and does not want to attack victims who display irregular behavior.

There are several ways a defender can act crazy. In the first case (Bittenbinder 1992) an old lady asked the would-be attacker "do I know your mother?" when facing the attacker, then the man hesitated and backed away because he was not sure if the victim really knew his mother. He certainly was not ready to attack someone who knows his mother. The second case was a female professor who acted like a mentally-ill patient when confronted with a small street youth gang on the street at midnight, and got away safely. The third case was a male who played like a drunk person and got away from the attack. The fourth case was a woman who acted like she had HIV and propositioned the attacker, causing the attacker to be scared away. The fifth case was an Asian student who acted like he did not speak English and could not understand what the attacker wanted. The sixth case was a male who acted like he just got fired at work and was ready to commit suicide.

There are some pros of this strategy. 1) It may set a psychological block for the attacker and stop the attacks because this is a situation the attacker does not have confidence to handle. 2) It may have an effect of delaying the attack because the attacker needs to find out what is going on and to make psychological adjustments to the situation. 3) It may ruin the attacker's chance.

There are also some cons of this strategy. 1) It is up to the attacker to make the final decision on attacking the victim or not, no matter how crazy a victim may act. 2) The defender may not have time to act crazy when the attack comes too suddenly. 3) It takes a lot of courage to act in front of an attacker. 4) The defender may agitate the attacker and make the situation even more violent.

Dealing with Different Crimes On-Site

Very often the defendants do not know what the attacker wants, and then it is very difficult to handle the situation. But if the situation is clearly a robbery or rape, then the following guidelines can be used to reduce the changes of injuries.

Handling Kidnaping

Kidnaping usually is conducted for money, political, or rape reasons. Being a victim of Kidnaping is dangerous, and the consequences are unpredictable. The victim might be released if the attacker gets what he wants, but might also may be killed. The victim may have more chance if there is a single kidnapper. The back-away strategies and the fighting option can be used depending on the situation. Snow (1995) advised people how to survive as a hostage. His tips include the following:

1. Do not do show sudden movements during the first half-hour.
2. Remain as calm as possible.
3. Do exactly as the kidnapper orders.
4. Do not speak to the kidnapper.
5. Tell the hostage taker if you are ill or need medicine.
6. Observe the area for potential opportunities.
7. Leave fingerprints or personal stuff.
8. Stay away from the window or door where police may enter or shoot.
9. Do not loose faith.

Handling Hijacking

Becoming a hijacking victim is dangerous and unfortunate. Escape options are very limited in terms of self-defense. What might happen includes three situations. The best solution is that victims get out safely when the hijacker is under control, or the hijacker lets them go after they have achieved their goals. The second one is that some victims will be killed when the hijackers try to put pressure on the government. The worst solution is that all victims are killed, such as in the 911 case.

The strategies to handle hijacking include the following rules. Both ways can be used to handle the hijacking. depending on the situation.

1. Remain calm and cooperate with the demands of the hijackers. Wait for the negotiation to be done, since most of the time the hijackers have their purposes and goals.
2. Do not try to fight or show sudden movements to avoid making the hijacker nervous then kill the passengers. Do not explore the airplane.

However, the 911 hijacking totally changed people's perspectives toward handling this situation. Out of the four airplanes, three followed the demands of the hijackers and crashed into buildings as bombs. Only one stood up and fought, but it was too late to get back the control of the airplane (although the fight avoided the plane being used as a bomb to the White House). Nowadays people feel they have no way to back up except to fight and win. There was a case of hijacking in China after 911. The security guards and the passengers all fought together to put the hijacker under control.

Handling Carjacking

1. If the attacker is still outside of the door and does not have a gun, you can take off suddenly to get rid of him.
2. If the carjacker hangs on the door, lock it and keep the window up if you can. Protect your face with one arm. Go by telephone poles to scratch him off, or stop and accelerate suddenly to get him off.
3. Smash into another car or tree where people are to get attention, and then run for help.
4. If a gun is pointed to you, you can follow the Kidnaping rules at the beginning, and then crash into something when the attacker is off-guard.

Handling Rapes

1. When the rapist threatens to kill you if you do not cooperate, then cooperate to save your life.
2. Scream to get help if you are not held or at gunpoint or knifepoint.
3. Run to a populated area for help if you are in good condition to run.
4. Warn, threat, and scare the rapist with your words or actions (such as a martial art stance or yell). Show him you are not a weak or easy victim.
5. Use any techniques or weapons to fight back.

Handling Murders

Dealing with murders depends on the situation. It is a tough decision since murders can be triggered by argument, gangs, revenge, robbery, and other reasons. If someone really wants to kill you, you may have to try the following strategies.

1. Run for your life. You may be shot but you cannot do much and you have to take your chances.

2. Fight for your life. You may make the killer mad and use more violence, but you will have some control of the situation and have a chance to win, depending on the situation.
3. Cooperate and hope the killer will change his mind. He may change his plan if you are lucky, but you have no control of the situation.

Handling Aggravated Assaults

Dealing with aggravated assaults includes the following strategies. The decision is made based on the situation.

1. Say "sorry" and walk away if it is argument oriented. Do not argue or talk if it is race oriented, just walk away.
2. Run to a public place to avoid being chased.
3. Give attackers an excuse to back up with dignity.
4. Threaten or warn to show the attacker you are a tough target, when you are sure there is no life-threatening risk.
5. Fight back if there is no other choice and when the attacker is attacking you.

Handling Robberies

1. Do not resist armed robberies. Do not say anything or try to identify the robber. Give him no reason to use more violence beyond the robbery.
2. Prepare money to give away in order to save your life.
3. Run or fight back if the robber wants to kidnap or kill you.

Handling Burglaries

1. Do not enter the house when you find it is burglarized. Go to a neighbor's to call police.
2. When you are inside the house and find a burglar is breaking into the house, you may turn on the TV loudly to scare him away, call a man's name, or point your gun or fake gun at the burglar. This way you may scare the offender away, but you may also expose yourself to him. Another way is to hide and call police or neighbors to help. This way, he will not know where you are and possibly avoid confrontations with him. But if the help is too late, he might still find you. Sneaking out of the house is a safer way.
3. If the burglar forces into the house when you are inside, then it is not just a burglary anymore. You should exit or may have to use force to resist.

REFERENCES

Bittenbinder, J. J. *Street Smart.* Illinois: Video Publishing House, Inc., 1992.

Brewer, J.D. *The Danger from Strangers: Confronting the Threat of Assault.* New York: Insight Books, 1994.

Dobson, T. Safe and Alive. Los Angeles: J.P. Tarcher, Inc., 1981.

Measows, R.J. *Understanding Violence and Victimization.* Upper Saddle River: Simon & Schuster/A Viacom Company, 1998.

Snow, R. L. *Protecting your Life, Home, and Property: A Cop Shows You How.* New York: Plenum Press, 1995.

Strong, S. *Strong on Defense.* New York: Pocket Books, 1996.

Chapter 10
Handling Everyday Arguments and Confrontations

Arguments, conflicts, and confrontations are common in everyday life. While some of them will not cause any severe consequences, some will lead to violence, such as murders, rapes, assaults, or fights. Handling everyday arguments, conflicts, and confrontations is an important part of self-defense. It has two functions in on-site responses in self-defense. The first function is to avoid motivating the real criminals or gang members to commit crimes against you. The second function is to avoid triggering crimes from regular people who may commit crimes resulting from confrontations over small things. The 2001 Uniform Crime Report indicated that argument is the leading cause (27 percent) of murders in the United States, and it has been the leading cause for several years. Many cases also indicated that everyday arguments and confrontations often result in violence.

What Do Arguments and Confrontations Create?

Arguments and confrontations create negative feelings on one side or both sides. Sometimes they create embarrassment, uneasiness, or loss of dignity, while sometimes they create hate and threat. The results of arguments or confrontations vary, depending on the situation or people. At the first level, nothing happens, since both sides back up or one side backs up due to uneven physical size or the location. The next level is the emotional or psychological injury on one side or both sides if the arguments or confrontations do not get to escalate, maybe due to the interference of bystanders. The third level involves the use of physical language to solve problems when the arguments or confrontations continue upgrade. Assaults, fights, rapes, or murders may burst out immediately on-site. But if one side is weak and is out-powered, then that person may temporarily back up from the scene but plan a revenge, such as calling a gang, getting a gun, or attacking unexpectedly.

Dangers of Arguments and Confrontations

The real dangers of arguments and confrontations include two aspects. The first aspect is that arguments and confrontations can trigger the real criminals or gang members to commit crimes against you. When victims get into arguments or confrontations with strangers, they often do not know whom they are arguing with. They would not start or continue the arguments if they knew they were arguing with dangerous gang members or criminals. These gang members or criminals did not plan to attack you at first. But when you start or continue the arguments or confrontations, they would not hesitate to attack you. The problem is that people never think about it until it is too late. The second aspect is that arguments or confrontations can trigger hate from regular people, then turn them into criminals who may commit crimes against you. Most people also never think about this possibility, otherwise they would not get into it or they would get out first to avoid the severe consequences.

Mechanism of Argument Related Crimes

Everybody has a temper, and the stress from everyday life in modern society makes people less tolerant. Therefore, arguments, conflicts, and confrontations occur very often in the society. Either the victim or attacker may trigger the confrontations, but sometimes the victims precipitate the trouble and make it worse. The problem is that everybody has ego and self-esteem issues and most people do not want to lose their dignity when backing up from these arguments and confrontations. This very often results in upgrading the confrontations, and violence usually follows up in order to solve the problem.

All people have both good and bad features. For most people, the good features dominate their behaviors, so they will not do anything bad to other people. But in some circumstances such as in arguments and confrontations, the bad features take over the control and dominate, and they can then do anything bad at the moment.

When people upgrade arguments or confrontations, they tend to get very mad at each other, and they do not think clearly anymore. In their mind, whatever they can do to hurt the opponents badly is their first priority and their actions outburst without thinking through the potential consequences. But at this moment, the actions do not go though the long thought process; instead they jump from emotion to action through a short circuit. Destroying the opponent becomes their only or ultimate goal. If they have access to a knife, they would use it right away and if they have a gun they would shoot immediately. They may wake up from the mad mental status after they commit the crime, but it usually is too late.

The argument oriented crime follows a pattern like this. People start an argument for small things, such as a parking space, due to different reasons such as being selfish or a bully or stressed. Both sides continue, and nobody wants to back up due to their ego and fear of losing their dignity. But the argument does not usually stay at the same level; instead, it tends to upgrade because both sides want to out-power the other side and win. Tension build up when they upgrade the arguments, and people get mad and hate each other badly. Since nobody backs up and there is no interference from the outside, one side or both sides have to use extreme methods to solve the confrontation. The solutions then include fighting, assault, rape, and the worst, the murder.

All arguments, conflicts, or confrontations have one thing in common: they all need two opposite sides. If one side backs up from these situations, none of these situations will be started or upgraded, and then there will not be a problem or severe consequences. As a famous Chinese proverb puts it "One palm cannot clap."

Factors Involved in Argument Oriented Crimes

Many factors impact the chances of argument oriented crimes. These factors include societal, psychological, and biological factors. Arguments and confrontations occur in almost every country and community, but the ways people handle these problems are different. Traditions and morals in a society have tremendous impact on the way people solve problems. In a society where people are highly educated, full of love, and peaceful, confrontations will be much less, and the ways they handle the confrontation tend to be peaceful too. On the other hand, however, if the government tends to use violence to solve conflicts with its neighbor countries or with its people, then people tend to follow the same pattern when they run into conflicts. It needs the effort of the whole society to reduce the impact of this factor on argument oriented crimes. The biological factor indicates that some people have genes which make them more aggressive, less patient, and violent. Reader's Digest reported that 20 percent of Americans have an angry personality and 60 percent more have this kind of personality sometimes. This factor is also out of our control in terms of self-defense.

The psychological factors can be reduced through proper education and this is the focus of this discussion.

One psychological factor is the life philosophy. As people grow up, they develop different types of life philosophies due to their growing environment and education. The life philosophy guides their behaviors and actions. A person who believes in peace will have less chance to get involved in arguments, and they tend to solve problems peacefully. These people will have less chance to become victims of argument oriented crimes. On the other hand, however, a person who is selfish and always tries to get something for nothing from other people or always fights for his/her own benefits by sacrificing other people will get more arguments and confrontations, thus have more chance to become a victim.

Another psychological factor is the personality factor. Some people are polite and friendly to other people and they often get the same friendly treatment in return. They rarely start arguments, and they tend to back up if there is a conflict. Some people have a bad temper sometimes or all time, and you can see these people everywhere. They get mad at small things easily and get a kick out of arguing with other people. These people create enemies easily and very often precipitate the crimes without knowing it.

Self-control ability is a key factor at reducing arguments and confrontations. When facing unfairness, challenges, conflicts, or an argument, people can demonstrate different kinds of reactions spontaneously, impulsively, aggressively, or peacefully. A strong self-control ability can give you more time to think, reduce the chance of getting involved in arguments about small things, or cause you to back up to avoid upgrading the tension. Sometimes, people may have a bad personality or temper, but if you can control yourself, then you still have less chance of becoming victims.

Thinking patterns and life goals have a strong influence on arguments and confrontations. People who have long-term ambitions and high life goals will not start arguments or confrontations over small things. Winning an argument over a small thing will not help them reach their life goal, but it may ruin your ultimate goal or your life. People with high life goals tend to have more tolerance and self-control, so that they will achieve their ultimate goals. From outsider's eyes, backing up seems like losing the argument and dignity, but actually you win in the long run since you did not let a small thing block your way to your life goal.

Understanding of the potential danger of arguments and confrontations is very important. Knowledge of the potential dangerous consequences from arguments, conflicts, and confrontations plays important role at reducing the chance of getting involved and help people get out of before severe consequences occur. As discussed above, people get involved in arguments and confrontations because they do not know the potential dangers. They would not get into them or they would get out fast if they knew what could happen to them.

Judgments of the situation can be another factor. People do not want to back up from an argument which will not cause any damage, but they do not want to risk their life for a small thing. The problem is that they do not know each other, and the result is very unpredictable. Decision making is hard when people do not have enough information and people cannot make good judgments.

Facilitating Factors

Besides the psychological factor, there are other factors that facilitate argument oriented crimes. Substance use is an essential factor. People tend to have distorted feelings, unclear minds, or less controlled behaviors when they use drugs or drink too much alcohol. The way they handle the arguments tend to go the hard way. The comparison of the physical sizes of both sides has some impact on the escalation of an argument. People who are strong, big, carry weapons, or have some fighting skills are more likely to upgrade their confrontations than someone who is more vulnerable. Location is another factor. People at familiar areas or in their own territories tend to have more confidence to continue the arguments than people in unfamiliar areas.

Major Confrontations and Triggering Factors

Family

Confrontations occur in families often, since there are more chances family members stay together. The problems mainly include three confrontations. One occurs between the wife and husband, usually on money related issues, child education issues, lack of respect and bullies, cheating, substance use, and romantic triangles. The second problems occur between parents and children, basically caused by lack of communication, generation gap, differences in expectations, and rebellion and the pulling root effect. The third problem is between siblings, mainly focusing on "unfairness," jealousy, opinion conflicts, and bullying.

Friends

Confrontations and arguments also occur among friends. They can be from differences in opinions, improper tones in talking, misunderstanding or lack of communication, competition of benefits, money, or cheating.

Neighbor

Relationships with neighbors can range from friendly to nasty, depending on people and how they get along with each other. Problems with neighbors usually arise from the invasion or harassment. Existing cases include, but are not limited to, the following: noise from music or repairing, jumping on the upper floors, tree branches reaching over fences, carelessness on shared fences or lawns, dropping stuff from high-stories to low-stories, children or pets invading or damaging property, borrowing things without returning them, and differences in religion, race and ethnicity.

Work

Arguments and confrontations in workplaces usually include problems between the boss and employees, among the co-workers or colleagues, and between employees and customers. Confrontations between bosses and subordinates usually arise from unfairness, excessive workload and pressure, lack of understanding and communication, racial or other ethnic issues, bossy behaviors from the bosses, rebellion behaviors from the employees, and layoffs. The problems among co-workers and colleagues usually start from unfairness, jealousy, racial and ethnic issues, competitions, cheating, and inconsideration. The conflicts between employees and customers often start with inappropriate attitudes, differences in expectations, misunderstanding and lack of effective communication, benefit conflicts, racial and other ethnic issues, and cheating.

School

Arguments and confrontations on school sites include problems between teachers and students and among students. Conflicts between teachers and students may arise from nasty and bossy behaviors from the teachers or rebellion from the students, lack of respect, misunderstanding and mis-communication, unfairness or the feeling of unfairness, or racial and ethnic conflicts. Conflicts among students involve immature behaviors, bullies, competitions, substance use, strong egos and dignity, rebellious behavior, romantic triangles, conflicts of groups (racial, gender, or gang), and jealousy.

Stranger

Confrontations and arguments with strangers can arise from almost anything, but mainly come from several aspects. The first is personal interest/benefit oriented, examples include fighting for a parking space or a better seat in the theater or in a subway, cutting the line, or blocking other people's way. The second is caused by misunderstanding of behavior patterns and traditions of different cultures, races, religions, and ethnic groups. The results of the differences and misunderstanding often create competition, jealousy, unfairness and renege, and hate. The third one is the inappropriate interaction patterns between people, and inexperience in solving these problems. Lack of tolerance with strangers also adds fuel to the fire in confrontations.

Prevention and Handling

Prevention Philosophy

These philosophies are guidelines for prevention of the arguments, conflicts, and confrontations from the self-defense perspective. These guidelines should become a part of one's thinking process and life philosophy which will guide their decision making in everyday life from the self-defense standpoint. This way, people will automatically behave in a safe way when facing arguments or confrontations without going through the thinking process.

1. Establish a safe thinking pattern. Think, think, and think before you act in the case of arguments and confrontations. Do not act on impulse, no matter how mad you are at the opponent of the upcoming argument, or how much you want to upgrade to win the argument. Explain the actions or results in positive ways. Avoiding confrontations does not mean you chicken out; instead it means you are smart. Furthermore, you may argue for things you think you are right but actually maybe wrong. Let time deal with it and heal the wound.

2. Establish your life goals and develop your tolerance. Remember always to look at the big picture, and do not let small things ruin your life goals. There may be a million small things during your life, and any of them can ruin your life easily. Therefore, one should develop tolerance to survive in this world. As an old Chinese proverb puts it "Intolerance of little things will ruin your ultimate goal."

3. Shape your personality. Know how you like other people to treat you, and then treat people in the way you like to be treated. As an old Chinese saying puts it "Do not do anything you do not like to other people." Respect other people. Do not be nasty to people, and do not always try to out-power others.

4. Improve your communication skills with other people. Be considerate, understanding, and caring. Talk in the way that will not insult or hurt other people. Forgive other people's faults. Focus on actions instead on people when you have to criticize other people.

5. Use potential consequences to guide your actions. Remember, there is no winner in the argument or confrontation in the long term, and remember the potential dangers of getting involved in arguments and confrontations.

6. Remember the law "everybody should try to avoid confrontations." Do not precipitate arguments and confrontations, as an old saying puts it: "Let the sleeping dog lie." Some con-

frontations can be smoothed out, but some will not let you go easily before something bad occurs to you. When you get involved, do not add fuel to the fire. Argument is a fire, any more talk or actions can be fuel at the moment when both sides do not think clearly.

7. Do not be a dead hero. Two Chinese proverbs have proven very effective at handling arguments or confrontations. One says "Even the strongest man does not risk their life for temporary winning for small thing." Another says "One step forward you will fall off the cliff, but one step backward you will have a free world." When you and an opponent are involved in a confrontation, you both stand on the edge of a cliff.

Handling Conflicts: On-Site Responses

Once people put these philosophies and guidelines in their mind and make these a part of their life philosophy and behavior guidelines, they will have the ability to avoid and handle arguments and confrontations more effectively, and the strategies can very simple. Furthermore, they do not have to think before they take their actions, since their decisions will be made automatically.

The basic strategies include both the soft style and the hard style. The soft style uses Tai Chi principles to handle the conflict. That is, always avoid use of equal power against opponent's power, such as shouting back when opponent is yelling at you. Instead, redirect opponent's energy by smiling, apologizing, and using jokes and humor to make it difficult to keep the confrontation going. The hard way is to be assertive, reasonable, and tough so that the opponent cannot find any opportunity to take advantage of you. The following strategies can help you handle on-site confrontations:

1. Back up from the cliff. Since all arguments and confrontations involve two sides, withdrawing from these confrontations can stop the process immediately. One palm is gone; the left one cannot clap by itself. You can find an excuse to walk away, such as going to the restroom or an appointment.

2. Make your opponent feel good. Even if it is not your problem when the argument or confrontation starts, you always can use the apology strategy. Saying sorry does not hurt you at all, but you make the opponent feel good and he/she has no reason to keep the argument or confrontation going. You actually give the opponent a stairway to step down with dignity. This way you may make the opponent calm down and rethink it. You can just leave or continue to talk with a better atmosphere.

3. Show a smiling face. An old Chinese saying puts it: "a smiling face will not be slapped." Showing a smile face can reverse the anger before the argument starts and reduce the tension during the process. The opponent has no reason to treat you as an enemy when you show your kindness and unwillingness for confrontation. Then it is up to you to decide to continue or to stop the interaction.

4. Talk friendly, with a friendly tone. No matter how mad the opponent is, keep your calmness and a friendly tone. Do not put yourself at the opponent's level by shouting or pounting the table. This way you will not upgrade the conflict, and your opponent may feel embarrassed when to keep a high pitch while you are calm.

5. Change the atmosphere by making a joke and showing humor. Often a good joke can make people laugh and relaxed, and the tension can be reduced right away.

6. Sometimes, the above strategies may not work since the opponent is trying to pick up a vulnerable target. In this situation, showing your assertiveness and out-powering the opponent can be a better way to solve the conflicts quickly.

7. Control your anger and emotion by taking a deep breath, using Tai Chi meditation, drinking a glass of cold water, or pinching yourself to remind yourself to keep calm.

PART FOUR

On-Site Responses: Fighting-Back Skills and Strategies

- ➤ Preparation for Learning Physical Skills

- ➤ Distance Fighting

- ➤ Open-Hand Close Fighting

- ➤ Throwing

- ➤ Floor Fighting

- ➤ Joint Locks

- ➤ Releasing Skills

- ➤ Special Fighting

Chapter 11
Preparation for Learning Physical Skills

This chapter focuses on how to prepare students mentally and physically for learning the fighting back skills in self-defense covered in the next seven chapters, and some factors relevant to learning these physical skills. Physical skill is an important part of the self-defense process. It gives students more confidence and experience in dealing with various attacks. Students will have the ability and the weapons necessary to control the situation instead of waiting for attackers to make decisions. This chapter includes discussions on self-confidence, body conditioning, the main principles in skill development and applications, safety guidelines and etiquette, and warm-up procedures, as well as injury prevention.

Self-Confidence

Many people have little confidence in fighting back for self-defense. They feel that it is useless for them (especially women) to fight back against a tall, strong, and armed male attacker. Therefore, they believe women should concentrate on other strategies such as talking their way out instead of developing physical skills. This is a big misconception due to several factors. First, not all attackers are so tall and strong that the defender cannot handle the situation. Actually, most attackers are regular size, maybe a little stronger than the average defender. Students should not scare themselves and become unnecessarily intimidated. Secondly, men generally have greater muscle mass than women, but women can develop good body conditioning and skills to reduce the difference dramatically. There have been many cases in sports where women have defeated men. Third, men have their weak body parts such as the head, groin, knees, et cetera, while women have some tough weapons such as feet, fists, elbows, and knees. When women use these tough weapons on men's weak spots, they are not weak anymore. Fourth, strength works only when the attackers grab or hold the victim. Strength has less effect when defenders keep a safe distance in fighting back by using particular fighting patterns such as distance fighting. Students usually have little self-confidence before they start learning self-defense, but develop confidence gradually as they gain more skills, knowledge, and hands-on experience.

Body Conditioning

Body conditioning is very important to the success of fighting back in self-defense. Since most of the time, the attacker is stronger than the defender, it is necessary for the defender to improve their body conditioning in order to reduce this discrepancy. Good body conditioning also makes it easier for the defender to learn and perform the physical skills. The body conditioning for fighting back includes reducing reaction times, while improving strength and power, speed, agility, and endurance.

Reaction

It is still controversial as to whether reaction times can be improved through training. But reaction time often is associated with judgment and anticipation which are essential to how fast the defender can react to a self-defense situation, and the ability of judgment and anticipation can certainly be improved. The common ways to improve include: 1) use of combative activities; 2) working with a combination of physical skills so that the defender can recognize the situation and react appropriately; and 3) having a partner perform the offensive skills, while the defender reacts to each attack.

Strength and Power

Proper strength gives the defender the opportunity to fight effectively using throws, joint control, floor fighting, and releases. Explosive power gives the defender the chance to fight more effectively with both distance and close fighting. Strength is the key to survival in situations involving grabbing, choking, or holds. The best way to improve strength and power is weight training activities.

Speed and Quickness

Speed is another important feature in physical skills. The defender needs to perform skills fast to avoid any attacks or to fight when the defender sees any opportunities. Everything in self-defense needs to be done in a fast pattern. The ways to improve speed and quickness include sprint running, fast weight lifting, and lots of repetitions of single and combination skill practice.

Agility

Good agility allows the defender to change motions fast and easily in order to respond to any potential attacking motions and to catch any opportunities. It also gives the defender a greater chance to use a variety of skills in a particular situation. There are many ways to improve agility, such as zig-zag running, changing from one skill to another, or shifting from one type of skill to another.

Endurance

Any fighting-back against an attacker using self-defense may last a very long time, and the defender should prepare for a long-lasting fight. Good endurance, therefore, is necessary for the defender to survive. The ways to improve endurance include long distance running, aerobic exercise, weight training, and long sparring in self-defense training.

Warm-Up and Cool-Down

A good warm-up can prepare the body for learning and performing the physical skills, as well as reduce the risk of injuries. A good warm-up routine should include the following activities: 1) running, jogging, or jumping activities to warm the muscles and raise the heart rate; 2) stretching activities to prepare all muscle groups to be used; 3) rotating activities to prepare all joints to be involved and 4) some combative activities related to the skills being performed.

Proper cool-down activities can relax the body and restore energy for the next workout, and prevent post-workout problems. A good cool-down process should include proper relaxation of all muscle groups involved and keeping the body clean and warm. Relaxation techniques include massage, shaking activities, and meditation.

Etiquette and Manners

Since students will learn all techniques with partners in self-defense classes, good etiquette and manners can make the learning process easier and more enjoyable. A lack of etiquette can make the learning very annoying. Good etiquette includes, but is not limited to, the following guidelines: respect classmates and the instructor, keep the gym clean, avoid using foul language, be considerate and helpful toward each other, perform to your best (both physically and mentally), control your temper, and keep proper personal hygiene.

Potential Risk of Injuries and Prevention

Learning and practicing physical skills in self-defense classes involves some risk of physical injuries. The possibilities of injuries, however, can be reduced to a minimum if both the instructor and the students follow the safety guidelines very strictly.

Potential Injuries

Injuries that occur in self-defense training may include, but are not limited to, the following: twisted finger muscles and tendons, twisted wrist muscles and tendons, strained elbow, twisted shoulder muscles or ligaments, twisted neck muscles, twisted upper back or lower back muscles, pulled hip and thigh muscles, sprained knee ligaments, twisted ankle muscles and ligaments, pulled Achilles tendon, being hit or scratched by your partner accidentally, and falling too hard.

Injuries occur most of the time due to the following reasons: previous injuries which have not yet healed, improper warm-up, incorrect performance of the techniques, going beyond your body limits, carelessness, accidents, being unprepared, and using quick or jerking motions.

How to Prevent Injuries

Many safety procedures can be used to reduce the chance of potential injuries in self-defense training. The following are commonly recommended: 1) Assess your health and consult your physician and instructor if you have any problems. 2) Do not practice if you are sick or injured. Report any injuries to the instructor immediately. 3) Wear sportswear and remove anything which may cause injuries to you or your partner, such as watches, jewelry, hard hairpins, and other similar objects. 4) Trim all long nails (hands and feet) to avoid potentially scratching your partner or breaking your nails. 5) Remove bubble gum before entering the gym, and bring no food or drink into the gym. 6) Absolutely allow no horseplay in the class. 7) Do not show off in the class or anywhere else with the skills you have learned. 8) Always warm up before practicing or learning. 9) Control your temper and do not become angry in the class. 10) Concentrate on class activities and avoid loud laughing and socializing during training. 11) Control your movements to avoid accidents. 12) Remain alert and be aware of what is going on around you.

Principles and Philosophies of Physical Skills

Fighting back in self-defense can be classified into various basic fighting patterns, but none of the variables (attacker, motive, pattern of attacks, timing, or location) is under your complete control. This feature determines the nature of fighting back methods used in self-defense: 1) it depends on the situation, 2) it is unpredictable, and 3) the situation may become quite violent. The defender should have a comprehensive preparation for the worst situations. Improper training of the physical skills may cause severe consequences to you. The following statements indicate the basic philosophy and the principles needed for the development and applications of physical skills presented in later chapters.

Overall Preparation

Applications of physical skills depend on the situation, but no one can predict how defenders will be attacked. Therefore, students should develop different kinds of skills for different kinds of situations. In another words, the defender should be well prepared with all the necessary basic skills for every potential situation.

Continuous Fighting Ability

When involved in fighting back and using physical skills, it is hard to predict how long a battle may last. It is nice if the defender can get out with one punch or kick, but that is usually not the case in reality. When both the attacker and defender are involved in fighting, it is not easy to get the opponent in one or two blows. The ability to fight continuously is very important for survival. The defender needs to develop the ability for continuous fighting with different skills, instead of expecting to win with one kick or strike.

Combination Skills

Situations change all the time in real fighting, such as fighting from two yards away to one-arm distance, from open hand fighting to grabbing or holding, and from standing or grabbing to floor choking. Defenders have to develop the ability to combine several fighting patterns together to deal with the changing situation in real fighting-back situations. Even though most skills from next seven chapters are introduced individually, students should always combine them together in different situations in practice sessions.

Variations of Skills

The skills introduced in this book are basic skills. Based on these skills, the defender can create more new skills by adding, changing, or reducing a couple of motions, and learning more advanced skills. The defender also should keep in mind that being able to use exactly the formal skills introduced here in real situations is almost impossible, since attackers will not set up precisely the way you want. Therefore, defenders should not only perform the formal skills, but also learn how to change motions to fit a particular situation.

No Limit to Applications of Skills

When defender's lives are threatened, they have the right to use any skills in order to protect themselves. Real fighting may require the use of many nasty skills, ranging from regular kicks and punches to bites and digs in the eyes. Any skill which can save your life is the best skill to use. Do not limit your mind to one or two skills or worry too much about the legal consequences of using these nasty skills. It is the attacker, not the defender, who should be responsible for any consequences in the fight they initiate.

Fight Back First

In real life-threatening situations, defenders have the right to use the physical skills first after they try to avoid the confrontation and give the attacker a warning. Defenders should not wait for the attacker to start the physical attack first and react to the attacker's movements because that is almost always too late. Remember, the best defense is a good offense. It is better, to put the attacker in a defensive situation than defenders use blocking and react to attacker's movement.

A Good Balance Between Defense and Offense

The real fighting in self-defense is not limited to attackers initiating the attack and defenders waiting to defend themselves. It is a battle in which both sides can use any necessary skills. It requires both good offensive and defensive skills to win. Students should be prepared with both offensive and defensive skills. Most skills introduced in the following chapters have both defensive and offensive applications.

Decision Making

Although defenders have to learn all the basic techniques, they do not necessarily use everything in all situations. The defender should make the decision of what skills to use in a certain situation. For example, defenders can dig eyes, strike the groin, or break the elbow in a life-threatening situation. On the other hand, defenders may only have to use a joint control move to deal with inappropriate touching or sexual harassment at work.

Mental and Physical Skills

The real fighting requires not only the physical skills but also mental skills. Mental skills can trick, distract, and scare attackers, and make the applications of physical skills more effective. The defender should keep in mind that anytime during fighting, they can use any back-away skills and fighting strategies introduced in the following chapters.

REFERENCES

Bittenbinder, J. J. *Street smart*. Illinois: Video Publishing House, Inc., 1992.

Strong, S. *Strong on Defense*. New York: Pocket Books, 1996.

Chapter 12
Distance Fighting

This chapter introduces the distance fighting pattern used in self-defense. The content includes basic concepts and implications of this pattern, basic offensive and defensive skills, applications of these skills, mental strategies, and hands-on experience. Most skills are demonstrated in the attached VCD in motion.

Introduction

Distance Fighting is a fighting-back pattern which uses movement, long kicks and punches, and blocks to counter the attack from a relatively safe distance (at least two-arms length distance). This pattern provides the defender less risks when fighting back against any attackers. It can and should be used in most self-defense situations whenever the defender has a choice. The chances to use the distance fighting pattern include situations such as before the attacker grabs the defender or after the defender releases from holds, whenever the attacker has a knife or other cold weapon (such as a knife, stick, or bottle), or when the attacker is much bigger or stronger than the defender.

There are several special features in distance fighting. It is relatively safe for the defender because the defender has less chance to be hit, held, or grabbed. The defender has more time and space for reactions, thinking, and decision making. The defender also can back up easily. The offense and defense are clearly separated in this fighting pattern.

Major Targets and Weapons

There are several vulnerable areas on a human body. These vulnerable areas should be the targets of offensive blows and should also be well protected from an attack. Since in most life-threatening situations the attacker is stronger than the defender, it is extremely important for the defender to use the strong parts of their body as a weapon against the attacker. The strong parts include hands (palm for strikes or fist for punches) and feet (the heel, top and outer edge for kicks). Of course the defender also can use other weapons, such as a chair or a stick. The major targets of attack include the primary vulnerable areas which include the head and groin, and the secondary targets which include the knee, elbow, low stomach, and ribs.

Hitting a primary target may totally disable the attacker so that he/she cannot continue the attack. Striking a secondary target may cause partial disability which will dramatically reduce the chances of a continued attack. Defenders should keep in mind that their vulnerable targets are also where the attacker will strike, and they should keep these areas well protected during the fight.

Basic Stance

Self-defense requires a correct stance which will allow the defender to move fast, to cover the body well, and to fight back easily. Although there are many different stances used in various martial arts, the basic stance for a beginner in self-defense is illustrated in Figure 12.1.

12.1. Basic fighting stance for a right-handed person

12.1a.
a. Defender is facing the attacker at a two-arm length distance
b. Feet apart about shoulder-wide weight on balls of the feet
c. Knees bent slightly
d. Trunk basically straight and turned halfway to the right
e. Head erect and looking into the attacker's eyes
f. Left hand in front at chin level
g. Right hand in front of the chest

12.1b.
a. A front look at the basic fighting stance

Basic Footwork

Correct and fast footwork will enable the defender to keep a safe distance from the attacker, to avoid any attacks (hit, kick, or grab), and to catch attacker's openings effectively. The basic footwork includes moving backward, moving forward, moving to the left, and moving to the right. The basic technique of moving is to move the leg which is at the desired direction first and the other leg follows, and still keep the same fighting stance after the move. For example, when you move backward, the back leg steps back first, and then front leg follows back. When you move to left, the left leg steps toward left side first, then right leg follows.

1. Move backward: Moving backward is used when the attacker throws a punch or kick, or moves forward. The defender uses this move to keep a safe distance (figure 12.2).

12.2. Move backward

12.2a. Fighting stance

12.2b. Right step back first

12.2c. Left foot follow back

2. Move forward: Moving forward is used when the defender wants to punch or kick the attacker. The defender uses this move to get closer to the attacker (figure 12.3).

12.3. Move forward

12.3a. Fighting stance

12.3b. Left step forward

12.3c. Right step follow up

3. Move sideways: Moving sideways is used when the attacker comes too strong or fast and it is difficult for the attacker to move back in order to avoid his momentum (figure 12.4).

12.4. Move to left

12.4a. Fighting stance.

12.4b. Left foot moves to left first.

12.4c. Right foot follows up.

12.4. Move to right

12.4d. Fighting stance.

12.4e. Right foot steps to right first.

12.4f. Left step follows up.

Offensive Skills

Offensive skills are used by the defender to disable the attacker or force the attacker to stay back. Although the defender does not need to disable the attacker for safety, it is often necessary for the defender to fight aggressively with these offensive skills since the best defense is a solid offense. Offensive skills in distance fighting include punches, kicks, and combinations. After performing each punch or kick taught in this chapter, students should immediately bring the striking arm or leg back to the basic fighting stance (to be ready for defense or to look for chances to strike again) in learning. All skills demonstrated here start from the distance fighting stance, and all skills should have the follow-up motions either to use more strikes at the attacker or back up for the next movement.

Punches

1. Jab Punch: The jab punch is a quick punch usually used to hit the attacker's face or to fake the attacker by forcing him to cover the face so that the defender can attack elsewhere. It is performed by the front (left) hand (figure 12.5).

12.5. A jab punch at the nose

12.5. Rotate the left shoulder forward to create power, extend the left upper arm and forearm forward to hit the target.

2. Cross Punch: The cross punch is a powerful punch usually used to hit the attacker's low stomach or ribs (or the face if the attacker is not very tall). It is performed by the back (right) hand (figure 12.6).

12.6. A cross punch at low stomach

12.6. Rotate right shoulder forward and pivot right foot to create power, extend the right upper arm and forearm forward to hit the target.

3. Hook Punch: The hook punch is a powerful punch usually used to go around the attacker's hand blocks and hit the attacker's ears (figure 12.7). It is performed by either hand.

12.7. A back-hand hook punch at the ear

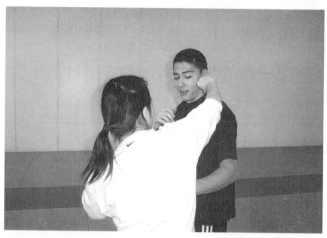

12.7. Rotate the right shoulder forward with a pivot motion to create power, extend the right upper arm and forearm in counter-clockwise motion to hit the ear with a curled pathway.

Kicks

1. Heel Kick: The heel kick is a powerful kick usually used to strike the attacker's low stomach or groin area to disable the attacker or force him to back up (figure 12.8). It is performed by either leg.

12.8. Heel kick at low stomach

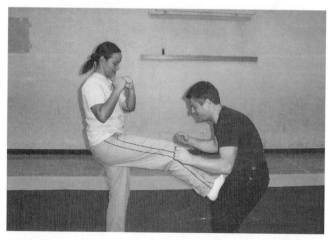

12.8. Pivot right foot and rotate right shoulder forward, then lift the right knee, extend right leg and point the heel to strike the target.

2. Side Kick: The side kick is also a powerful kick, mainly used to strike the attacker's front knee (figure 12.9). It can be performed by either leg.

12.9. Side kick at front knee

12.9. Curl the front leg and point the heel, and then extend left leg and use the heel or outer edge of foot to strike the target (toes pointed sideways).

3. Back Kick: The back kick is also a powerful kick usually used to strike the attacker's low stomach and groin (or sometime ribs) when the attacker is behind the defender (figure 12.10). It can be performed by either leg.

12.10. Back kick at stomach

12.10. Curl the back leg and point the heel, and extend the back leg to strike the target with the heel (toes pointed downward).

4. Snap Kick: The snap kick is a quick kick usually used to strike the attacker's groin area (figure 12.11), or sometimes the hand holding a knife or stick. It can be performed by either leg.

12.11. Snap kick at groin

12.11. Curl the leg, and extend the leg and hit the target with the top of the foot (toes pointing forward).

5. Round-House Kick: This kick is a quick kick used to disable attacker's knee or kick the face (figure 12.12). It can be performed by either leg.

12.12. Round house kick at knee

12.12a. Lift the knee sideways and bring leg in, extend the leg and hit the target with the top of the foot (toes pointing sideways).

12.12b. Back view

6. Spin Kick: The spin kick is a powerful kick usually used to strike the attacker's low stomach or ribs (figure 12.13). It is similar to the back kick except a spin motion is added so that the defender can kick the attacker. It is used to pretend that the defender is running away and then the defender kicks when the attacker is off guard or tries to chase the defender.

12.13. Spin kick at stomach

12.13a. Start from fighting stance.

12.13b. Pivot on left foot, rotate the body clockwise, turn your back to the attacker.

12.13c. Curl right leg and point the heel, extend back-leg to strike the target with the heel.

7. Floor-Sweeping Kick: The floor-sweeping kick is a powerful kick usually used to throw the attacker down (figure 12.14). It is similar to the spin kick, except that the defender stays on the floor. It is not recommended to use often unless the defender catches the chance or has to do it. It can be performed by either leg.

12.14. Floor-sweeping kick at ankles

12.14a. Lean backward.

12.14b. Knee down and spin on left leg.

12.14c. Rotate the body clockwise and sweep at the attacker's ankle or knee.

12.14d. Keep the low stance and keep sweeping.

Combinations

In real fighting situations, it is difficult to get the attacker by one punch or kick. The combination skills work more effectively. For example, when the defender throws a punch at the attacker's face, the attacker usually has to block it, and at the same time he tends to leave other parts open, such as the stomach. The defender thus can take this opportunity to catch that opening.

1. Side Kick, Jab Punch, Cross Punch Combination: Use a side kick to attack the attacker's knee (figure 12.15a), and follow up with a jab punch at the face (figure 12.15b) when the attacker is avoiding the kick, then use a cross punch to hit the stomach if the attacker is covering his face (figure 12.15c).

12.15. Side kick-jab-cross punch combination

12.15a. A side kick at knee.

12.15b. A jab punch at face.

12.15c. A cross punch at stomach.

2. Side Kick, Spin Kick Combination: Use a side kick to attack the attacker's knee (figure 12.16a), and follow up with a spin kick at the stomach (figure 12.16c).

12.16. Side kick-spin kick combination

12.16a. A side kick at knee.

12.16b. The kicking foot lands.

12.16c. Use right leg for a spin kick.

3. Hook Punch, Spin Kick Combination: Use a hook punch to attack the attacker's face (figure 12.17a), and follow up with a spin kick at the stomach (figure 12.17b).

12.17 Hook punch-spin kick combination

12.17a. A left hook punch at face.

12.17b. Turn clockwise.

12.17c. A spin kick at privates.

There are many ways defenders can put skills into combinations. Examples include a jab punch followed with a cross punch, a fake jab punch followed with a side kick, or a round-house kick followed with a floor sweeping kick.

Defensive Skills

These skills are used by the defender to counter the attacker's punches or kicks. In real life-threatening situations, fighting back is just like a sport event in which offense and defense switch very rapidly. Therefore, the defender not only needs to learn how to disable the attacker but also needs to know how to counter the punches and kicks used by the attacker.

Counter a Punch

1. Block: The block is the easiest way to counter a punch. The easiest motion a defender can do is to keep the basic fighting stance which makes it hard for the attacker to strike the face since the defender's hands are in the way (figure 12.18a). To make it safe, the defender sometimes can block the punch sideways with a small motion (figure 12.18b).

12.18. Natural block and a push block

12.18a. Arms up in the way as a natural block.

12.18b. Quickly push the punch slightly sideways but keep your hands in front.

2. Body Movement: Body movement is an intermediate skill in distance fighting. The basic idea is to keep the body a moving target which makes the attacker's strike difficult to aim. The basic body movements include leaning backward (figure 12.19a), ducking downward (figure 12.19b), and slipping sideways (12.19c). These movements work best when combined with the arm blocks. Boxers actually tend to use many of the body motions in their boxing games.

12.19. Lean, duck, and slip at a punch

12.19a. Lean back at a jab punch with both hands in position.

12.19b. Duck at a punch with hands up to cover the face.

12.19c. Slip at a cross punch with front hand up.

3. Throw: Throwing is a soft way to counter punches (figure 12.20). It works effectively in intermediate and advanced fighting. However, throwing requires more strength, quickness, courage, and skill.

12.20. Counter a punch with a tackle throw

12.20a. Block the punch.

12.20b. Lock the knees with both hands.

12.20c. Shoulder rushes forward to push attacker down.

Counter a Kick

1. Step Back: The safest and easiest way to counter a kick is simply stepping back in order to be out of the attacker's reach. If the defender detects the kick early and steps back, it is hard for the attacker to touch you. The step back skill was introduced previously in the movement section.

2. Leg Block: The leg block is the main skill used to counter kicks when the attacker kicks fast, before the defender can react and step back. The defender lifts up the front leg to cover the groin area and to prevent a broken knee (figure 12.21a). The defender may need to leap backward, maintaining the defensive stance, if the attack comes too close (figure 12.21b).

12.21. Leg block and leap back

12.21a. Lift the front leg to block the kick, keep both hands in position.

12.21b. Leap backward, remaining in the same block position.

Strategies

Effective fighting-back and winning in self-defense requires more than just the physical skills introduced above. It demands mental strategies to effectively apply these skills in real situations. The strategies in distance fighting include defensive fighting strategies and offensive fighting strategies.

1. Fight defensively. This is the strategy defenders should use when the attacker is much stronger, has a knife, or is eager to finish the battle and puts the defender under control. Moving around to keep a safe distance for a long-lasting fight is the main idea. The basic strategies when fighting back defensively include the following.

- a. Keep moving and maintain a safe distance.
- b. Save energy and do not attack unless necessary.
- c. Strike aggressively if the attacker tries to approach you.
- d. Be alert and notice the environment (is there any available assistance nearby?).
- e. Hit and run (attack when there is a chance and back up for the next movement).

2. Fight offensively. This is the strategy the defender should use when he/she is eager to finish the battle, when the defender has to disable the attacker in order to get away, or when the attacker has no obvious advantage. The basic idea is to put the attacker into a defensive situation where the attacker is busy covering himself instead of attacking the victim. The basic strategies include the following:

- a. Use back-away skills to get the attacker off guard (such as pretending to be scared), then attack fast.
- b. Use fake motions to trick the attacker and use combination skills.
- c. Attack aggressively, even when the defender has to take a couple of punches or kicks.
- d. Yell and demonstrate a scary fighting stance to show high fighting-back spirit.

Improve Distance Fighting Skills

Learning the above skills is just the first step. Students should keep practicing these skills until they become automatic and effective motions. There are three ways students can continuously improve their distance fighting skills. The first is to work on the quality, such as speed, power, accuracy, timing, anticipation and judgment, variations, and applications of these skills in imitative situations.

The second way is to combine distance fighting with other fighting patterns. Due to the fact that there are no limits for both the defender and the attacker and that there will be many unpredictable changes in life-threatening situations, the defender may have to combine other fighting patterns such as freehand close fighting, throwing, and floor fighting. For example, the defender throws a punch at the attacker, but the attacker took the punch and grabs the defender. The defender then has to use throwing skills. The defender should not limit his/her thinking to one fighting back pattern only. Instead, defenders should learn how to combine the distance fighting pattern with other patterns for the best results.

The third way is to develop advanced skills through learning a particular martial art. The distance fighting skills introduced in this chapter are basic skills. To learn more advanced distance fighting skills beyond the basics, students may select a martial art which uses the distance fighting pattern and skills. This will allow the student to continuously improve their distance fighting abilities. The martial arts which use the distance fighting pattern and skills include Karate, Boxing, Tae Kwon Do, Southern and Northern style of Chinese Kung Fu, Thai Boxing, Kickboxing, Shoot Boxing, and San Shou.

REFERENCES

Chen, Z. K. *Practical Kicks in Wu Shu.* China: Tour and Education Publisher, 1989.

Dong, Z. H. *Thai Boxing.* China: Beijing Physical Education University Publisher, 1994.

Ji, F. L. *Chinese Shuai Jiao.* China: Beijing Physical Education University Publisher, 1990.

Mattson, G. *The Way of Karate.* Japan: Charles E. Tuttle Company, 1993.

Park, Y. H., & Gerrard, J. *Tae Kwon Do.* New York: Facts on File, 1989.

Pu, S. W. *Capturing Skills for Police Officers.* China: Beijing Physical Education University Publisher, 1991.

Zhang, W. G. *San Shou.* China: Canton Science and Technology Publisher, 1983.

Chapter 13
Open-Hand Close Fighting

This chapter introduces skills and strategies used for fighting back at a closer range with open-hand techniques. Included are basic offensive and defensive skills, applications of these skills in fighting-back situations, and basic fighting strategies. All skills are demonstrated in the Attached VCD in motion.

Introduction

The open-hand close fighting pattern provides the defender with skills to fight back during life-threatening situations using elbow strikes, knee strikes, short punches, shoulder shovels, head butts, and blocks. This pattern is used when the attacker is very close to the defender (usually at one-arm length distance or closer), or when the attacker is grabbing or trying to grab or hit the defender, or when the attacker has openings. The defender has some chance to disable the attacker, yet there is much more risk of being hit or grabbed.

The open-hand close fighting has several special features. The situation is very violent and dangerous because the defender may be hit or grabbed anytime. The chance of injuries also increases. The defender has no time or space for reactions or thinking. The offense and defense are not clearly separated, and it is usually a messy fight.

The major weapons the defender uses include the elbow, knee, hand, and head. The major targets to aim at in the attacker (also the vulnerable areas for the defender to cover if the attacker uses this pattern) include head (nose, chin, and ears), neck, groin, ribs, and low stomach.

Basic Stance

The basic stance for freehand close fighting is similar to, yet also a little different from, that used in distance fighting. The defender should tuck in more for better protection. This stance is illustrated in figure 13.1.

13.1. Open-hand close fighting stance (left-handed)

13.1. Similar to distance fighting but at one arm-length distance and keep both arms in front of the face for full coverage.

Offensive Skills

The following skills are used to fight back from a close distance. All skills are performed from the close fighting stance, and all skills should have follow-up motion, either to further disable the attacker when the target is hit or to back up into the basic stance and get ready for the next movement.

1. Knee Strike: The knee strike is a powerful strike toward the attacker's groin or low stomach. Knee strikes require good timing and quick motion, and they can be performed by either knee. A knee strike is shown in figure 13.2.

13.2. Knee strike at groin

13.2. Grab the attacker's shoulder or hands and pull him toward the defender, and then lift the knee to strike the attacker's groin.

2. Elbow Strike: The elbow strike is a powerful hit toward the attacker's head or rib/low stomach. The elbow strike can be performed by either elbow, and can be used when the attacker is in front or back. The elbow strike also can be used in other situations to attack the back, kidney, elbow, or other weak parts of the body.

2-1. Forward strike at the head. This strike is used when the attacker is in front and he is not very tall (figure 13.3). The motion is more like throwing a punch, and it has a swinging motion.

13.3. Forward strike at the head

13.3. Rotate the body toward the left, and at the same time, swing the elbow at the attacker's head.

2-2. Forward strike at the ribs. This strike is used when the attacker is in front and he is tall (figure 13.4). The motion is more like stabbing your elbow into attacker's ribs.

13.4. Forward strike at the ribs

13.4. Duck the body and point the front-elbow toward the ribs, and then strike the ribs by the combination force of the back leg, trunk, and back-hand.

2-3. Back strike at the head. This strike is used when the attacker is behind the defender and his head is low (figure 13.5).

13.5 Back strike at the head

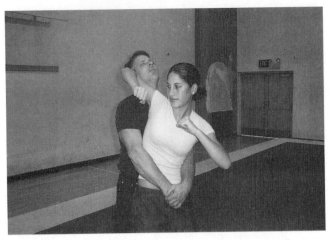

13.5. Rotate the trunk, swing the elbow toward attacker's head with full power.

2-4. Back strike at the ribs. This strike is used when the attacker is behind the defender and he is tall or his ribs are unprotected (figure 13.6).

13.6. Back strike at ribs

13.6. Rotate the trunk, swing the elbow, and strike the ribs with full power.

3. Short Punches: Short punches look like the hook punches in distance fighting, but do not reach out far. Short punches aim at the head, chin, or stomach. To fight back effectively, the defender should always use body power to punch and keep the arms in front as protections. Short punches include two types of hits: high punches at the head and chin, and low punches at the ribs or stomach.

3-1. High short punch. This punch is used to hit the attacker's ear or face when the attacker is not very tall and his head is not well protected (figure 13.7).

13.7. High punch at the head

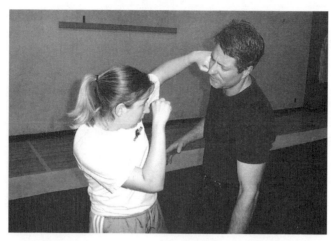

13.7. Twist the trunk clockwise and hit the head sideways (palm pointed downward).

3-2. Uppercut punch. This punch is used to hit the chin when it is not well protected (figure 13.8).

13.8. Uppercut-punch at the chin

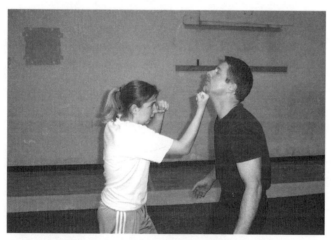

13.8. Rotate the trunk to right and hit the chin upward (palm pointed to the defender).

3-3. Low punch. This punch is used to hit the attacker's low stomach or ribs when the attacker is tall and his ribs are not well protected (figure 13.9). The problem with this punch is that sometimes it will not cause enough damage to the attacker, especially when the attacker is big.

13.9. Low-punch at the ribs

13.9. Rotate the trunk and hit the ribs upward
(palm pointed upward).

4. Head Butt: The head butt is used to strike the attacker's nose or chin. It can be performed either forward (figure 13.10) or backward depending on the situation.

13.10. Front head butt at the attacker's nose

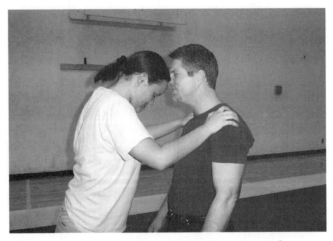

13.10. Grab the attacker and hit the nose with your forehead.

5. Short Kick: The short kick is used to damage the knee or the shin when the attacker is concentrating on the upper body motions (figure 13.11).

13.11. Short kick at knee or shin

13.11. Use the back leg to kick the knee
fast and powerfully.

6. Shoulder Shovel: The shoulder shovel is used to push the attacker away so that the defender can keep a safe distance or use other fighting skills (figure 13.12).

13.12. Shoulder shovel

13.12. Rush forward and keep arms up and tight to shovel attacker away.

Defensive Skills

When the attacker uses the offensive skills to attack the defender in freehand close fighting, the defender also has to use defensive skills to protect himself. Three types of defensive skills are introduced here.

1. Block and back up into distance fighting: The defender blocks the punches, elbow strikes, or knee strikes with their arms and legs first, then quickly backs up to a safe distance for distance fighting. This is an easy way to counter the close attacks (figure 13.13).

13.13. Counter elbow strike and back up

13.13a. Block the short punch.

13.13b. Push and step back fast.

2. Block and strike back: The defender blocks the punches, elbow strikes, or knee strikes with her/his arms and legs a couple of times, then quickly strikes back to force the attacker into a defensive situation. This is the aggressive way to counter close attacks (figure 13.14).

13.14. Counter a short punch and perform a knee strike

13.14a. Block the short punch.

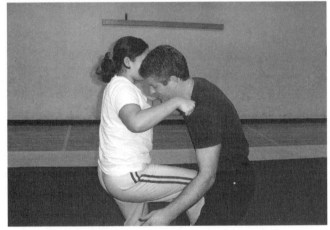

13.14b. Grab the shoulder and strike the groin.

3. Duck and throw: The defender gets close to the attacker so that the attacker will not have time or space to start elbow or knee strikes, and then quickly throws the attacker on the ground (figure 13.15). This throw, if performed well, is very effective at close fighting situations. This countering skill is better dealing with knee strikes and elbow strikes before the attacker starts the swinging motion.

13.15. Counter an elbow strike, and then throw.

13.15a. Block a strike before it starts.

13.15b. Grab attacker's arms and bock the leg.

13.15c. Push attacker back.

Fighting Strategies

1. Back up for distance fighting whenever there is a chance because this is much safer for the defender.
2. Be aggressive with the opponent if there is no chance to back up. Use all striking skills nonstop to force the attacker into a defensive situation. This way the attacker will worry about his own safety instead of attacking the defender.
3. Use lots of combinations and fight continuously. Show the attacker that you are not afraid of the fight and you dare to sacrifice everything to save yourself.
4. Use any skills possible for the defender to get out of this situation.

Improve Open-Hand Close Fighting Skills

After learning the basic close fighting skills, students should practice these skills until they can be used effectively for self-protection. Like the distance fighting pattern, there are three ways students can continuously improve their close fighting skills. The first step usually is to work on speed, power, accuracy, timing, anticipation, and judgment, variations, and applications of these skills in imitative situations.

Combining close fighting techniques with other fighting patterns is the second way to improve close fighting skills. Due to the fact that there are no rules for both the defender and the attacker and that there will be many unpredictable changes in life-threatening situations, the defender may have to combine other fighting patterns such as distance fighting, throwing, and floor fighting in order to survive. It is essential that the defenders do not limit their mind to one pattern and that they can apply other skills during the close fighting. The defender may have to use such skills such as biting, digging the eyes, and grabbing the groin.

Students should take one further step in order to develop their advanced skills through learning a particular martial art. The martial arts which use the freehand close fighting pattern and skills include Thai Boxing (knee strikes and elbow strikes), Boxing (short punches), Ultimate Fighting (head butt, elbow strikes, knee strikes, short punches), and Kung Fu (elbow strikes, knee strikes, head butt).

References

Dong, Z. H. *Thai Boxing*. China: Beijing Physical Education University Publisher, 1994.

Du, Z. G. *Controlling Skills for Police Training*. China: Beijing Physical Education University Publisher, 1993.

Haislet, E. L. *Boxing*. New York: Barnes & Company, 1980.

Pu, S. W. *Capturing Skills for Police Officers*. China: Beijing Physical Education University Publisher, 1991.

Wu, Z. N. *Chinese Qin Na*. China: Zhejiang Publisher, 1985.

Zhang, W. G. *San Shou*. China: Canton Science and Technology Publisher, 1983

Chapter 14
Throwing

This chapter introduces skills and strategies used when the attacker and defender are grabbing each other in self-defense. Included are falling and rolling, offensive and defensive skills, applications, and basic fighting strategies. All skills are demonstrated in the attached VCD in motion.

Introduction

Throwing is a fighting-back pattern which uses grabbing and avoiding skills, breaking out and keeping balance skills, falling and rolling skills, and throwing skills and countering throwing skills. The basic purpose of this fighting pattern is to develop knowledge, skills, and strategies in dealing with grabs, falls, throws and counters in self-defense situations. Throwing skills are usually used to get away from the attacks when the attacker is trying to grab the defender, or when the attacker has already grabbed the defender's shoulders, or when the attacker is trying to throw the defender down on the ground.

Special characteristics of this fighting back pattern include several aspects. The defender is at a greater risk because very often the attacker is stronger and has more control when he grabs the defender. Muscle strength plays a key role in this fighting pattern. The defender has no chance for thinking or decision making. Offense and defense are not clearly separated, and the fighting will be messy and dangerous.

Falls and Rolls

Falls and rolls have two important purposes in physical skills. The first purpose is to protect the defender from injuries when being thrown on the ground so that the defender still can fight back on the ground. The second purpose is that while learning the throws and counter moves, students usually develop more self-confidence and perform much better when they can fall and roll correctly. These skills include three falls and two rolls.

1. Fall backward: This skill is used to protect the defender's head and spine when falling backward (figure 14.1).

14.1. Fall backward

14.1a. Place one leg behind and fall backward.

14.1b. Tuck the chin and extend arms sideways (palms down) to take the shock off the back.

2. Fall forward: This skill is used to protect the face and chest when falling forward (figure 14.2).

14.2. Fall forward

14.2a. Move one leg slightly forward to reduce the force and get arms ready.

14.2b. Use palms and forearms to keep head and body off the floor.

3. Fall sideways: This skill is used to avoid potential injuries when falling. It is much safer to fall sideways than forward or backward, since the side of the body is strong (figure 14.3).

14.3 Fall sideways

14.3a. Attacker pushes defender sideways.

14.3b. Fall on the right side, keep your head off the floor, and right palm hits the floor (palm downward) to keep the balance.

14.3c. A look at the left fall.

4. Roll forward: This skill is used to prevent potential injuries when the defender is falling forward fast and cannot stop for a decent forward fall (figure 14.4).

14.4. Roll forward

14.4a. Bend knee and place palms down.

14.4b. Hands touch the ground first, and head moves toward the hip to make a ball shape.

14.4c. Roll over the shoulder.

14.4d. Get up for next movement.

5. Roll backward: This skill is used to protect the head and spine when falling backward with a great force and you cannot stop (figure 14.5).

14.5. Roll backward

14.5a. Left step back.

14.5b. Tuck chin and palms hit side.

14.5c. Roll over one shoulder.

14.5d. Get up for next movement.

Avoid, Break, and Balance

These skills are used to counter the grabs or attempted grabs from the attacker. These skills help the defender to avoid the disadvantage of being grabbed. The main skills used include pushing, grabbing, and movement. The defender, however, also can use any other skills such as punches, kicks, or strikes while performing the avoidance, breaking out, or maintaining balance.

1. Avoid before being grabbed: This skill is used to block the hands away and move out of the way when the attacker is trying to grab the defender (figure 14.6).

14.6. Avoid the grab

14.6a. Block attacker's hand to right.

14.6b. Step to left side and keep the fighting stance.

2. Break out when grabbed: This skill is used to put pressure on the attacker's weak joint to force a release when the defender is grabbed (figure 14.7).

14.7. Break the grab

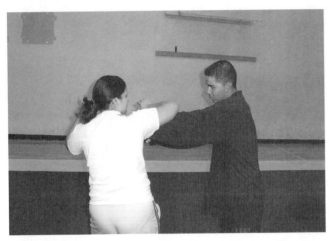

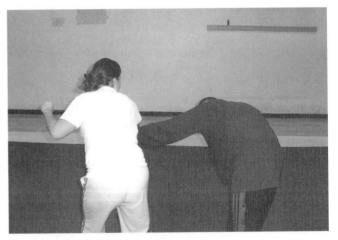

14.7a. Turn to strike the attacker's wrist or elbow to left.

14.7b. Step to left and continue to press on the joint until released.

3. Balance: This skill is used by the defender to keep the balance and look for chances to break out or throw when the attacker is grabbing the defender and trying to throw the defender down (figure 14.8).

14.8. Keep balance

14.8. Hold onto the attacker, move with the attacker, and look for a chance to break out, kick, or throw.

Throwing Skills and Counters

Throwing skills are fancy and are easy to learn in the class. However, they are not easy to perform in life-threatening situations, especially when the attacker is strong. Furthermore, throwing does not disable the attacker and thus gives him more chances to come back. It is recommended that beginners avoid using throwing skills unless necessary or the defender has good throwing skills and decent strength. Due to these considerations, this chapter only introduces two throwing skills and they are face-to-face type throws. The face-to-face type throw is used when the defender tries to throw the attacker while they are facing each other. It is much safer since the defender can see what the attacker is doing and can keep her balance easily.

1a. Tackle throw: This skill is used to lock the attacker's leg and shovel him off balance (figure 14.9).

14.9. Tackle throw

14.9a. Hold onto the attacker.

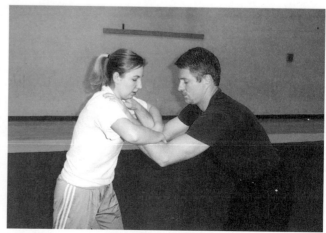

14.9b. Break the hold.

14.9c. Lock the knee, shoulder rush forward.

14.9d. Push the attacker down.

1b. Counter a tackle throw: An easy way to avoid the tackle throw (figure 14.10) is to step back. The attacker cannot throw the defender if he can not lock defender's knees. The defender also can perform a knee-strike at the face or elbow-strike down on the head, or simply step back.

14.10. Counter a tackle throw

14.10a. Attacker tries a tackle throw.

14.10b. Both legs jump back, and push attacker's head back.

2a. Reap throw: This skill is used to trip and push the attacker off balance (figure 14.11).

14.11. Reap throw

14.11a. Grab the attacker to keep balance.

14.11b. Twist the attacker's left shoulder forward, left steps forward toward attacker's right leg.

14.11c. Place right leg behind the attacker's right knee.

14.11d. Kick the knee up and push forward.

2b. Counter a reap throw: The defender can use two skills to deal with a reap throw from the attacker (figure 4.12). Figure 14.12a and 14.12b show the defensive way to avoid a reap throw by withdrawing the leg targeted, and 14.12c shows that the defender uses the same skill to throw the attacker before the attacker starts the throwing process.

14.12. Counter a reap throw

14.12a. Attacker is trying to lock defender's knee.

14.12b. Defender takes right leg back to avoid.

14.12c. Defender kicks attacker's right leg back and pushes his shoulders backward.

14.12d. Continue to kick up and push attacker off balance.

Strategies

Strategies in the throwing pattern are not very complicated. The defender should try to avoid being grabbed and to keep a safe distance. The reason is simple: most attackers are stronger, and stronger muscles play a key role in throwing. If being grabbed, the defender should always try to break out from the grabs and get into distance fighting or other fighting patterns unless the defender has more skill and confidence in getting the attacker down. The defender also can use any available skill such as distance or close fighting skills to disable the attacker or force him to release.

Improve Throwing Skills

After learning the basic throwing skills, students should practice these skills to a degree that they can use them effectively for self-defense. Like the other fighting patterns, students can continuously improve their close fighting skills through three steps. The first step usually is to work on speed, power, accuracy, timing, anticipation, judgment, variations, and applications of these skills in imitative situations.

Combining throws with other fighting patterns is the second way to improve these skills. Due to the fact that both the defender and the attacker will use any available skills, and that there will be many unpredictable changes in life-threatening situations, the defender may have to combine other fighting patterns such as distance fighting, close fighting, and releasing skills in order to survive. To fully prepare for actual fighting, defenders also need to practice other possible skills including biting, digging the eyes, grabbing the groin, etc.

Students should take one further step forward developing advanced skills through learning a particular martial art. The martial arts which focus on throwing skills include Judo, Wrestling, Shuai Jiao (Chinese wrestling), Aikido, and Jujitsu.

REFERENCES

Ji, F. L. *Chinese Shuai Jiao.* China: Beijing Physical Education University Publisher, 1990.

Kirby, G. *Jujitsu—Basic Techniques of the Gentle Art.* Bubank: Ohara Publication, 1993.

Nishioka, H., & West, J. R. *The Judo Textbook.* Burbank: Ohara Publication, 1988.

Pu, S. W. *Capturing Skills for Police Officers.* China: Beijing Physical Education University Publisher, 1991.

Yohei, K. *Aikido with Ki.* Japan: Ki No Kenkyukai, 1984.

Zhang, W. G. *San Shou.* China: Canton Science and Technology Publisher, 1983.

Chapter 15
Floor Fighting

This chapter introduces students to basic floor fighting skills. Included are floor distance fighting skills, floor releasing skills, applications, and fighting strategies. All skills are demonstrated in the attached VCD in motion.

Introduction

Floor fighting is an important type of skill in self-defense. Very often, the defender ends up falling on the ground first within several seconds during the fighting back process (Quigley 1995). In rape situations, the victims will definitely be facing more floor fighting. When the defender is down on the floor, the attacker is more likely to either knock the defender out or hold and choke the defender. However, falling on the ground does not mean the battle is over, because the defender still can fight from there. Therefore, defenders have to learn how to fight back on the ground. Floor fighting provides defenders with three kinds of skills: 1) floor distance fighting which is used when the attacker is not grabbing the defender, 2) floor kneeling fighting which combines boxing skills and throwing skills, and 3) floor releasing which is used when the defender is held, grabbed, or choked on the ground.

Floor fighting has several features. The defender is usually at a great disadvantage on the floor and the situation is in very dangerous. There is no chance for thinking or backing-away, and the chance of getting out safely is reduced. The defender has to use defensive movements most of the time.

Floor Kneeling Fighting

Floor kneeling fighting is used when the attacker is dragging the defender in kneeling positions. The defender can hold on the attacker to keep balance and avoid punches, then catch chances to punch the attacker (figure 15.1).

15.1. Floor kneeling fighting

15.1a. Hold on to keep balance.

15.1b. Punch attacker's face.

Floor Distance Fighting

Floor distance fighting is used when the defender is on the ground and the attacker tries to grab or choke. Several skills are designed to counter potential grabs, chokes, or holds by using pushing, moving, kicking, and punching skills. The defender also can use many other skills in distance and close fighting patterns. The floor distance fighting usually includes the following several steps (figure 15.2).

15.2. Floor distance fighting

15.2a. Fall properly.

15.2b. Push or kick to prevent a grab or hold when the defender is on the floor.

15.2c. Roll away from the attacker.

15.2d. Set up a floor fighting stance and move to keep a safe distance from the attacker, two arms are on the floor as legs and point a foot toward the attacker for a side kick.

15.2e. Kick or punch to force the attacker to back up.

15.2f. Catch the chance to roll out and get up when the attacker is stepping back.

Floor Releasing

Floor releasing skills are used to fight back while the defender is on the ground being choked, held, or grabbed. The defender usually is in a very difficult situation, and the chance to get out safely is reduced. Therefore the defender has to fight to the limit using any regular skills such as punches or kicks, or nasty skills such as digging eyes, biting, tearing ears, scratching the face, or twisting the groin. Floor releasing skills are categorized into several situations to make them easy to remember. By the way, learning these skills can be very easy and fast, but the key in floor releasing is not how to perform just a single skill. Instead, it is much more important for the defender to be able to recognize how they are being attacked in order to react quickly and correctly. Therefore, lots of practice on combinations of different choking and holding situations is essential to success.

1. Side Choke Release: Press-scratch face-lock elbow. The purpose of this skill is to protect the defender's neck, scratch attacker's face for a release or to distract him, and then press his elbow to force the attacker to release the choke (figure 15.3).

15.3. Floor side-choke: press-scratch-lock

15.3a. Defender is side choked.

15.3b. Press attacker's arm down tight.

15.3c. Scratch attacker face.

15.3d. Right hand holds attacker right wrist, left hand presses attacker right elbow hard.

15.3e. Push or strike the elbow hard to force a release.

2a. Top Choke Release: press and turn. This skill is designed to lock the attacker arms down and use body motion to throw him sideways (figure 15.4). It is used when attacker's arms are bent.

15.4. Floor top-choke: Press-turn

15.4a. Floor top-choke.

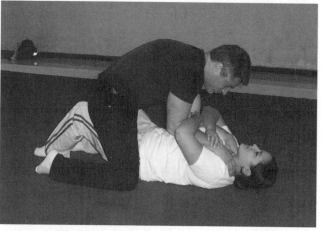

15.4b. Press the attacker's arms close to the defender's chest.

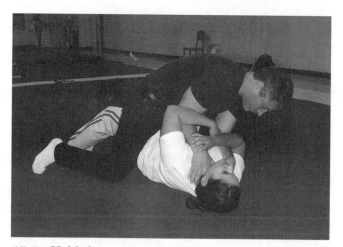

15.4c. Hold that position, and twist your body sideways to throw the attacker off.

2b. Top Choke Release: drag and push. This skill is used when the attacker's arms are straight and firm. The defender then can push attacker's arm overhead and then push him off sideways (figure 15.5).

15.5. Floor top-choke: Drag-push

15.5a. Both hands push the attacker's arms overhead with a knee bumping attacker's hip.

15.5b. Push the attacker sideways.

3. Top Arm-hold Release: slide-push. The top arm-hold situation puts the defender at a great disadvantage. The defender's arms and legs are both held down and the defender's choices are very limited. The attacker may use head butt or punches anytime. The following slide-push combination is used to deal with the top arm-hold (figure 15.6). This skill was developed based on the observations of weight training activities (lateral-pull down). The sliding motion gives the defender the maximum strength in release.

15.6. Floor top-arm-hold: Slide-push

15.6a. Defender's arms are pinned down.

15.6b. Slide the left arm down.

15.6c. Push attacker sideways with the left arm and body power.

4. Top Punching Release: block-grab-lock elbow. The floor top punching is a violent form of top attacks. The attacker may use any holds, chokes, punches, or strikes. The chance of survival is reduced dramatically. The defender may have to take some punches or strikes when fighting back in this situation. The major skill introduced to counter the top beating is the block-grab-lock elbow combination demonstrated in figure 15.7.

15.7 Floor Top-punching: Block-grab-lock elbow

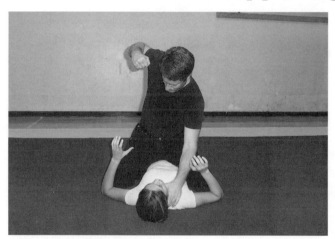

15.7a. Attacker is punching.

15.7b. Block the punch and grab the hand.

15.7c. Right hand grabs the wrist, left hand presses the elbow.

15.7d. Force him to fall to side.

5. Top Stabbing Release: Grab-lock elbow: The top stabbing is probably the worst floor fighting situation. The attacker has all the advantage being on the top with a knife and the defender has a very limited chance. The main skill introduced to counter the top beating is the grab-lock elbow combination demonstrated in figure 15.8. However, it is not guaranteed that it will work for everyone every time due to the difficulty of performing this situation.

15.8. Floor Top-stabbing: Grab-lock elbow

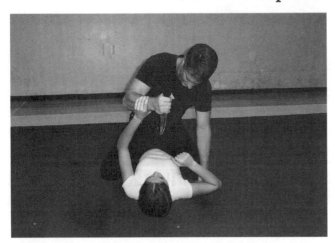

15.8a. Block and grab the knife-arm.

15.8b. Both hands grab the attacker's knife-arm

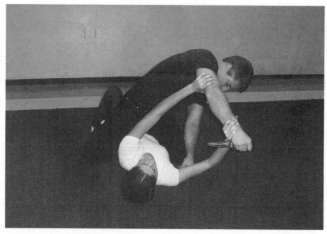

15.8c. Lock the attacker's elbow to push the attacker away.

6. Top back-choke Release: pull-tuck-flip. The top back-choke is a difficult situation for the defender, since the defender loses the leverage to fight back, and the neck is choked and can be broken easily. The attacker has all the advantage being on the top, and the defender has a very limited chance. The main skill introduced to counter this situation is the pull-tuck-flip combination demonstrated in figure 15.9. However, it is not guaranteed that it will work for everyone every time due to the difficulty of performing this situation.

15.9. Floor Top back-choke: pull-tuck-flip

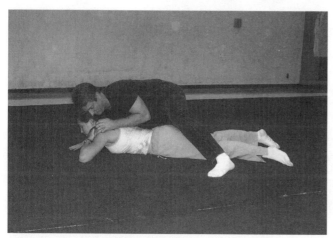

15.9a. Hold attacker arm to protect the neck, and then tuck chin in and bite.

15.9b. Pull attacker arm tight, left leg pushes up.

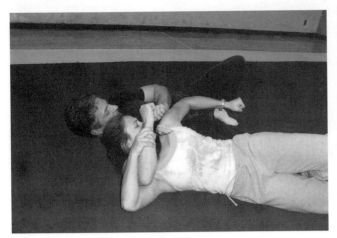

15.9c. Rotate body to right to flip attacker out.

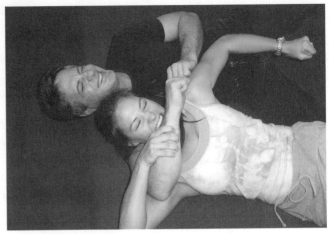

15.9d. Bite or hit the private.

Fighting Strategies

The basic floor fighting strategies can be classified into several aspects. 1) The most important one is to avoid ending up in the floor fighting situation. 2) The defenders should fight aggressively, even when the defender sometimes has to take some punches or scratches. 3) The defender should fight to the limit and use any nasty skills, such as grabbing the groin, biting, digging eyes, etc.

Improve Floor Fighting Skills

To be able to apply these basic throwing skills for real fighting-back, students should practice these skills to improve speed, power, accuracy, timing, anticipation, judgment, variations, and applications of these skills in imitative situations.

The most important drill for floor releasing is to have a partner or several partners to attack with all different floor attacks so that the defender can react to the changing situations and apply proper techniques. Actual fighting-back involves more fighting patterns than just floor fighting. Floor fighting is always connected with other skills such as punches, kicks, strikes, throws, or releases due to the unpredictable patterns in life-threatening situations. To prepare for the actual fighting which usually uses all possible skills, defenders need to develop the ability to combine these fighting patterns together.

There are many more skills in floor fighting included in some martial arts which can help students to improve their floor fighting ability. The martial arts which use floor fighting skills include Jujitsu, Aikido, Judo, Kung Fu, Military Training, and Wrestling. Other martial arts may also have some floor fighting skills, but it is not a major part of their disciplines.

REFERENCES

Chen, Z. K. *Practical Kicks in Wu Shu.* China: Tour & Education Publisher, 1989.

Du, Z. G. *Controlling Skills for Police Training.* China: Beijing Physical Education University Publisher, 1993.

Kirby, G. *Jujitsu—Basic Techniques of the Gentle Art.* Burbank: Ohara Publication, 1993.

Nishioka, H., & West, J. R. *The Judo Textbook.* Burbank: Ohara Publication, 1988.

Pu, S. W. *Capturing Skills for Police Officers*. China: Beijing Physical Education University Publisher, 1991.

Quigley, P. *Not an Easy Target*. New York: A Fireside Book. 1995.

Sun, B. Y. 91 *Skills for Self-Defense*. China: Beijing Physical Education University Publisher, 1994.

Wu, Z. N. *Chinese Qin Na*. China: Zhejiang Publisher, 1985.

Chapter 16
Joint Locks

This chapter focuses on skills and applications of joint control. Included are basic offensive and defensive skills in joint control, applications of skills, and basic strategies.

Introduction

Joint control is a fighting back pattern which applies pressure on weak parts of the attacker's body (usually the joints, including fingers, wrist, elbow, shoulder, neck, and ankle) in order to release from holds and chokes or to put the attacker under control. It causes pain and fear of sustaining a broken joint, and it makes the attacker stop the attack. No matter how strong an attacker is, these joints are relatively weak and easily become the targets for defenders. These skills are best used in easier situations such as sexual harassment. In life-threatening situations, however, it is a little hard to use since joint control uses many advanced skills. It requires some strength, good skill, and perfect timing. Furthermore, these skills work effectively only when the attacker is off guard. It does not work when the attacker tightens up muscles and resists and these skills are not quick solutions like knee strikes or kicks. Using these kinds of skills also has more risk if it fails because the defender is close to the attacker. This chapter will introduce three basic joint lock skills: elbow lock, wrist lock, and finger lock.

Elbow Lock and Counter

1. Elbow lock: A common elbow control skill is introduced as following. The defender can lock the attacker's elbow with her hands if the attacker is not very strong (figure 16.1), or lock the elbow under the armpit to increase the force if the attacker is resisting (figure 16.2). The defender should keep one hand on the elbow all times during the action so that the attacker will not get away. There will be some applications of this skill in later chapters.

16.1. Locking elbow with hands

16.1a. Step in and grab the attacker's elbow.

16.1b. Right hand grab attacker wrist and left hand lock the elbow.

16.1c. Press the elbow down and keep the wrist high for more pressure.

16.1d. Force the attacker to the ground and use left knee to press down attacker shoulder.

16.2. Use armpit to lock elbow

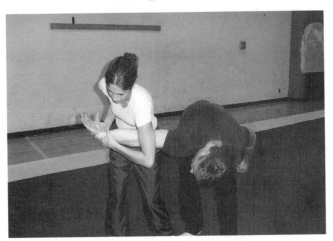

16.2. Press attacker's elbow under your armpit and keep his hand up for more force or control.

2. Counter elbow-lock: The defender can use any skills such as kicks, punches, or strikes to get out when the attacker is trying an elbow lock if the defender can recognize the attacker's intention early, or they can just tighten up muscles and withdraw the arm. Otherwise, the defender may have to use a forward roll to get out at a later stage of the attack (figure 16.3).

16.3. Countering the elbow-control: Roll out

16.3a. Attacker is locking the defender's elbow.

16.3b. Lean forward and roll out.

Wrist Lock and Counter

1. Wrist lock: There are several ways to control a wrist and a commonly used skill is introduced here (figure 16.4). It is also called as wrist wrap

16.4. Lock wrist

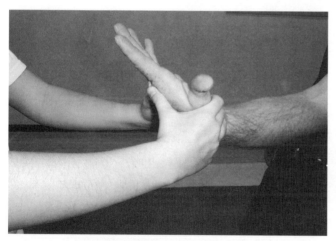

16.4a. Hold the attacker's palm like a hamburger, and fold the wrist toward the forearm.

16.4b. Keep the folded position and twist the wrist outward.

16.4c. Right step back to drag the attacker down at the same time.

2. Counter wrist lock: Defender can tighten up muscles and withdraw her arm if she can identify attacker intention early (figure 16.5). She can use the locking-elbow skill at late stage (figure 16.6).

16.5. Counter wrist lock: Withdraw

16.5. Defender grabs her own hand under attack, tighten up muscles and withdraw the hand.

16.6 Counter wrist control: lock elbow

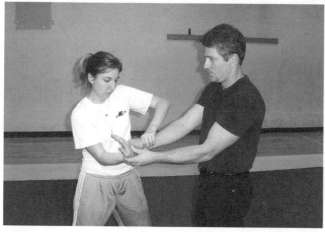

16.6a. Use left hand to grab attacker's right arm and left step in.

16.6b. Lock attacker's right elbow under armpit.

Finger Lock

1. Finger lock: The following is a demonstration of finger lock skills (figure 16.7). The defender grabs attacker's small and index finger and bends them backward toward his forearm. To prevent the attacker from releasing the lock, the defender also needs to hold attacker's arm in position.

16.7. Finger lock

16.7a. Grab attacker's small and ring fingers.

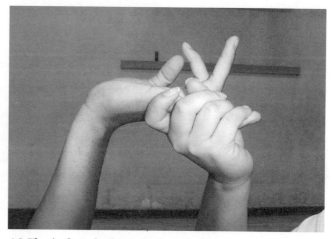

16.7b. A close look at the bending motion.

16.7c. Use elbow to push attacker elbow up, and pull his fingers backward.

16.7d. Keep pulling on fingers and use left hand to hold attacker arm.

2. Counter finger lock: The easy way to counter finger lock is to tighten up muscles and withdraw the hand with the help of the other hand (figure 16.8). Of course, the defender can use any close or distance fighting skills such as knee strike and elbow strike.

16.8. Counter finger lock: Withdraw

16.8. Defender grabs her right hand and withdraws.

Strategies

The joint control and pressure point lock skills are difficult skills, and sometimes they are not effective to force the attacker to release if the attacker tightens up muscles. Furthermore, using these kinds of skills places the victims closer to the attacker and may create more risk. It is not highly recommended for defenders to use these techniques in life-threatening situations. It is better to use these methods in dealing with harassment or acquaintance rapes. When using these kinds of skills, the defender should try to take the opponent off guard and catch the chance to attack fast, or combine back-away skills and other fighting-back skills together to make them more successful. For example, the defender can slam attacker's face and then attack the fingers while attacker tries to avoid the slam.

Improve Joint Control Skills

Like the other fighting patterns, students should continuously improve their joint control skills to a level that they can use them effectively for self-defense. The first step is always to work on quickness, strength, accuracy, timing, anticipation, judgment, variations, follow-ups, and applications of these skills in imitative situations.

Students also should combine joint lock skills with other fighting patterns together to prepare for many unpredictable changes when fighting back in life-threatening situations. Joint lock skills may have to rely on other skills to set up, and the applications may not work on certain attackers. Therefore, students have to learn how to change from joint lock to other patterns or from other patterns to joint locks in order to be prepared for different situations.

Although many martial arts teach some joint lock skills, several martial arts use joint locks as their major combative pattern. These martial arts usually have more systematic and in-depth skills and training. These martial arts include Jujitsu, Aikido, Qin Na, Hapkido, Police Training, and Military Training.

REFERENCES

Du, Z. G. *Controlling Skills for Police Training*. China: Beijing Physical Education University Publisher, 1993.

Kirby, G. *Jujitsu—Basic Techniques of the Gentle Art*. Burbank: Ohara Publication, 1993.

Pu, S. W. *Capturing Skills for Police Officers*. China: Beijing Physical Education University Publisher, 1991.

Spear, R. K. *Hapkido—The Integrated Fighting Art*. Burbank: Unique Publications, 1988.

Sun, B. Y. *91 Skills for Self-Defense*. China: Beijing Physical Education University Publisher, 1994.

Chapter 17
Releasing Skills

This chapter focuses on releasing skills and applications in four types of situations in which the defenders may be attacked: arm-hold, hair-pull, bear-hug, and choke. The releasing skills used include, but are not limited to, those introduced in previous chapters. These skills are demonstrated in the attached VCD in motion.

Introduction

Holds, chokes, and hugs are common ways defenders are attacked before they can recognize the situation and keep a safe distance. Defenders usually have no chance for thinking or decision-making, and they have to use defensive movements most of the time. These kinds of attacks often put defenders at a great disadvantage, since attackers are usually stronger and control the weak parts of the defender's body. Releasing skills provide ways to allow defenders to fight back during these situations although the chance to get out safely is very limited. But no matter what chance they have, defenders need to fight back instead of giving up. These releasing skills are categorized into several types based on the ways the defender might be attacked. The situations include arm-holds, bear-hugs, hair-pulls, chokes, and joint locks. The skills used include many fighting skills described in previous chapters. The releasing skills are presented according to the situations in which victims are attacked.

The applications of releasing skills include three kinds of movements. First, grab the attacker's arms to protect the weak body parts if the hold or choke is life-threatening. Secondly, use strikes, punches, and kicks to strike back since it is quicker and more effective in solving the problem. Third, use other skills such as twisting, withdrawing, controlling joints to release, but defenders may have to use the second kind of skills more often in order to get the attacker's attention and to release effectively.

Release from Arm-Holds

1. High arm-hold: When the attacker holds the defender's arm(s) in a high position, the defender can use a simple twist to get out (figure 17.1). The defender also can punch, kick, or knee strike the attacker to force a release or to create other opportunities.

17.1. High arm-hold: Twist release

17.1a. Grab the attacked arm and step in.

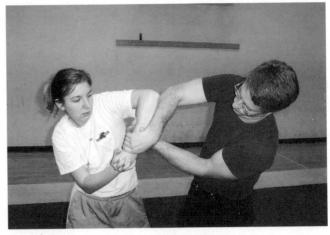

17.1b. Turn the body to right and twist the attacker's arms to force a release.

17.1c. Keep twisting and press down attacker's wrist at same time.

17.1d. Rotate fast to release.

2. Low Arm-hold: When the attacker holds the defender's arm(s) in a low position, the defender can use a similar twist motion as dealing with the high-hold to release (figure 17.2). The defender also can use any punches, kicks, strikes, or throws learned earlier, depending on the situation. The defender will need to decide how much force to use in each case. She may need to kick the attacker's groin in life-threatening situations, but probably just need a gentle release in attempted date rape.

17.2. Low arm-hold: Twist release

17.2a. Punch or scratch the face to distract him.

17.2b. Grab the attacked hand and step in.

17.2c. Bring the left hand up, and twist body to right.

17.2d. Rotate fast to release.

3. Back arm-hold: When the attacker twists the defender's arm backward, the defender can use a strike-trip (figure 17.3) when the defender can maintain their balance, or use a front roll to roll-out when the attacker is twisting the arm up to force the defender to bend forward and the defender loses leverage to fight back.

17.3. Back-arm-hold: Strike-trip

17.3a. Strike attacker's head with the free elbow, and then move the leg (free-arm side) behind attacker's legs.

17.3b. Push attacker's face backward, or strike the groin if the attacker refuses to release.

4. Back wrist-hold: When the attacker locks defender's wrists behind her back, the defender can releases with a back-kick and follow up with turn-strike (figure 17.4). Other skills also can be used.

17.4. Back wrist-hold: Back-kick and strike release

17.4a. Lean forward and back kick at the attacker's groin.

17.4b. Turn to left and left foot lands open.

17.4c. Knee strike to groin or head butt the attacker nose.

Release from Hair-Pulls

Hair-pulling is also a bad situation for defenders. The attacker easily controls the defender's head when he grabs the defender's hair. The basic skills to counter hair-pulling include: 1) grabbing the attacker's arms to take the control of the head and block further potential chokes or strikes, 2) using hard strikes, kicks, and punches to force the attacker to release, and 3) using throws and control skills.

1. Front hair-pull: Front hair-pull can be released by a series of motions. The skill introduced is a three-motion release (figure 17.5).

17.5. Front hair-pull: Hold-kick-lock elbow release

17.5a. Grab attacker's arms to protect the head and avoid punches.

17.5b. Strike the groin at the same time.

17.5c. Lock or break elbow.

2. Back hair-pull: Before the attacker drags defender down or adds a choke, the defender can try to injure attacker elbow or attack the private, depending on which side she turns. She will hit the elbow when she turns one way, and use knee strike if she turns the other way when she can not get the elbow (figure 17.6).

17.6. Back hair-pull: Hold-hit the elbow-or knee strike

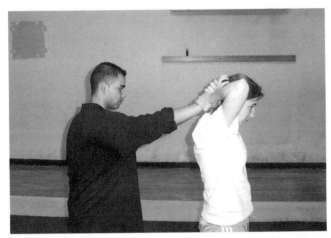

17.6a. Grab the attacker's arms to protect her neck and prevent choking.

17.6b. Rotate to right to hit attacker's elbow hard with tightened arm.

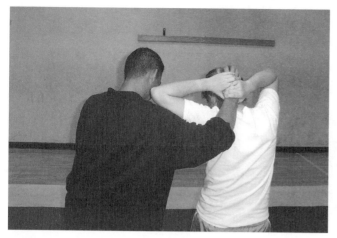

17.6c. If turned the other way and you don't get the elbow, get left foot settled down.

17.6d. Knee strike the groin.

3. Back hair-pull down: This combination is used when the attacker pulls the defender backward and downward, and the defender is not in a good balance to fight back. The defender can follow the attacker's pull to fall and at the same time kick the face unexpectedly, and then get into floor distance fighting (figure 17.7).

17.7. Back hair-pull down : Fall-kick-floor fighting release

17.7a. Attacker is pulling defender down.

17.7b. Defender falls backward and kicks the attacker's head.

17.7c. Defender rolls out for floor distance fighting.

Release from Chokes

Choking is a bad situation for the defender since the attacker is controlling a weak and vital part of the defender's body, and the defender can be in immediate danger if the attacker chokes too hard to cause fainting or a broken neck. However, the attackers will create some openings when they choke the defender due to the fact that their hands are occupied. The defender should take this chance and use any skills to force a release. Two movements are usually used in releasing from chokes. The first movement is to grab the attacker's arm(s) in order to protect the neck and allow breathing. Secondly, the defender can use hard punches, kicks, strikes, throws, or joint locks to force the attacker to release.

1. Front choke: The defender can use a combination skill to deal with this choke (figure 17.8). She may only need one motion and should know how to continue if the first one does not work.

17.8. Strike and lock-elbow release

17.8a. Press attacker's arms down.

17.8b. Strike the private.

17.8c. Left hand grabs attacker's right wrist, right arm or shoulder hits the elbow hard.

2. Back choke release: Back choke is hard to counter, especially when the defender loses her balances. This attack can be released using the following combinations (figure 17.9):

17.9. Back-choke: Pull-tuck-bite-strike-trip

17.9a. Pull the attacker's arm down and tuck chin to protect the neck.

17.9b. Bite attacker's arm.

17.9c. Strike the groin.

17.9d. Left step behind the attacker's leg.

17.9e. Push him backward.

3. Head Lock Release: This attack can be released using a combination skill (figure 17.10). Attack the private first if the attacker is a man, and attack eyes first if the attacker is a woman.

17.10. Head lock release: Grab-dig-trip

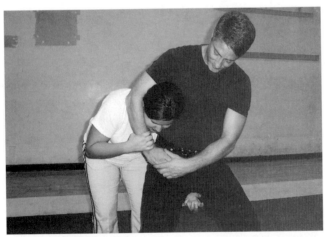

17.10a. Pull attacker's arm down and grab the attacker's groin.

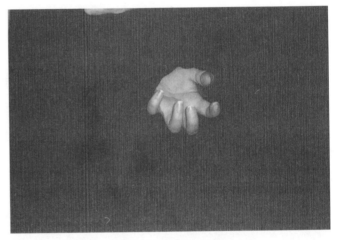

17.10b. A close look at hand motion.

17.10c. Dig eyes when attacker tries to bring legs together.

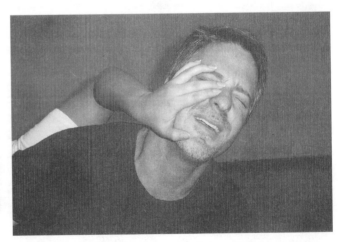

17.10d. A close look at hand motion.

Release from Bear-Hugs

Bear-hugs are a common tactic attackers use against a victim, and it gives the attacker an advantage in the fight. Mostly the attackers try to drag the defenders onto the ground or into some place. To release from the bear hugs, defenders need to keep their balance first, and then create chances to use other skills to release. Bear-hugs include front hug or back hug with arms free or arms locked. The basic skills used to release from bear-hugs include many skills learned earlier as well as scratching or biting. When attacked by bear-hugs, the defender should hold onto the attacker and lower the center of gravity to keep the balance, and then look for an opportunity to attack attacker eyes, head, or groin.

1. Back bear-hug with free arms: Many skills can be used to release from this situation and the defenders have more choices when their arms are free. The following is a strike-trip release (figure 17.11). The defender strikes the head to force a release, and follows up with a trip when the attacker blocks the strike or the strike fails.

17.11. Back bear-hug with free arms: Strike-trip

17.11a. Grab attacker's arms to keep balance.

17.11b. Elbow strike(s) at the attacker's head.

17.11c. Move left leg to block the attacker's leg.

17.11d. Push him backward.

2. Back bear-hug with locked arms: Defender has less freedom for using skills when arms are locked up. The releasing skill (figure 17.12) introduced here has been tried and found to be effective as demonstrated, and by the way, Bruce Lee also demonstrated the same skill in his self-defense book published in 1970s. There are other skills such as kicking back at the legs or stepping on the toes. They are not very practical since the kick can not be powerful, and it is very hard to use a small weapon (your heel) to step on the small target (the attacker's toes) during real fighting (by the way, toes and legs are not especially vulnerable targets).

17.12. Back bear-hug with locked arms: Strike-trip

17.12a. Grab the attacker's arms and keep a low position.

17.12b. Strike groin with a firm palm or grab.

17.12c. Move left leg behind the attacker's legs.

17.12d. Push the attacker backward.

3. Front bear-hug with free arms: Defenders have great risk to be attacked by a front bear-hug, especially in rape cases. The situation can be very bad when the defender's arms are locked up and the body is forced to bend backward. But it may give the defender a chance to do a knee strike or head butt or bite. Skills for countering the front bear-hug include digging eyes, striking the private, and tripping.

When the defender hands are free, they should dig into the attacker's eyes, and at the same time push the attacker's head backward and strike with a knee to force a release (figure 17.13).

17.13. Front bear-hug: Dig-push release

17.13a. Use both thumbs to dig into the attacker's eyes and push in.

17.13b. Add a knee strike at the same time.

4. Front bear-hug with locked arms: When defender's arms are locked up, she can hold onto the attacker and then use a knee strike followed by a trip (figure 17.14).

17.14. Front bear-hug with locked arms: Strike-trip release

17.14a. Hold on and strike the groin.

17.14b. Place right leg behind the attacker.

17.14c. Push hard to throw.

Strategies

Usually when the defenders are in the above situations, they are at disadvantage and they have to react to the attacks. The strategies they can use are very limited too. The defenders should identify if the situation is life-threatening or harassment and use skills accordingly. The defenders most often will have to use any nasty technique available and fight back aggressively and continuously. Many combination skills may have to be used to force a release.

Improve Releasing Skills

To be able to effectively apply these basic releasing skills in real life-threatening situations, students must develop the speed of the performance, the timing, and applications of these skills dealing with different attackers in imitative situations.

There are several essential factors to improve releasing skills. Students need to develop the ability to recognize the attacks and respond with proper skills. Learning these skills is very easy, but to be able to recognize the situations and use proper skills to get out takes a lot of practice. The best way to develop this ability is to have your partner attack in different ways and react to these attacks by using the skills you have learned. Students also need to develop the ability to use any skills learned to deal with various holds, chokes, and grabs. Another ability students need to develop is to switch from using releasing skills to using other fighting-back patterns to fit the changing fighting situations. The four-on-one practice is where each attacker is responsible for one type of attack (such as hair-pull or choke) and all four attackers attack randomly and continuously to develop defender judgment and reaction ability.

Students can further learn more releasing skills for other situations. These skills can be developed through taking martial arts or special training. The martial arts which can help students improve their releasing skills include Jujitsu, Aikido, Qin Na, Police Training, and Military Training. Other martial arts will also introduce some releasing skills even if that is not their major focus.

REFERENCES

Chen, Z. K. *Practical kicks in Wu Shu*. China: Tour & Education Publisher, 1989.

Dong, Z. H. *Thai Boxing*. China: Beijing Physical Education University Publisher, 1994.

Du, Z. G. *Controlling Skills for Police Training*. China: Beijing Physical Education University Publisher, 1993.

Kirby, G. *Jujitsu—Basic techniques of the Gentle Art*. Burbank: Ohara Publication, 1993.

Pu, S. W. *Capturing Skills for Police Officers*. China: Beijing Physical Education University Publisher, 1991.

Spear, R. K. *Hapkido—The Integrated Fighting Art*. Burbank: Unique Publications, 1988.

Sun, B. Y. *91 Skills for Self-Defense*. China: Beijing Physical Education University Publisher, 1994.

Wu, Z. N. *Chinese Qin Na*. China: Zhejiang Publisher, 1985.

Zhang, W. FG. *San Shou*. China: Canton Science and Technology Publisher, 1983.

Chapter 18
Special Fighting

This chapter focuses on dealing with special situations in self-defense, including self-defense at gunpoint, self-defense at knife-point, and self-defense against multiple attackers. This chapter will provide basic information on the chances of survival, decision-making fighting-back skills and strategies, and applications in real life. Most skills are also demonstrated in the attached CD in motion.

Introduction

Knives and guns are widely used by criminals in violent crimes in the United States. Based on the 2001 Uniform Crime Report, guns were used in 65 percent of murder cases, 40 percent of robbery cases, 26 percent forcible rapes, and 18 percent of the aggravated assault cases, while knives were used in 13 percent in murder cases, 8 percent of robbery cases, 40 percent of forcible rapes, and 18 percent of aggravated assault cases. More than half a million Americans have already become victims of these three crimes at gun-point or knife-point. Guns and knives were also used in other crimes, such as burglary, rape, and carjacking (77 percent of attackers used weapons). About 95 percent of the attackers in school settings used knives or other weapons against victims in aggravated assaults (Bureau 1995). In more than 50 percent of Car jacking cases, victims were facing two or more attackers. Guns, knives, and multiple attackers put defenders at a greater disadvantage.

Since a large percentage of the violent crimes involved guns, knives, and multiple attackers, teaching students self-defense to deal with these situations should be a major and critical part of the self-defense curriculum, and quality instruction of self-defense has significant implications to the lives of millions of university students at campuses and in their workplaces. However, although different fighting-back skills have been taught in different classes in nationwide self-defense courses (Chen 1998) and in self-defense textbooks as well as in martial arts books, and police training books, there are only two studies conducted on chances of injuries using these skills or on the effectiveness of these skills (Chen 1999, Chen 2000). Teaching self-defense at gun-point concerns the lives of millions of people annually, and more research on this topic is absolutely critical and urgent.

When facing guns, knives, and multiple attackers, the defender is at a big disadvantage and the chance to get out safely is very limited in these situations. Staying away from these situations is the best strategy, and running away from the scene probably is second best. Special training provides students with knowledge and skills to make correct decisions and to fight back in these situations. The basic ways recommended by experts to deal with these dangerous situations include: 1) cooperate, 2) run away, and 3) fight back. The skills used include all of the fighting skills introduced in the previous chapters.

Remember that the defender is at a tremendous disadvantage and has a great risk of injury or death when they face guns, knifes, and multiple attackers. No self-defense skill or strategy is guaranteed, and the chance of survival is very unpredictable. Making right decisions at the scene is the key to survival, but it is very difficult to make the right decision. Fighting back in these situations requires perfect judgment, skill, and timing. The best strategy for these situations still is "DO NOT PUT YOURSELF IN THERE!".

Chapter 18

Self-Defense at Gunpoint

The number of cases of serious crimes which involve the use of guns by criminals stay the same every year. The threatening power of guns make most people feel very vulnerable and scared when facing gun-point, and even police officers and martial arts experts are not exceptions, although these people usually have more preparation and skills in dealing with guns. Self-defense at gun-point is probably the most difficult situation for any individual, due to the unknown motivation, behavior, and decision-making of the attacker. The defender does not know if the attacker will shoot or just try to threaten the defender to make the crime easier. The defender hardly knows how accurately the attacker can shoot, if the gun is real or fake, or if the gun is loaded. That is why no skill or strategy is guaranteed to work, and the chance of survival is very unpredictable.

The basic self-defense at gunpoint includes three types of strategies and skills. 1) Cooperate with the attacker in the hope that they will simply get what they want and leave the defender unharmed, or cooperate first and then look for a chance to run away or fight back. 2) Run away immediately to avoid being taken to an isolated area and shot. 3) Fight back to control the gun in order to run away or put the attacker under control when the defender has no other choices.

Cooperate

Cooperation with the attacker's demand is probably what most victims want to do and what most self-defense instructors teach in their classes. The chance of survival, however, is unpredictable due to the unknown intention of the attacker. There is no research on the percentage of victims who survived or got shot using the cooperation strategy. In some case studies, some victims got away safely after they cooperated with the attacker's demand, while other victims still got shot or killed even after they did everything the attacker said (Bitternbinder 1992). It is very individualized, situational, and unpredictable. Experts suggest several situations in which the defender may have to cooperate: 1) when the defender has no time, space, or leverage to run or fight, and cooperation becomes the only solution; 2) the attacker grabs tightly or sits on the top of the victim while pointing the gun at the defender, and the chance to run or fight is limited; 3) the attacker is very nervous and it looks like any attempted movement will make him pull the trigger, and any potential move will put the victim in immediate danger; and 4) when the attacker has shot other people who tried to move or fight. In these situations, any movement may make the attacker angry and drive them to shoot. Therefore, defenders should take no immediate action. Instead, they should wait for their best chance, hoping that the attacker will be off guard at some point. Other strategies such as talking, lying, or acting may work with some attackers but not with all of them. As discussed earlier, the cooperation should have a limit. When the attackers want to take the defenders to a different place or tie them up (both may have unpredictable consequences), the defenders need to make a decision if they will continue to cooperate or run away or fight. All strategies here involve taking chances.

Run Away

Running away is probably scarier than cooperating, since defenders tend to believe that the attacker will become angry and shoot them. It is true that some attackers may shoot, but others will not. Some experts suggest that defenders run away as soon as they find themselves at gun-point. There are several rationales for this suggestion. 1) Most attackers do not intend to shoot at all, and they just want to frighten the defender and make their crimes easier. 2) The attackers do not like to shoot and chase a defender who is running away because they are afraid that their chasing and shooting may be seen by witnesses. 3) Even when attackers shoot, the bullets may not hit the defender, or sometimes it will not hit severely when the defender may gee hit on the arm or leg. The only statistics on the chances of survival were given by detective J. J. Bittenbinder in his

204

lecture "Street Smart." Based on his statistics, the chance of being shot severely when the defender is running away at gunpoint is 2 percent. That means 98 percent of the time the defender will not be in serious trouble at all (Bittenbinder 1992).

Experts suggest several situations in which the defenders should run: 1) when the defender is in a public place with other people nearby; 2) when it is possible to head away from the attacker in various directions; 3) when there are obstacles nearby that will block the shot; 4) when the defender is able to run fast and is dressed properly for running; 5) when the attacker tries to take the defender to an isolated place; or 6) when the attacker is at a distance, such as 10 yards away.

Running away at gunpoint requires the use of several skills. The defender may run around the obstacles, run in a zig-zag pattern, throw obstacles to block the attacker, and fake fainting and roll out to run.

Fight Back

Fighting back at gunpoint is probably the most frightening action a defender may take, and it has advantages and disadvantages. Fighting may increase the possibility of getting shot because the attacker is forced to protect himself, while on the other hand, fighting back at gunpoint may give the defender more control of the situation instead of waiting for the attacker to make the decision.

The defender has the opportunity to get out of danger even though pulling the trigger is easier and faster than fighting. A study (Chen 1999) was conducted with 174 university students in which a water handgun was used and the defenders utilized a skill demonstrated later in this section. Defenders chances to get away safely when fighting back was about 42 percent, while the chance of being shot was about 58 percent when the attacker shot every time. In general, if the attacker shoots every time when the defender fights back, the chance to be hit severely (head, belly, and chest) is 41 percent. However, the chance to get out safely is very individualized. About 8 percent of subjects were shot every time and 3 percent got away every time in the same study. Therefore, it is very individualized and the chance depends on the defender's experience as well as the attacker's skills and intentions. Defenders should try the skills with many people to find out his or her chances of injuries in order to make right decision. If the defender is shot most time, the fighting option is probably not good for her/him or she/he needs to work more on his skills. This research was done in a lab situation in order to provide a basic idea about the chance of survival at gunpoint, and the chance of survival probably is different in real-life situations.

It is much easier to fight back when the attacker is very close to the defender. A distance less than one arm-length gives defenders a greater advantage to control the gun-arm fast. The defenders can push the gun away or move their body away to avoid the first shot if they act fast and effectively. The defender, however, needs to control the gun-arm immediately after avoiding the first shot. Otherwise the attacker can easily get the defender with a second shot. If the attacker is far away, the defender should run instead of fight. The worst situation is when the defender is at a distance that is too far to fight and too close to run, such as three or four yards away. Based on author same study at gunpoint, the chance of being shot at two yards away is 95 percent. The situations where the defender may choose to fight back include the following: 1) when the defender has to choose between fighting and death; 2) when the attacker is distracted or off guard momentarily; and 3) when the attacker is very close and the defender can feel the gun easily, such as when the gun is pointed at the back or chest.

There are many ways defenders can fight at gunpoint, even though the chances of survival have not been tested. The technique recommended in textbooks is using the joint control skills. People usually feel safe when they can control the attacker's arm which holds the gun. The common process to fight back at gunpoint involves several types of movements: 1) using a quick block to avoid the first shot while slip the body or head off the gun-point; 2) controlling the attacker's gun-arm immediately; and 3) disabling the attacker or taking the gun away. These movements may occur at the same time or one after another.

When fighting at gun-point, the defender should not show any intention to fight back so that the attacker will not be able to identify your reaction. When the defender is ready to fight, she/he needs to act fast.

1. Gun pointing at belly: When the gun is pointed at the belly, the defender can suddenly use one hand to hit the gun to side and turn the body sideways to avoid the first shot, and then immediately step in and control attacker gun-arm to avoid more shooting. The combination technique is demonstrated in figure 18.1.

18.1. Gun at belly: Hit-turn-grab-control elbow

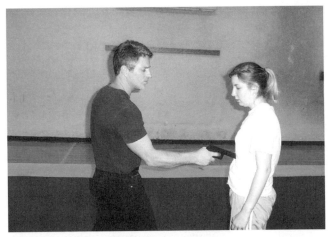

18.1a. Show no sign of fighting back.

18.1b. Hit the gun-arm to right and turn body to left.

18.1c. Step in to grab the gun-arm.

18.1d. Use body to break the gun-arm elbow.

2. Gun pointed at back: When the gun is pointed at the back, the defender can suddenly rotate body to right and right hand swings back at the gun-arm to get the body off gun-point. Then defender immediately rolls into the attacker and controls attacker gun-arm to avoid more shooting. The combination technique is demonstrated in figure 18.2.

18.2. Gun pointed at back: Turn-roll in-control gun-arm

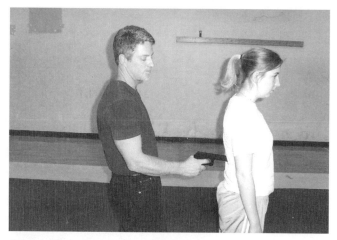

18.2a. No movement at gunpoint.

18.2b. Quickly turn to right and right arm swing clockwise.

18.2c. Roll into the attacker as close as possible and use arms and body to keep the gun-arm locked between the defender and attacker.

18.2d. Knee strike groin.

3. Gun pointed at head: When the gun is pointed at the back, the defender can suddenly duck and push the gun-arm up to get the body off gun-point. Then defender immediately steps in and controls attacker gun-arm to avoid more shooting. The combination technique is demonstrated in figure 18.3.

18.3. Gun pointed at head: Duck/push-step in-break gun-arm

18.3a. No movement at gunpoint.

18.3b. Quickly duck and push the gun-arm up.

18.3c. Step in and grab the gun-arm.

18.3d. Break the elbow.

There are several basic guidelines for fighting back at gunpoint. 1) Do not show any pre-movement which will indicate your intention of fighting. 2) Act suddenly without any hesitation to avoid the first shot. 3) Control the attacker gun-arm immediately so that the attacker can not pull back the gun and point at you again. 4) Disable the attacker with any available skills.

Self-Defense at Knifepoint

A knife is a very dangerous weapon which gives the attacker a great advantage, even when the defender has a martial arts background. The most difficult process when facing a knife is still what decision to make due to the unknown factors: the attacker's motivation, intention, and skill level. The defender does not know if the attacker will kill or just try to threaten the defender to make the crime easier. Therefore, the chance of survival is very unpredictable. The basic self-defense at knifepoint includes several types of strategies and skills similar to the self-defense at gunpoint. 1) Cooperate with the attacker in the hope that the attacker will get what they want and leave the defender unharmed, or cooperate at first and then look for a chance to run away or fight back. 2) Run away immediately and avoid being taken to an isolated area. 3) Fight back to avoid being stabbed or to put the attacker under control. The defender can fight barehanded or use other weapons such as a chair or stick.

Run Away

Most martial arts experts suggest that self-defenders or martial arts practitioners run away immediately when they face an attacker with a knife. Running away and leaving the danger behind probably is the best self-defense strategy at knifepoint due the unpredictable consequences. However, dealing with a knife depends upon the specific situation. The following situations usually provide a good chance to run away: 1) before the attacker is ready to attack, 2) when confronted by the attacker in public, 3) when the defender can run fast and is dressed for running, 4) before the attacker forces the defender to an isolated place, or 5) when the defender has no experience or ability to fight.

Running away can be done in many ways, and these skills have been explained in the back-away chapter. The defender also should be ready to fight if they can not outrun the attacker.

Back Up

Some attackers will stab their victims while others will not hurt the victims, depending on the attacker's motivation. The defenders may have an opportunity to use other back-away skills, such as negotiation, cooperation, or bluffing. Back-away skills do not agitate the attacker, therefore there is a possibility to avoid being stabbed or killed. However, an attacker who is dedicated to kill a witness will not let the victim go, even though the victim cooperates. The chance of survival is unpredictable, and the defender should be ready to fight or run anytime during the process. The necessary back-away skills have been presented in the early chapter.

Fight Back

Fighting-back may agitate the attacker and motivate them to use more violence, but it gives the defender a little more control of the situation than cooperation. Still, the chance of survival is unpredictable, and the defender needs the fighting option in case other strategies do not work. A lab research project (Chen 2000) indicated that when fighting back at knifepoint, there is a great possibility of injuries to the defender. In another word, fighting back against a knife is very dangerous. Every time the attacker is determined to stab the victim, the chance of injury to the defenders (males and females) is about 80 percent. The chance of injury is 84 percent with male attackers and 78 percent with female attackers, and this indicated that it is equally dangerous when attacked at a knifepoint by male or female attackers. If the subjects were attacked by male attackers, 57 percent of the time the subjects were cut severely, and 43 percent of the time the subjects were cut on arms or legs. If the subjects were attacked by female attackers, about 50 percent of the time the subjects were stabbed severely and about 50 percent of the time the subjects were stabbed on arms or legs. All defenders were cut more than three times out of ten trials and as high as about 40 percent of defenders were injured every time when they were attacked by male attackers. About 33 percent of subjects were injured every time when they were attacked and about 94 percent defenders were stabbed more than five times.

There are many situations in which defenders end up facing a knife, and the skills used in these various situations should be different. The most dangerous situation is when the attacker is holding the defender and pointing the knife at the neck or chest, either in a standing position or on the ground. The attacker can stab the victim any time while the defender is not in a good position to fight back or run. Temporary cooperation is highly recommended to avoid agitating the attacker, but the defender should be ready to control the knife when spotting an opening or when the attacker is off guard.

The second situation is when the attacker is close to the defender but not holding the defender, and the knife is pointed at the defender's back or chest. The defender has a relatively better chance to fight or run in this kind of situation. The two basic ways to fight back are to push the knife away and back into distance fighting, or to control the attacker's knife-arm.

The third situation is when the attacker is a couple of yards away from the defender. The defender is out of the reach of the knife and is temporarily safe. The basic ways to fight back against a knife in this kind of situation include distance fighting, joint control, and the use of another weapon.

1. Distance fighting: Distance fighting seems to be relatively safe, since there is a space between the attacker and defender. The defender is at immediate danger and can run away at any time. According to Chen's study, it actually is dangerous from the above statistics (80 percent chance of injury) when the attacker started the attack first. Even Bruce Lee felt that he would not fight back barehanded against a knife unless he had a weapon to use. The common skills when fighting a knife are movements and blocks together with kicks to the groin and knees. The defender should avoid using punches so that the upper body will be fully protected all times. There are several guidelines for using distance fighting against a knife include the follwing: 1) Keep your open palms in front to block or redirect the stabs. The defender may have to take some risk of being cut on their arms or legs in order to successfully protect the vital parts of their body. 2) Keep moving, stay away from the knife, and fight defensively. 3) Focus on breaking the attacker's knee. 4) Back up and run away whenever there is a chance. Figure 18.4 demonstrates a basic skill of dealing with a knife using distance fighting. The floor sweeping technique demonstrated in the chapter of distance fighting can also be used to deal with a knife.

18.4. Knife-point: Distance fighting

18.4a. Move to keep a safe distance with both palms in front.

18.4b. Hit the knife sideways and kick the knee when attacker comes close and stabs.

2. Joint lock: Joint lock is a good skill to use in dealing with a knife and the situation will certainly be easier if the defender can control the joint. However, it is very difficult to apply because it is very difficult to grab the knife-arm in real fighting-back situations when the attacker usually keeps swinging the knife and the defender has to avoid being stabbed. Joint control does not work effectively either whenever the attacker tightens up their muscles. Therefore, it is not recommended for most people, especially the beginners, unless there is a good chance or they have no other choices. The joint control skills are better used when the knife is pressed at defender's belly or back where the defender can reach the knife-arm. When the defender starts the defense action first when the knife is pointed at the belly, the chance of injury is about 52 percent (Chen 2000). The two common skills used to deal with a knife are elbow lock (figure 18.5) and wrist lock (figure 18.6) introduced in a previous chapter. Another technique similar to these two is also introduced in Figure 18.7.

18.5. Knife-point: Lock elbow

18.5. Right hand grab attacker's wrist and lift up, left arm press down the elbow.

18.6. Knife-point: Lock wrist

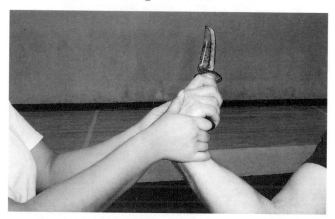

18.6. Grab the wrist when catching the chance, fold in and twist outward, step back and drag attacker down.

18.7. Knife-point: Grab and stab back

18.7a. No motion at knifepoint.

18.7b. Grab attacker's knife-arm and right foot steps in.

18.7c. Left step in and keep knife-arm up.

18.7d. Stab the attacker.

3. Use other weapons: A knife gives the attacker more threatening power and advantage in the fighting. To compensate for the disadvantage, a defender certainly can use some weapons to fight back. These weapons can be anything at hand. The common weapons that the defender can use include: 1) a sweat shirt (figures 18.8), 2) a chair (figure 18.9), 3) a trash can or similar objects, and 4) a stick (figure 18.10), or 5) a broom.

The chances of injuries when defenders use the above equipment were indicated by Chen's study. While the barehanded fighting has 80 percent chance of injury, using a sweat shirt has 65 percent chance, using a chair has a chance of 54 percent, and using a stick has a chance of 44 percent. The reason is that using the above stuff block attacker's way to stab and chairs and sticks also can cause injuries on the attackers and that make the attacker scared.

18.8. Knife-point: Use a sweat shirt

18.8a. Hold shirt tight in front.

18.8b. Block the knife sideways when attacker stabs.

18.9. Knife-point: Use a chair

18.9. Use the chair to keep the attacker away, do not let the attacker grab the chair, and kick back when attacker comes in.

18.10. Knife-point: Use a stick

18.10a. Point the stick toward the attacker at a safe distance and keep moving.

18.10b. Poke the attacker face or groin when he comes in, do not let the attacker grab the stick.

4. Deal with chop knife: A chop knife is a very dangerous weapon, and it is used often by criminals in China. Dealing with a chop knife is very scary, and it is much safer to keep a safe distance by using distance fighting. But if the defender has no room to back up, then she/he has to use joint lock skills (figure 18.11).

18.11. Dealing with chop knife: lock elbow

18.11a. Try to back up.

18.11b. Grab the knife-arm.

18.11c. Use a knee strike.

18.11d. Break elbow.

Self-Defense against Multiple Attackers

Self-defense against multiple-attackers puts the defender in an extremely dangerous situation. It is very difficult to react to the attacking movements of two or more attackers at the same time, even for a martial arts expert. Based on the observation in self-defense classes over years, when faced with multiple attacker's, the chance to get out safely is very limited and unpredictable when facing with multiple attackers. The basic self-defense against multiple-attackers includes several types of strategies and skills: 1) run away immediately to avoid being held or taken from the scene; 2) cooperate with the attackers in the hope that they will get what they want and leave the defender alone; 3) cooperate first and then look for a chance to run away or fight back; or 4) fight back, then run away.

Run Away

Some martial arts books demonstrate how a master handles a one-on-four situation in which the master deals with the attackers one by one while the other attackers are watching and waiting for their turn. This is for show only and definitely is not true in real life. The real situation will be that all attackers come to the defender at the same time, and it is almost impossible for a defender, sometimes including martial art experts, to handle them at the same time. Most martial arts experts suggest that self-defenders or martial arts practitioners should run away immediately when they face multiple attackers. This is probably the best self-defense strategy. The situations for the defender to run include: 1) whenever there is a chance, 2) when the attackers try to take the defender away to an isolated place, 3) when the defender has no experience or ability to fight, 4) when the defender can run fast and is dressed for running, and 5) before the attackers are ready to attack. The running away strategies and skills are introduced in the chapter on back-away skills.

Back Up

Sometimes attackers commit crimes in groups in order to make the defender scared and make it easier to get what they want instead of intending to kill the defender. This possibility leaves the opportunity for the defender to use other back-away skills, such as cooperating to calm down the attackers, negotiate, play dumb or use the skunk model. Back-away skills do not agitate attackers, therefore there is a possibility to avoid more or severe potential harm. However, the attackers who are dedicated to killing a witness will not let him/her go, even though the victim cooperates. The defender should be ready to fight or run during the entire process. The back-away strategies have been introduced in the chapter of back-away skills.

Fight Back

Fighting-back may agitate the attackers and increase their motive to use more violence, but the defender may have some control of the situation. The defender needs the fighting option in case other skills do not work. The basic fighting pattern in dealing with multiple attackers is distance fighting combined with other fighting patterns. The defender should try their best to keep a safe distance from the attackers and try to avoid being grabbed, thrown, or involved in floor fighting. The fighting strategies and skills include: 1) move constantly to keep at a safe distance, 2) move to keep one attacker in front and deal with one at a time, 3) combine other strategies such as yelling, deception, or bluffing together with fighting, and 4) use any weapons at hand. No statistics on the chance of fighting against multiple attackers is available, and more research on this topic is certainly valuable and urgent. The basic fighting skills against multiple attackers are demonstrated in Figure 18.12.

18.12. Dealing with multiple attackers: move and fight against one at a time

18.12a. Two attackers try to trap the defender.

18.12b. Move away and attack one first.

18.12c. Move to keep the attackers in a line of front and back.

18.12d. Keep eyes on both attackers and move.

18.12e. Keep moving and keep attackers in one line.

Household Objects as Weapons

Since attacks always come suddenly and leave defendants no preparation, defendants may have to use any possible things nearby to increase their ability to fight backs. Practically there is no limit on what can be used and everything may become a weapon. These weapons include, but are not limited to, fire extinguishers, kitchen knives, umbrellas, pens, sticks, bricks, and bottles, etc.

Improve Special Fighting Skills

To effectively handle these special life-threatening situations, students must develop the ability to apply skills very accurately with quickness and perfect timing. A lot of practice with different partners is probably the best way to improve these skills. Students also need courage to take the chance when they fight back in these situations. More advanced skills and hands-on experience certainly give students more power and alternatives in dealing with these situations. These advanced skills and hands-on experiences can be developed through martial arts or special training. The martial arts which can help students improve releasing skills include Jujitsu, Aikido, Qin Na, Police Training, and Military Training. Other martial arts also introduce some releasing skills even though this is not their major focus.

REFERENCES

Bittenbinder, J. J. *Street Smart*. Illinois: Video Publishing House, Inc. 1992.

Chen, G. (March, 1999). Fighting-Back at Knifepoint in Self-Defense: What Is the Chance of Survival. A research paper presented at 1999 CAHPERD Annual Conference, Monterey, CA., March 1999.

Chen, G. "Self-Defense at Knifepoint Using Different Techniques." A research paper presented at the 2000 CAHPERD Annual Conference, Long Beach, CA., March 2000.

Du, Z. G. *Controlling Skills for Police Training*. China: Beijing Physical Education University Publisher, 1993.

Lee, B., & Uyehara, M. *Bruce Lee's Fighting Methods: Self-Defense Techniques,* Santa Clara: Ohara Publiocations, 1976.

Liu, H. C. *Wudang Traditional Tai Chi*. China: Shanxi Science and Technology Publisher, 1991.

Pu, S. W. *Capturing Skills for Police Officers*. China: Beijing Physical Education University Publisher, 1991.

Wu, Z. N. *Chinese Qin Na*. China: Zhejiang Publisher, 1985.

PART FIVE

Lifetime Learning and Applications in Self-Defense

➤ Lifetime Learning and Applications

➤ Martial Arts and Self-Defense

Chapter 19
Lifetime Learning and Applications

After you have learned self-defense, there are two important steps you need to take to follow up. The first step is to apply what you have learned from the class into your life so that these skills, strategies, and principles will actually work for you. What you have learned will be worthless unless you use it. The second step is to continuously sharpen your physical skills, work on your body conditioning, and improve mental skills and strategies to prevent crime and prepare for the potential attacks during your lifetime. Meanwhile it is very important that you monitor the new trends of crime and develop new self-defense strategies and skills.

Applications in Everyday Life

Put Prevention Strategies and Skills into Action

Prevention strategies and skills have been introduced in the previous chapters. Students should use these skills in their everyday life to reduce the chance of becoming a victim of crime. The end of a self-defense does not mean the end of self-defense; instead it indicates the beginning of self-defense for your life in the next 60 years. Self-defense is a lifetime activity, not a single or momentary experience. An effective way to carry out the prevention is to make a checklist on the prevention strategies and techniques/skills which you feel proper for you and plan a schedule to put into practice. For example, you will install a security alarm for your house and hook up with the law enforcement system next week, or join your neighborhood watch program this month. Another way is to write a short list of self-defense tips for each location on a flashcard and post out to remind yourself. For example, you can post a home safety card by the door, a driving safety card on the steering wheel or dashboard, and workplace safety on your office computer. Having good communication and reminding each other of safety with family members, friends, and roommates is also a good idea to implant the awareness of self-defense into your lifestyle. It is also suggested that students creatively adjust these strategies to fit into their personal situation.

Watch Trends of Crimes

The trends and patterns of crimes change over time, and so do criminals and their attacking patterns. It is very important that students remain on guard at all times and watch where the trends of crimes are going. Students should have a clear idea about the status of crime at the national and local levels such as: what is happening around your neighborhood (any gangs moving into this area?), what is happening at your workplace (any tensions or layoffs at work?), what is going on nationwide (school shooting or terrorism attacks?), or what is the crime situation in China where you are going to do business for your company. Students can get the information from the newspaper, television, radio, talking to people, or at meetings. The prompt information will help people be prepared to take actions dealing with the new trends of crimes.

Family Involvement

An important way to apply what you have learned in self-defense is to get your family, your relatives, and friends involved in self-defense. This could be your best contribution to your family. You may be the first and only one who has learned formal self-defense in your family, and it is your responsibility to motivate your beloved family members to learn this important life-saving skill. You will feel guilty if your family member becomes the victim of violent crime because you never help them learn self-defense.

There are several ways you can get your family involved. 1) Share this information with your family to make them aware of the danger of becoming a victim of violent crimes and the importance of self-defense to them, and help them develop the basic concepts in crime prevention and self-defense. 2) Teach them prevention strategies and skills, help them develop a plan, and assist them to start immediately. Besides the common prevention strategies, you may teach them specific strategies based on their status. For example, your younger brother in high school may focus more on avoiding gangs and drugs as well as avoiding confrontations, while your young sister in high school may work on preventing date rape and party safety. 3) Teach them basic skills in back-away and fighting: meanwhile it is a good opportunity to review these skills for yourself by teaching your family members. 4) Encourage your family members to take self-defense classes and receive more systematic training on self-defense if you do not feel you are qualified to teach them. 5) Give them special gifts for birthdays and holidays. These gifts can be personal alarms, pepper spray, a self-defense book, or a video tape on self-defense and crime prevention.

Continue to Learn Self-Defense

Reading

Numerous books are produced each year which cover many aspects of self-defense and crime prevention. Each book usually focuses on one topic in depth and often provides important information and strategies. The existing books include workplace crime prevention, rape prevention, terrorism prevention, driving anger management, self-defense for women, children self-defense, self-defense for elderly, gang crimes and prevention, self-defense for disabled population, hate crime prevention, school violence prevention, traveling safety, international crimes, and of course different kinds of martial arts. Reading these books brings additional information to your existing knowledge and helps you become better prepared for the crimes. The reading can be very selective based on what you need. These books can be easily found in bookstores, local libraries, and university libraries. You can consult experts on which book is best for you if you are not sure which one is useful for you. Again, it is important that what they learn from the reading is applied into actions, otherwise the reading will be useless.

Physical Skill Training

After students learn the physical self-defense skills in a comprehensive university self-defense class, most students with decent body conditioning usually should be able to develop basic fighting-back skills, hands-on experience, and self-confidence to deal with common unarmed attacks based on the classroom observation. However, feedback from students in previous classes indicated that students tend to forget their skill after the class is over if they do not continue to practice, and it is difficult for them to practice their skills by themselves due to the lack of opportunity and motivation. Self-defense is a lifetime learning process, and students definitely should continue their skill training to a degree that they do not forget anymore.

There are two ways students can continuously develop their physical skills. One way is to follow the formal class format which works on overall fighting-back patterns for all potential attacking situations. Intermediate self-defense classes and some martial arts such as Jujitsu, Kungfu, Street Fighting, and Shoot Boxing can provide further overall training on most of the physical skills students learned in class and very often they can and will learn more intermediate and advanced skills and develop more hands-on experience at applying these skills.

Another way is to develop personalized skills and styles based on their individual needs, their neighborhood, work environment, personal interest, body conditioning, and availability of classes, etcetera. The philosophy behind this is that although self-defense is situational and students should be prepared for different attacks, it is very difficult to be very good at every type of fighting-back patterns, and students should focus on the development of a couple of fighting-back patterns that are best for each individual. People are different and the development of personalized self-defense skills makes self-defense more specific and individualized. The best way to get this type of training is to practice martial arts which focus on specific combative patterns as introduced in the previous physical skill chapters. Students may visit some martial art studios to observe their classes before they make decisions. Self-defense instructors can also help each student choose the styles they want to establish. However, there will be some problems learning martial arts for self-defense, and the next chapter will have detailed discussion and suggestions.

Using Modern Technology in Self-Defense

To increase your winning chance in fighting-back against criminals, you can further develop skills on using special devices and weapons, such as personal alarms and pepper spray. These devices, if used properly with a good background of physical skills and mental strategies, can give you more threatening power over attackers. However, these devices also can have some negative effects. Therefore, it is necessary to use them carefully. The major tools which most defenders like to use include the following types.

Types of Devices

1. Spray Devices

Mace This is a small device which can shoot poisonous gas causing itching eyes and creating temporary breathing problems when aimed at the attacker's face directly at a short distance (it works best within a yard). It is small and works well when the attacker is not ready for it. However, it does not work when missing the face or when you are too far away from the attacker. The worst is that you do not have time to take it out of your pocket or purse or that the mace does not work due to mechanical problems. Remember that in some states (for instance, California), a license and training is needed in order to carry mace. Defenders must attend a special training class and receive a certificate before they can legally carry mace. Many organizations offer mace training classes and provide different kinds of mace for the students to purchase because it is not available in regular stores. You can use other similar devices such as hair spray or a fire extinguisher if mace is not available in your area.

Pepper Spray Pepper spray has the same function as the mace, except that it sprays hot-pepper liquid. It also has limits which are similar to mace, and besides, it usually expires within a year and has much less power after you shoot once. Yet carrying pepper spray does not require a license, and it can be purchased in many stores.

Paint Spray This type of device shoots paint at the attacker's face which causes visual difficulty. It works much like the mace and pepper spray, and it does not require a license. You can purchase this at hardware stores.

Repel This is a small device similar to a necklace. Whem the defender breaks it, a stinky smell like skunk is generated in order to drive the attacker away. However, Repel is not yet on the market, and it works more like the skunk model and does not have much power to stop the attacks.

2. Electric Devices

Stun Gun A stun gun is a small device which can generate high-voltage electricity which can cause the attacker to suffer partial paralysis from forty minutes to several hours. An example of the stun gun is the baton police officers use against criminals. It works by touching the attacker's skin directly or across clothing; therefore, it should be used at a close distance only. But defenders have to put themselves at greater risk when they have to use the stun gun at a close range. In recent years companies manufactured a couple new types of stun gun which can shoot up to five yards away. One type of the new stun gun advertised by a company not only works by touching the attacker but also shoot a "T" electric wave toward attacker's body to cause the same effect. However, the author purchased one and it did not work at all. Another type of the new stun gun shoots metal balls or darts (called tasers) which are connected with two thin wires to the gun. The effectiveness of these two types of stun gun remains unknown since it has not been documented in the literature. A stun gun should have stronger threatening power to deter the attacker, help build up defender's courage and confidence, and enhance defender's fighting-back ability, more than mace and pepper spray. However, it also has its limits, such as the availability on-site, potential battery and mechanical problems. Stun guns can be purchased at special stores or through the mail. Some states have requirement for carrying these devices.

Personal Alarm A personal alarm is a small device which can make a very load sound. Personal alarms do not cause injuries on attackers, but the loud sound can attract attention of police and other people passing by so that the attackers can be scared away since attackers do not want people's attention when they attack their victims. Another alternative to the personal alarm is a whistle which has the similar function as the alarm. Both personal alarm and whistles work better in the evening and nights when it is quiet, than in the daytime , and at places where people or police may pass by. Both personal alarms and whistles can be purchased at stores, and there is no requirement for carrying a personal alarm.

House alarm and car alarm These alarms are very popular and many people are using them for their house and car safety. The major function of these alarms is to attract attention to scare the offenders, the same as the personal alarm. It works well as a deterrent to the burglars and auto thieves according to Mantice (1992).

Closed circuit video camera This device has been used by banks and stores as a deterrent to robberies and burglaries, and also help chase the criminals. Most burglars and robbers do not want to be recorded and recognized, so they tend to hesitate when they commit their crimes under the camera. But sometimes, it does not work effectively when the criminals wear ski masks. This device is getting popular for home safety, since it is effective and less expensive. Some companies manufacture fake video cameras for crime prevention purpose. It is much less expensive, and it may work well at scaring the burglars because the burglars do not know whether it is a real one or not. Using a real camera or a fake one depends on the purpose of the user. The real camera is usually used to record the burglar and the user usually tries to hide it from the view of the burglars. But it can be used as a deterrent to threaten the burglars if the user puts a sign showing that this house is protected by camera. The fake camera with a sign is usually used as a deterrent to scare burglars away.

Cellular Phone Cellular phones have changed our life dramatically, and it is also a great self-defense device. Although it can not be used to cause any physical harm to the attackers, the victims can get help fast and can report to the police fast. In emergencies such as a car problem which might result in trouble since it is late or at a bad location, cellular phones can get help easily. It is strongly recommended to have one for self-defense purpose.

3. Wearing protections

Bullet-proof vest This type of vest has been used by police officers and other law enforcement officers and by army soldiers. It is made of steel wires, and it can prevent the penetration of bullets into the body. It usually works well dealing with small handguns but not bigger and more powerful guns. Another problem is that this type of vest only protects the trunk of the body, not the head and limbs. Bullet-proof vests can be purchased at a very high price (ranging from several hundred to several thousand dollars). Furthermore, it is not very common that regular people wear them daily. The Chinese army developed a thin vest made of metal pieces in 1985 and the new vest works well during lab experiments based on the news report, but it has never been on the market for self-defense purpose. A recent invention of wearing protection was reported by the Time Magazine as one of the ten important inventions. This new jacket is more like a stun gun and the attacker will be shocked when they touch it. This new jacket is worth about $900.

Techno-bra This is a new self-defense device for women. This device installs a radio transmitter in the bra and monitors the heartbeat of the person wearing it is attacked. When the person is attacked, her heartbeat suddenly becomes fast, then the transmitter can send help signals to the station to indicate where the victim is. This device is not very popular yet, probably due to the reasons that many other events can cause the change of heartbeat, and it may be too late for the helper to get on site.

Wristband transmitter This is a new technology developed a couple years ago. Its mechanism is similar to the Techno-bra. The transmitter sends a radio message to the station continuously so that the station can monitor the exact location of the person wearing it. It may work well in the kidnaping and missing situations, especially for children. But again this is not popular in the public yet although they are sold in stores.

Veri Chip This is the newest technology which is still waiting for the approval from the FDA. The Applied Digital Solution Company in Florida is exploring the possibility to install this little chip inside the skin. With a GPS system, the police can locate where a person is in case of a kidnaping. This chip has the similar function as the wristband transmitter, but it cannot be removed by the kidnappers (*The Spoch Time* 2002).

Pros and Cons of Self-Defense Devices

As discussed above on each device, modern technology can add some advantages for self-defense. Some devices make the defender look tough and armed, show the attacker that the defender is prepared to fight back, and give the defender more self-confidence. Some make the targets hardened to deter the offenders by making the targets very difficult to get and threaten to record the offenders. Some can get help and attention fast. All these functions help self-defense in one way or another, and defenders may use as much as they can to minimize the chance of becoming a victim.

On the other hand, however, these devices from modern technology may also have some problems. The major problem is that no device can prevent all different kinds of attacks in different situations, and all above devices are very limited at their functions on self-defense. There is no sign that a perfect self-defense device will be invented in the near future, and it is impossible to make such a perfect device with the technology we have at present. The second problem is that the devices discussed above can only cover a very small part of people's needs in self-defense, and furthermore some of them are not on the market yet. The third problem is that these devices may have manufacturing problems, and their effectiveness has not been tested. For example, when you purchase a stun gun or mace, there is no way that you know it will work for you or not unless you try on yourself or someone else—but who wants to try? You cannot even try it on animals in this country either. The fourth problem is that even though the defender may have a device on site of the attacks, the defender may be grabbed before they can get the device out, or the mace or pepper spray may miss the attacker's face, or the device may not work at the moment (broken or inactive batteries). Police officer Snow (1995) indicated that these devices rarely work in real life because attackers will not stand there to let you shoot them. Snow also felt that even as a police officer with full training on self-defense and usage of the device, these devices do not work effectively all the time. A worse situation is that the attacker may snatch the device and use it against the defender. If the burglar cuts off the telephone line, a house alarm will not work. The worst scenario is that defenders rely on the devices too much, thus they fail to develop enough strategies and skills because they think the device is the only or best self-defense, and the only solution to the violent crimes. Some companies also over-exaggerate too much about the functions of their products, and they make people believe that the device is self-defense. The author watched a one-hour television show on a self-defense device several years ago. When the manufacturer asked the audience the question "What is self-defense?" the audience all yelled the name of the device. This type of advertisement is completely misleading the public and consumers in a very dangerous way, and may cause severe consequences if customers really believe the advertisement. It is not ethical for these companies to try to make money while risking customers lives, and students need to be seriously aware of the danger. The last but not least problem is that these devices may make criminals know that you have something they want from you and that may trigger their motives and pick you as a target (Sliwa and Schwartz 1982).

Guidelines for Using These Devices

Since there are problems with the modern technology on self-defense devices, several guidelines are provided to help students learn how to handle the problems concerning these devices. Students should read these guidelines carefully before they step forward to buy them.

1. Keep in mind that the main function of these devices is to extend your physical limits, not to replace self-defense training. It is only a small part of self-defense and the last part in self-defense education. It is extremely dangerous to bet your life on these devices because they may not work well, or you may not have a chance to use them. Defenders should first develop comprehensive mental strategies and physical skills to be prepared for any attacks, and then go one step further to use these devices.

2. Ask experts (police officers, self-defense instructors) when they want to obtain these devices. Be sure you have a full understanding of the device you want to get, including the major functions and limitations of the devices, the availability of the brands and their features, and the laws regarding carrying and using the device. It is your responsibility to have a clear understanding of these advertisements.

3. Learn how to use the device properly first, and then check if it works. Then practice as much as you can to make yourself an expert on using it.

4. Keep the device at a place you feel you might need it and make it easy to pull out and use. Be sure to avoid the misuse of the device by children.

5. Keep a good maintenance of device and check regularly to make sure it is in a good working condition. Keep a record of the date of purchase or when you put in the battery because you have to change the battery or purchase a new one when it is expired.

REFERENCES

Mantice, J. *Bug Off!* Evanston: Walnut Grove Publishers, 1992.

Quigley, P. *Not an Easy Target.* New York: A Fireside Book, 1995.

Sliwa, C., & Schwartz, M. *Street Smart.* Menlo Park: Addison-Wesley Publishing 1982.

Snow, R. L. *Protecting Your Life, Home, and Property: A Cop Shows You How.* New York: Plenum Press, 1995.

The Spoch Times, March 31, 2002.

Chapter 20
Martial Arts and Self-Defense

This chapter explains the relationship between martial arts and self-defense and introduces different types of martial arts and their characteristics related to self-defense. The discussion includes the pros, cons, and guidelines of taking martial arts for self-defense, and a brief introduction of the main martial arts practiced in the United States.

Major Martial Arts and Developmental Trend

There are many different types of martial arts in the world, but only more than a dozen are popular or well known. These popular martial arts include Chinese Martial Arts (Wushu, or Kungfu); Korean Tae Kwon Do, Kuk Sul Won, Hapkido, Japanese Karate, Judo, Jujitsu, Aikido, Sumo, Thailand Thai-boxing, American Kickboxing, wrestling and boxing in Western and Middle East, Europen Savate, Phillipino Kali and Doce Pares, and Russian Sambo. Many martial arts also have their own different styles. For example Chinese Wushu has the biggest collection of styles and Aikido has twelve different sub-styles. Some martial arts are sports (competions) while some are activities.

Each martial art has its own unique style and combative pattern. But in recent years, there is a trend that most martial arts learn from each other and add more combative patterns to their mainframes toward a more comprehensive pattern which include most combative styles and skills. There are several reasons behind this trend. The first reason is that most martial arts use self-defense as their advertisement. However, most of them do not fit into the self-defense model because self-defense needs a variety of comprehensive patterns, while martial arts are limited by their unique combative patterns. To compensate for this problem, they have to add more patterns to their mainframes. The second reason is that the Ultimate Fighting competition represents the highest level of martial art competition in the world, and most participants have black belts in several martial arts or at least have mastered several combative patterns before they have a chance to win or to survive there. This popular competition pushes martial arts toward becoming more comprehensive.

Relationship between Martial Arts and Self-Defense

Many people have a misunderstanding of the relationship between martial arts and self-defense, and they use these two terms interchangeably. They very often see these two activities as one, therefore many people go to martial arts classes for self-defense, and other people go to self-defense classes to learn martial arts. Even many physical educators look for martial arts classes to prepare themselves for teaching self-defense. This confused impression may mislead students and the public.

Self-defense is not a martial art, and martial arts are not self-defense. They have some things in common, yet they are different from each other. Martial arts basically include two major parts: the physical combative skills and the theories. Their physical skills are further divided into two parts: the practical applications in self-defense/competitions and forms/shows. Self-defense is developed based on two parts: the mental strategies and applications of physical skills in fighting back situations. The only overlap between martial arts and self-defense are the applications of certain types of physical skills, with the theoretical aspects having little in common. Furthermore, each martial art only focuses on one or two fighting patterns, with well developed in-depth skills and applications. On the other hand, self-defense covers all possible fighting patterns and the skills include a variety of areas used in different martial arts. But martial arts and self-defense intervene and help each other on their development. The major benefits of this intervention is that martial art skills are a major source of self-defense skills and martial arts are the major way for continuous development of self-defense physical skills after students take a self-defense class. On the other hand, all martial arts need to advertise self-defense as their major instruction purpose.

Benefits of Learning Martial Arts for Self-Defense

Martial arts can help self-defense in several ways. First, most martial arts have more in-depth physical skills which may help defenders develop advanced skills and have a greater chance of defending themselves successfully. For example, Karate can help defenders develop more distance fighting skills, and Wrestling can help develop throwing skills. Secondly, martial arts studios probably are the only places where self-defense students can go to maintain and further develop their physical skills after they take a self-defense class. Third, martial arts can motivate defenders to continuously practice physical skills due to their advanced skills and promotion. Most self-defense classes last only several months, and students tend to forget what they have learned after a period of time if they do not follow up. In addition, there are few places defenders can go to continuously practice self-defense after their classes end, while most martial arts have a ranking system and advanced skills for the defender to continue learning. Fourth, martial arts are the major source of self-defense physical skills.

Potential Problems of Learning Martial Arts for Self-Defense

There are potentially negative aspects in learning martial arts for self-defense. First, as discussed above, martial arts are arts, not self-defense. Many martial arts spend more time on content which is not relevant to self-defense, such as meditation, form, and honoring the instructors. Usually only a very small percentage of the time will be used for learning physical skills or applications for self-defense. Therefore, students may spend several years in a certain martial art but learn very little about self-defense. Secondly, some martial arts studios are handled by someone who has little background in self-defense education, and whether or not these instructors can teach self-defense will remain as a question. Furthermore, many instructors lack formal education in physical education and their knowledge of teaching is limited to what they have learned from their teachers. Third, martial arts are a business at the present time. Many martial arts studios keep students in these programs as long as they can, not for teaching purposes, but for making money.

Guidelines for Taking Martial Arts for Self-Defense

Since there are the above potential problems and the lack of formal information and research on martial arts, choosing a proper martial art for continuous self-defense training can be a difficult task for students. When choosing a martial art club for continuous self-defense skill training, the following factors need to be taken into consideration. First, the school should be registered, formal, responsible, and professional. A school that only focuses on taking your money instead of focusing on teaching certainly is neither responsible nor professional. A club which is unregistered or informal may be less expensive but has greater risks of losing money or get into further trouble. Some martial art practitioners who paid their fees for a three-year program in California several years ago got into big trouble when their martial art club ran out of business shortly and the students somehow still had to pay the State Franchise Board every month while the owner ran away. Second, you should decide what you need before choosing a martial art. You should find a martial art in which either you like the fighting pattern or it fits your particular needs in self-defense. You may consult with experts through document research, on-line searches, observation of classes or training, talking to the instructor, and telephone inquiries. Third, you should find a decent school or studio or club which really focuses on the applications of skills for self-defense and one which has instructors who are experts in self-defense and who know how to teach. You may consult experts and people who are in the clubs or shop around to find the best one for yourself.

Brief Introduction of Major Martial Arts

The skill chapters have had a brief introduction to martial arts which can be used to develop different self-defense skills. There are many different kinds of martial arts in the world, and the following introduction will provide some basic information on major martial arts in terms of self-defense for students to use as a reference.

Aikido

Originally from Japan, Aikido is very popular in the United States and throughout the world. Several years ago, a former Japanese Priminister even hired a female Aikido expert of fourth dan black belt as his body guard. Other martial arts similar to Aikido include Jujitsu, Qin Na, and Hapkido. Aikido is well known to the public due to the films involving the applications of Aikido such as the movie "Under Siege." The major actor Steven Siegel is a six-dan black belt in Aikido; his performance in that film certainly is a good advertisement for this martial art. Aikido is a pure martial art which is performed for movement and self-defense purposes, and it does not allow formal competitions in public. It is popular at universities, community centers, and private clubs. Aikido is a gentle martial art which stresses defensive movements without hurting opponents. Aikido combines several types of combative patterns, including joint lock, joint control-type throws, throws, and floor fighting. Aikido uses hands most of the time to lock joints and catch opponents off balance, and rarely uses kicks or punches. From the self-defense standpoint, Aikido is great at improving the joint control skills and some releasing skills. However, it is not a proper martial art for overall self-defense training due to its limited skills. As discussed in the previous chapter, the effectiveness of Aikido skills in self-defense really depends on long-term training and the defender has to catch the opponent off guard, and that is very difficult in real fighting-back situations. Its philosophy of "not hurting the opponent" does not fit into self-defense situations because in life-threatening situations it will give the attacker more advantages.

Boxing

Boxing is practically a universal martial art, even though it was originally from Europe. Boxing was very popular years ago since it was one of few martial arts practiced in this country (another one is wrestling), but now it is only practiced at the professional and club levels. NCAA dropped boxing out of NCAA sports due to the severe injuries in the games, and it has a bad image in the public as a bloody sport which lacks morals. Boxing is a combination of distance fighting and open-hand close fighting, but it uses only long and short punches and blocks; no other skills are allowed. No other martial art is similar to boxing, but many martial arts use similar punches and countering skills in boxing. Boxing is an international competitive sport, even though most people are reluctant to call it a martial art. From the self-defense perspective, boxing is a good martial art for improving punching and defending skills only. When boxers compete against other martial arts where other skills are allowed, boxing certainly is at disadvantage. For example, American boxing teams had several competitions with Chinese San Shou (a style using punches, kicks, and throws) team the first time in the United States in 2000 and a second time in China in 2001. The boxing lost badly. It was commended that boxing versus San Shou is more like a knife versus a gun.

Hapkido

Originally from Korea, Hapkido is not a very popular martial art in this country. It is mainly taught in some clubs. Other martial arts similar to Hapkido include Aikido, Qin Na, and Jujitsu. Hapkido uses similar patterns as Aikido and focuses on joint control, although other techniques are also taught. Its advantage and disadvantages are similar to Aikido. But another problem is that there are not enough studios or classes for people to participate.

Judo

Originally from Japan, Judo is very popular throughout the world and there are regular international competitions. Famous tournaments include the Olympics and the World Championship. Other martial arts similar to Judo include Wrestling, Chinese Shuai Jiao, and Sumo Wrestling. Judo competitions range from six-year-olds through professional games. It is relatively popular in this country at universities and in Judo studios. The San Jose State University in California has the best Judo teams in NCAA, and the team took the most championships since Judo started at this level more than thirty years ago. Judo is a combination of a throwing combative pattern, which concentrates on catching opponents off balance, and floor works, which holds or pins the opponent on the floor for a period of time to win the competition. The combative pattern of Judo is very similar to that of Wresting but allows some choking and joint locks. Judo uses three kinds of skills in competitions: hand skills (pulling, pushing, dragging, and lifting), combined with leg skills (sweeping, tripping, and blocking), and ground control (holding, locking joints, pinning, and choking). Judo is very effective at improving throwing skills and counters, falling and rolling skills, dealing with grabs, and some floor releasing skills for self-defense. However, there are two problems when using Judo for self-defense. One problem is that Judo is limited at throwing and floor skills and practitioners need to develop other fighting-back patterns as well. Another problem is that Judo practitioners usually practice it in a Judo way based on the rules and regulations of Judo competitions instead of in a self-defense way; therefore, some skills and applications may not be proper for self-defense situations.

Jujitsu

Originally from Japan, Jujitsu is the father of Judo. It has declined since Judo became a sport a half century ago, but is becoming popular again in this country due to its effectiveness in sparring and good reputation as a winning martial art for several years at the Ultimate Fighting in 1990s. Other martial arts similar to Jujitsu include Aikido, Qin Na, and Hapkido. Mainly taught at private settings, Jujitsu focuses on different kinds of joint control skills, throwing skills, releasing skills, and floor fighting skills. The floor fighting techniques make Jujitsu a unique martial art, and even Bruce Lee admired the effectiveness of Jujitsu's floor techniques and street fighting. Jujitsu has a ranking system from white to black belts, and the testing for promotion of belts usually contains more than a hundred skills and applications. Jujitsu training is very effective at improving self-defense ability, and it is highly recommended for students who want to continue self-defense training after taking a self-defense class. The only consideration is that the Jujitsu training process is very hard on the body due to the twisting of joints and throwing and flipping. A real tough mind and strong body are required for joining Jujitsu training.

Kali

A Philippino martial art, Kali is mainly taught in private studios in some areas in this country. Kali uses short weapons as the major form of combat although it also combines other combative patterns such as kicking and punching. Another form of Philippino martial art is Doce Pares which has similar pattern as Kali. Kali and Doce Pares both can be used for self-defense training on how to use and how to deal with short weapons in self-defense. The problems include its limited combative patterns and lack of enough studios for people to participate.

Karate

Originally from Japan, Karate is one of the most popular martial arts in the United States, Europe, and some Asian countries. Other martial arts similar to Karate include Tae Kwon Do, Kickboxing, Savate, and boxing. Karate has competitions from local through international levels. It is taught at private settings, community centers, afternoon school programs, and universities. Karate (meaning bear hand combating) is basically a distance fighting pattern, although some patterns are also taught in some studios and classes. The basic skills of Karate include punches, low kicks, and hard blocks. Karate has been used in many films, starting in Bruce Lee's Era. The most famous figure in Karate film is Chuck Norris. Karate has rankings from white belt (beginners) through black belt (experts). It usually takes a student at least three years to get a first-degree black belt. Karate's skills are very simple and practical for combat and it is recommended for students who focus on improving the distance fighting ability in self-defense after taking a self-defense class. However, students should keep in mind that Karate only works on one pattern in self-defense, and sometimes Karate has a lot of Kata (form) training which is useful only for self-defense if students take Karate for a long time.

Kickboxing

Kickboxing is popular in the United States. Other martial arts similar to Kickboxing include Karate, Tae Kwon Do, and in partial, boxing. Kickboxing has competitions similar to Karate, but it does not require a karate uniform. It actually is a combination of boxing and some kicking skills from Eastern martial arts, and it takes the form of a distance fighting pattern. Kickboxing is an international competitive form of martial arts, but it is only taught at some clubs and studios in this country. It does not have rankings like Karate or Tae Kwon Do. Kickboxing has similar functions and problems as Karate when used for continuous self-defense physical skill training. In recent years, movements and skills in Kickboxing have been adopted by aerobic dancing as a unique form of cardio exercise. People taking this new "Kickboxing Aerobic" as an exercise usually expect to get fit while getting training on self-defense as the inventor advertised. This new exercise mainly is good for aerobic dance, even though students may learn some kicks and punches. However, this new exercise is more aerobic exercise than self-defense since it only teaches a very small part of self-defense physical skills, and its training of these skills are not self-defense oriented. Furthermore, it has no mental training for self-defense.

Kuk Sul Won

A Korean martial art, Kuk Sul Won is a very small martial art in this country. It is mainly taught at private settings. Kuk Sul Won uses many combative patterns, such as distance fighting, joint control, and weapons. Kuk Sul Won has a ranking system and skills similar to many other martial arts. Kuk Sul Won is useful for continuous self-defense physical skill training on above patterns. However, this martial art is not popular, and it is difficult to find a studio to participate.

Qin Na

As a branch of Chinese Martial Arts, Qin (pronounced as "chin") Na is not a competitive martial art, but it is widely used in police training, military training, and self-defense training in China. In the United States, Qin Na is mainly taught at some Kung Fu clubs. Other martial arts similar to Qin Na include Aikido, Jujitsu, and Hapkido. Qin Na basically uses two kinds of patterns in combat: the joint control and pressure-points control. Qin Na is very useful for continuous self-defense physical skill training on joint control and releasing skills and its pressure-point control can be used in dealing with harassment. But, like Aikido, Qin Na's skills only represent a part of self-defense skills and it usually takes long time to master and apply these skills in real self-defense.

Sambo

As a Russian martial art, Sambo is not very popular in this country and it is not a competitive martial art. Sambo uses different kinds of skills in combatives, including distance fighting, throws, joint control, and dealing with weapons. This martial art does not seem to have a historical background, instead it is more like a collection of skills from other martial arts. It does not seem to have a system of training or promotion like other original martial arts, although skills are similar to that used in self-defense. This martial art can be used for self-defense training but its effectiveness is unknown and availability is very limited.

San Shou

Originally from China, San Shou started in the late 1970s and has become an international competition. San Shou is mainly taught in China and in Kung Fu clubs in Chinese-American communities in the United States. Some countries like France and Brazil also have San Shou teams. San Shou is a combination form of martial art which applies distance fighting, close fighting, throwing, and joint control in competitions. But in San Shou competitions, distance fighting and throwing are the two major combative forms used most of the time. San Shou has its annual competitions in China, but in recent years started its competitions against other martial arts in other countries in the effort to make it competitive and popular at the international level. In 1998, the Chinese San Shou team competed against American kickboxing team with some advantages. In 2000 and 2001 Chinese San Shou teams won the competitions over American boxing teams with big advantages. But in 2002, the Chinese San Shou team lost to a Thai Boxing team. In 2003, Chinese San Shou defeated Karate. San Shou training can be a good form of continuous self-defense training, although its skills and patterns are limited (for example, no floor fighting) and training is needed on other combative patterns to make it more effective in self-defense.

Savate

Savate is a martial art popular in European countries. It is actually a different name for Karate, since its system and skills as well as competition pattern are the same as Karate. Therefore, its features and benefits for self-defense skill training are same as that of Karate. However, it is not popular in the United States.

Shoot Boxing

As a new style of Japanese martial art, Shoot-boxing (also called Shoot-fighting) is mainly taught in Japan but has just started in this country. Shoot Boxing has already established some reputation due to its status in recent Ultimate Fighting competitions. Shoot Boxing combines distance fighting, close fighting, throwing, floor fighting, and joint control patterns used by other martial arts, and it is a much more comprehensive martial art. Since its combative pattern is similar to the self-defense pattern, Shoot-boxing is highly recommended for continuous self-defense physical skill training. However, Shoot-boxing is not as popular as other martial arts such as Karate, therefore it is difficult to locate a studio or a class to participate at present.

Shuai Jiao

Originally from China, Shuai Jiao has a very long history as a form of combat and it is an international competition form. Shuai Jiao is mainly taught in China and other Asian countries, even though some countries in Europe and South America also have Shuai Jiao teams. In the United States, Shuai Jiao is taught in Kung Fu clubs in the community and some universities. Shuai Jiao as a combative martial art is similar to Judo and wrestling, but it mainly uses throws as the combative pattern without any floor fighting skills. The major skills used in Shuai Jiao include grabs, pulls, pushes, twists, trips, and sweeps. All of these skills can be used in San Shou training as well. Shuai Jiao is useful for continuous self-defense physical skill training on throwing and countering only, and it is also difficult to find a studio for practice.

Tae Kwon Do

Originally from Korea, Tae Kwon Do is a popular martial art form in the United States and some Asian countries. Tae Kwon Do is taught in private settings, community centers, and universities. Tae Kwon Do (meaning kicking and punching art) is basically a form of distance fighting. The basic skills in Tae Kwon Do are kicks, punches, and blocks. The traditional Tae Kwon Do uses high kicks, and the international competitions require kicks above the shoulder to receive points. The modified Tae Kwon Do popular in this country is similar to Karate. Tae Kwon Do is an international competitive martial art, and it was a demonstrative event in the 1992 Olympics and became an official event in the 2000 Olympics. Tae Kwon Do also has rankings from white belt (beginners) through black belt (experts) like Karate. It usually takes a student at least three years to get a first-degree black belt. Skills in Tae Kwon Do are very simple and practical for combat and it is recommended for students who wish to focus on improving the distance fighting ability in self-defense after taking a self-defense class. However, students should keep in mind that Tae Kwon Do only works on one pattern in self-defense and sometimes Tae Kwon Do has a lot of Kata (form) training which is useful only for self-defense if students take it for a long time.

Tai Chi

As a Chinese martial art, Tai Chi in modern times is practiced by most people in China and throughout the world as an exercise for internal health, rather than a martial art. People tend to forget that Tai Chi started as a martial art about 400 years ago, and it is still practiced as a martial art by Chinese martial arts experts in Kung Fu studios. Tai Chi is more like a defensive martial art which is used for self-defense only, not for hurting opponents. The basic combative patterns in Tai Chi include joint and pressure point control, using the opponent's power to force them off balance, distance fighting, throwing, tripping, and close fighting. Among martial arts, Aikido has some philosophy and skills similar to Tai Chi. Tai Chi is very popular in the United States and in the world as an exercise, but many classes advertise that Tai Chi is for both exercise and self-defense while Tai Chi is only taught as an exercise. It may mislead the public to believe that they will learn how to defend themselves while they are learning Tai Chi for health purpose only. Tai Chi is not recommended for self defense physical skill training since it takes much more training and much longer time than regular self-defense classes before one can apply Tai Chi skills in real self-defense, therefore it is not an effective way to learn self-defense. In reality, only Tai Chi experts who practice at least six years or more on Tai Chi as a martial art (not as an exercise) may use their skills in self-defense. By the way, Tai Chi's philosophy "being defensive" in combat gives Tai Chi some disadvantages in combating, since Tai Chi tends to throw opponent down but the opponent can come back easily, and they always use more violent patterns against Tai Chi. A perfect example is the competition between Tai Chi and Thaiboxing in Hong Kong years ago, and Tai Chi lost badly. However, Tai Chi's principle "avoiding direct confrontations with opponent" is very effective in the prevention of violent crimes.

Thai Boxing

Originally from Thailand, Thaiboxing is popular in east-Asian countries and it is still developing its reputation in the United States. Thai boxing is basically taught in private settings. It is a combination of distance fighting (such as in Karate, Tae Kwon Do, and Kickboxing) and close fighting. The basic skills include not only kicking, punching, and blocking, but also elbow and knee strikes. Thaiboxing is an international competitive martial art, and its competition format is similar to that of Kickboxing, Karate, and Tae Kwon Do. Thaiboxing has a record of defeating Tai Chi, Karate, San Shou, and has scared boxers away before the competition. Thai Boxing is a very tough martial art which requires a strong mind and body for the stressful training. Thaiboxing is highly recommended for continuous self-defense physical skill training because of its effectiveness on distance fighting and close fighting. The problems of utilizing Thaiboxing for self-defense are the availability of studios and its limit on the combative patterns.

Wrestling

Wrestling is a Western martial art popular in American, Europe, and some Asian countries. Wrestling is very popular (even though it is diminishing to some extent) at high schools in the United States, and it is an international competitive sport. Wrestling is a combination of a throwing combative pattern which concentrates on catching opponents off balance and floor fighting which focuses on pinning opponents on the floor to win the competition. No punches, kicks, or joint locks are allowed in wrestling. Judo is another martial art similar to Wrestling, even though there are differences in rules and skills. Wrestling uses three kinds of skills in competitions: 1) hand skills (pulling, pushing, dragging, and lifting), 2) leg skills (sweeping, tripping, and blocking), and 3) ground control (holding, pinning, and locking). Wrestling is very effective at improving throwing skills and counters, falling skills, dealing with grabs, and some floor fighting skills for self-defense. However, there are two problems when practicing wrestling for self-defense. One problem is that wrestling is limited at throwing and floor skills, and practitioners need to develop other fighting-back patterns for self-defense. Another problem is that wrestling practitioners usually practice it in the wrestling way based on the rules and regulations of wrestling competitions instead of in a self-defense way; therefore some skills and applications may not be proper for self-defense situations.

Wushu

Wushu is usually known as Kung Fu in the United States, and Wushu is the general term for all Chinese martial arts. The four martial arts mentioned above (San Shou, Shuai Jiao, Qin Na, and Tai Chi) are only a small part of Wushu. Wu Shu is the most comprehensive martial art system in the world, and no other martial arts have a similar system. The representatives of Wushu in modern films are Bruce lee, Jacky Chan, and recently, Jet Lee. Wushu includes all fighting patterns in other martial arts used throughout the world and has much more on weapon combatives. Besides San Shou, Shuai Jiao, Tai Chi, and Qin Na, there are Nan Quan (styles using punches and low kicks), Bei Tui (styles using more kicks), Imitative styles (styles using imitative movements of animals in combatives, such as the Tiger style or Praying Mantis style), Jeet Kune Do (Bruce Lee's style), Wing Chun (a style for close fighting), ground fighting style, Qi Gong (styles of using vital energy to resist attacks of the hand, feet, and weapons), and much more styles. Wushu started its ranging system in 1997. All styles have their forms and combative patterns, but the general combative competition of Wushu is San Shou. Wushu system is too big to be recommended for self-defense training, and students should choose the styles which fit into their needs and available one. For example, Nan Quan and Bei Tui can help improve distance fighting skills, and ground fighting style can improve floor fighting skills. A problem of Wushu is that the development of each pattern is not as deep as some other martial arts; for example, the floor fighting skills in Jujitsu are much more developed than that in Wushu. A major reason is that Wushu experts tend to be developed laterally on many patterns instead of developed vertically on a few specific patterns like in Jujitsu. Another reason is that Wushu people still refuse to change because they believe Wushu is the best martial art in the world.

Other Martial Arts

There are some other martial arts practiced by relatively smaller populations in the United States or in the world. They are not introduced here due to the reason that there is not enough information on them, or the lack of availability to the public for self-defense students, or their systems or skills are from other well-known martial arts and do not have a system, or their skills are not proper for self-defense. Examples include Capoira, Tae Bo, Kendo, Vega (Israeli martial art), Vietnamese Martial Art, Malaysian Martial Art, and Indian Martial Art.

REFERENCES

Bennett, G. *Aikido Techniques and Tactics*. Champaign: Human Kinetics, 1998.

Chen, Z. K. *Practical Kicks in Wu Shu*. China: Tour and Education Publisher, 1989.

Dong, Z. H. *Thai Boxing*. China: Beijing Physical Education University Publisher, 1994.

Du, Z. G. *Controlling Skills for Police Training*. China: Beijing Physical Education University Publisher, 1993.

Ji, F. L. *Chinese Shuai Jiao*. China: Beijing Physical Education University Publisher, 1990.

Kirby, G. *Jujitsu—Basic Techniques of the Gentle Art*. Burbank: Ohara Publication, 1993.

Liu, H. C. *Wudang Traditional Tai Chi*. China: Shanxi Science and Technology Publisher, 1991.

Mattson, G. *The way of Karate*. Japan: Charles E. Tuttle Company, 1993.

Mysnyk, M., Davis, B., & Simpson, B. *Winning Wrestling Moves*. Champaign: Human Kinetics, 1994.

Nishioka, H., & West, J. R. *The Judo Textbook*. Burbank: Ohara Publication, 1988.

Park, Y. H., Park, Y. H., & Gerrard, J. *Tae Kwon Do*. New York: Facts on File, 1989.

Shaw, S. *Hapkido: Korean Art of Self-Defense*. Tokyo: Charles Tuttle Company, 1996.

Soet, J. S. *Martial Arts Around the World*. Burbank: Unique Publications, 1991.

Spear, R. K. *Hapkido—The Integrated Fighting Art*. Burbank: Unique Publications, 1988.

Sun, B. Y. *91 Skills for Self-Defense*. China: Beijing Physical Education University, 1994.

Ueshiba, K. *The Spirit of Aikido*. San Francisco: Kodansha International, 1984.

PART SIX

Skill Demonstration in Video Compact Disc

➤ Distance Fighting Skills

➤ Close Fighting Skills

➤ Throwing Skills

➤ Floor Fighting Skills

➤ Joint Lock Skills

➤ Releasing Skills

➤ Special Fighting Skills

➤ Practice Patterns, Class Assignments, and Skill Tests